IF SOMEONE IS KILLED AND THE OFFICIALS REFUSE TO INVESTIGATE...

IS IT STILL
MURDER?

A family conspires to protect a mother's murderer,
however, they overlook one crucial element...

A daughter who loves her

Sherry Lewis Henry, Ph.D., MSW
Cecelia A. Maurer, M.A. & Aubrey J. Harness, B.S.

20 Twenty
Literary Group

ISBN
978-1-961250-94-9 (Paperback)
978-1-961250-95-6 (eBook)
978-1-961250-93-2 (Hardcover)

DEDICATIONS

This work is first and foremost dedicated to my mother, Olive Lewis. Secondly, to both my parents, who did a remarkable job with their lives despite their circumstances, and to my Sister and Brother, whom I hope read this book and know I have a special place in my heart for them.

Further dedication goes to all humans who "Try to help somebody," as Dr. Martin Luther King, Jr., wisely stated and demonstrated.

To Jackie Kennedy Onassis who preceded me by one year in combining two opposites: nightmares of a loved one executed and the successful rearing of two small children, never losing sight of which was the higher priority. Her strength was strengthening to me and her example gave me hope that it could be done. My love is among many who cherish the memories of the nation's First Son, John F. Kennedy, Jr., and pray for his sister, Caroline in her present family.

TABLE OF CONTENTS

ENDORSEMENTS

"Sherry's quest for truth is a compelling account of children living in fear and a loving wife's submission to the alcoholism of her husband, yet it is more than that. It shows the spiritual and intellectual growth of the author as she channels her own pain, fear and oppression into a ministry to help others. This book clearly conveys how being a victim does not equate into victimizing others – rather, life can be rewarding and productive even after such a loss as, 'murder in the family.'"

Michael Latimer, *Attorney, San Antonio, Texas*

"This is an excellent illustration of how one's life course can be determined by the events that occurred in childhood. Childhood abuses leave lasting scars along with an implicit need to resolve and master overwhelming experiences. Sherry's work reads like a mystery novel, weaved in social corruption, personal guilt, anguish and intrigue."

Anne Courso -Johanson, *Ph.D., Cerritos, California*

"Most of what is worthy and of value is either born of pain or strongly associated with it. Through her personal and profound pain, Dr. Lewis has elucidated, distilled and explained a syndrome, distinct and differentiated, that identifies the horrific experience of a particular category of victims. The term 'Survival Syndrome' explains what for many sufferers has been wordless, captivating, enslavement. With Dr. Lewis' seminal work, the victim and the treating clinician are given the conceptual tools, the optimism and a poignant and inspirational example of recovery. I highly recommend this book to those serious in their study of the devastations of trauma."

Robb Johanson, *Ph.D., Cerritos, California*

"There is no greater existential struggle in life, than the pulling free from the dysfunctionalities of one's own family. Dr. Sherry Lewis' shocking autobiography is one such heroic struggle."

Robert M. Anthony, *Ph.D., California*

Aubrey, Cecelia and I extend our special appreciation to
Dr. Robert H. Schuller's Crystal Cathedral
in Garden Grove, California.
We discovered that truly it is the Ministry that puts
"Strong Wings on Weary Hearts."

ACKNOWLEDGMENTS

I am grateful to my children, Cecelia and Aubrey, for their assistance in writing this book. Cecelia's editing and consultation contributed enormously and Aubrey's artwork and book cover are lovely enhancements. They helped me to survive the events and to record them. They are the most quintessential people I know and have been the joy of my life.

Further gratitude goes to the National Organization of Parents of Murdered Children and Other Survivors of Homicide Victims, for their support and the Second Opinion Service, "Autopsy Review," by Harry Bonnell, M.D.

I sincerely appreciate the integrity of the gracious ladies who shared their testimonies with me – testimonies they expected to share at the Coroner's Hearing, which never occurred. Also thanks to the other individuals who contributed valuable information on my mother's behalf, assisting me in my investigative efforts.

I also want to thank these individuals who assisted in my personal and professional quest, which ultimately resulted in this book's completion:

Robert M. Anthony, Ph.D.
the late Viktor Frankl, M.D.
Robert Merkle, Ph.D.
Rex Rook, M.D.
Robert H. Schuller, Ph.D.
Stan Terman, Ph.D., M.D.
Andre Weiss, M.D.
and the late Paul Tournier, M.D.

A TRIBUTE TO ROY ROGERS AND DALE EVANS

America has her problems, but I wonder, is she even aware
Of what her most serious one may be, which abounds for many, despair?
It's the lack of American Heroes, the kind of heroes we need...
The kind that marches to the beat of Love, that all humans long to heed.
Not the sports and entertainment names,
nor politicians, rebels and such,
But the guys and gals who live Values, who
master smiles and tears and touch,
Those who call upon Jesus, to strengthen and guide them through,
Those are the ones kids can follow, and adults still need them too.
For these are the Quality People, who make life worth learning to live.
These are the people we humbly salute, for
these are the people who Give.
They give us a reason to follow... and they show us the route to go.
They nurture through the strength of their
spirit, many whom they never know.
And because they're authentic and lasting, in all they say and do,
Truth and Beauty and Goodness and Hope, become our visions too.
So we thank you for your loving Endurance...
and we thank you for your Smiles...
We thank you for being Quintessent, worth
our travel and trust, these miles.
For we need people to believe in, people who prove 'tis
true, That Jesus is our greatest Hero, and secondly...

You and You.

MISSING YOU

I think of you Mama, so often each day,
Of things I would show you and things you would
say. Oh! How you should see the kids growing so fast
Who speak of you daily, remembering the past.
The places we go, the people we meet.
We want you to know and good times to repeat.
My heart bleeds inside from need of your love -
Tears fall I can't hide. Do you see from above?
Do you know of the heartache, the agony felt,
With each passing daybreak,
from the deed that was dealt?
So often I forget you're gone
and see you waiting there
For us to come running in home,
in answer to your prayer.
I ache to write you letters;
ache more, for yours to me.
But the ones that lie in my bureau drawer
Are all there'll ever be.
I want to buy you dresses,
when I see the kind you wore,
But the ones you had, boxed beneath my bed
Tell me you'll need no more.
It's so empty now without you,
I can hardly find the way.
But oh Mama, do remember

that we'll meet again someday,
And because you were so good to me,
This prayer will e'er be mine,
That like you were I'll learn to be
And they who silenced you will see
That you live on and on in me
And thanks to God, eternally,
Our love is still entwined.

"LIFE'S GREATEST COMPLEXITY
IS ITS UTTER SIMPLICITY."

Robert Merkle, Ph.D.
Methodist Pastor

CHAPTER ONE

AN OMINOUS PRESENCE SEEMED to surround her as she hurried up the front sidewalk to her parents' home. Shari inserted her key in the lock and swung the door wide open. There on the living room floor was her mother, lying in a pool of blood, dead. A large revolver lay a few inches away.

Shari screamed and woke up, realizing that it was only a nightmare.

First thing the next morning, she called Mama on the telephone. She wanted to tell her about the ridiculous dream and rid herself of the gloom it had cast on her. But when she heard her mother's voice on the line, she knew she couldn't speak of her dream. She'd have to wait until they were together. She couldn't bear the thought of losing Mama.

"Oh, Shari, I'm so glad you called. I'm looking forward to having you and my babies come home for the holidays. I can hardly wait for their eyes to light up when they see the surprises I'm making for them."

"You really spoil Aubrey and Cecelia, Mama. I sure hope we can make it for Christmas, but you know construction work. We're not told yet if Nat will be off for Christmas or New Year's."

Her mother's sweet voice offered comfort. "Now, don't you worry, honey. Whether we have our Christmas on December 25th or on January 1st, the babies won't know the difference—just whenever you all get here."

Shari smiled, hearing her mother's excitement and love.

"How is everything, Mama?"

There was a pause. "You know, Shari, it's not easy with your Daddy. Every day it seems he's filled with more venom." She sighed. "He doesn't want me to talk to anyone or go anywhere."

"You can't do that, Mama," Shari said.

"Oh, I won't. I told him so, too. I told him that he could live like a hermit if he chose to, but that I wasn't going to. No, I won't do that."

"I worry about you, Mama," Shari said softly.

"Don't, honey. You know, with you kids being older, I won't be putting up with him much longer. Robbie's a senior now and even engaged. Isn't that something!" She was so happy for her youngest child.

"How are Robbie and her beau doing?" Shari asked.

"Oh, just fine. They're both so cute and bashful. He's a good boy from a good home. I'm real proud of Robbie. I still like to baby her, though, while I can, so I have her a hamburger cooked when she gets off the school bus each day. She seems to like a little spoiling. You and Ellis had it better in some ways than she has. Daddy don't give her much spending money or car privileges. He's a lot tighter than he was with you both, but she don't fuss. She's a good little gal."

"Is Ellis coming home for Christmas?" Shari hadn't seen her brother much since marrying and moving away from Clinton four years ago.

"Oh, you know Ellis. He does whatever he feels like at the time. He'll probably open presents with us, then be off on his way. He's still mad at me about his diabetes, but I don't take any lip from him. It's in our family, and he has to deal with it the same as I do. At least he seems to like this new college he's in. Maybe he'll make a go of it this time."

The two chatted a little longer, both growing more and more excited to see each other in the next couple of weeks. Then, with the dream still vivid in her thoughts and memory, Shari made a point of ending the conversation with words she wished she said more often: "I love you, Mama."

She had no idea this was to be her very last conversation with her mother. The nightmare would soon become a gruesome reality.

Over the next few days, the dream would not leave her. It had such a powerful effect that she began to systematically collect all of Mama's letters. She didn't want anything of hers to be accidentally thrown away. Every morning she woke up with that same image in her mind of Mama lying on the living room floor. *Get over it*, she told herself. *You've got a lot to do. It was only a dream. Mama's fine.*

Shari knew she wouldn't be telling Nat about her phone call to Mama, because he had given her explicit orders not to make any more long-distance phone calls. They would soon be disconnecting the phone and all the utilities, preparing to move once again. She didn't like moving so often and particularly dreaded leaving this town where her friends and church were. But with her husband in construction work, they had to move often, and she tried to make the best of it.

Nat liked having his own truck. It enabled him to unhook the utilities himself and move their trailer home whenever he wished. There were occasions when his wife wished this wasn't so easy for him to do. One Saturday morning in particular stood out in her mind. They had just finished eating breakfast—dishes were still on the table—when Nat said it would be a good time for her to go buy groceries. He had other things to do later in the day and would need the car. Shari left immediately, since they were out of milk and other necessities for the kids.

To her horror, when she returned to their trailer space, it was vacant! Nat had unhooked the utilities and moved the trailer right after sending her away. She had no idea where their home had gone. She wondered whether he had taken the time to pack appropriately. Somehow, she doubted that he had. A simple chore, really, yet it made a profound difference in securing their belongings. A few pillows stuffed into the cabinets, and tape on the doors, closets, bathroom medicine chest, and drawers tended to protect most things well enough. He probably hadn't taken the time to do that, though.

After a number of phone calls she learned that he had moved the trailer to another town not far away. When she eventually got there, groceries still in the car, Nat enjoyed her reaction too much. Inside their trailer home were breakfast dishes strewn across the floor, coffee spilled, glass dishes broken, food smeared into the carpet. No doors had been secured, so the refrigerator door had swung open, food had toppled out, and dishes had been thrown from the cabinets.

"This'll teach you to leave without washing the dishes first," he scoffed, watching his wife closely in her bewilderment of the whole trashy mess.

"I left because you told me to go right away. You were still at the table." Her words were useless in defense, but they nevertheless seemed important for the simple reason that they were true. Her entire life she had valued the simple truth, whether it changed the situation or not. She knew that she would still be blamed, but she felt the need to hear the truth in her own words.

They had started to go to church, and Mama was so happy about that. She was certain that they would be a happy family now. Shari hoped she was right. She geared her letters toward that impression, which wasn't difficult to do. They were in church, after all, and she was happy about that. Yet there were many signs that something was wrong, which even her pastor and other couples noticed as they interacted with them.

Nat demanded a leadership role, but he wasn't willing to humbly invest himself in preparation for leadership. He wanted to be seen as an expert in every class discussion, yet he seldom had his facts straight. Everyone was aware of it but him.

He was dictatorial with his wife, and it seemed important to him to deny her anything that he knew she valued. This wasn't lost on their children. Shari had seen young Cecelia and Aubrey emulate their dad once in play, saying, "Shari, you see that little bug? You like that little bug? You want that pretty little bug?" Then with their feet they smashed the bug, symbolizing his dual enjoyment of destroying her interest and eliciting a reaction.

Shari knew that Nat had been given his nickname in childhood for being so vulnerable to input from others. He had been seen as a gnat, eager to be an associate with other, older boys. They, of course, had recognized this trait and had taken advantage of it, making him do silly things, amusing themselves with his blind faith in them.

None of Nat's ideas seemed to originate with him, and he always prefaced them with "Bill says" or "John says," which to Nat, was unquestionable. Shari was never allowed input into any decisions. But she hoped that now, in the church, he would learn a humility that would put their family on solid ground. She was also glad that Mama felt so happy about them, and she thought that, just perhaps, time would prove her right. She would have to answer to Nat later about defying him and phoning Mama, but oh, how that phone call helped!

She had a great deal to do, as they were moving again, this time to a new state. Her days were spent packing and taking care of the children: Aubrey, now a three-and-a-half year old, and Cecelia, one year younger. Although Mama called them "her babies," Shari knew they were growing quickly, and she valued every day and every experience with them.

So much happened in so short a time. They made the move, and immediately in came a heavy snowstorm. They were exhausted. Shari barely found time to get out to the Green Stamp store to purchase a Christmas purse for Mama. Five days after they had talked on the phone, she was wrapping the purse when someone knocked on the door.

"Yes?" she said, looking at an elderly woman she'd never seen before.

"Your mother is dead."

"What?" she asked in disbelief. Her confusion turned into anger, anger at this stranger who had the audacity to deliver such a message.

"You can use my phone," the woman said, pointing to her mobile home across the street.

"You must be mistaken. I just spoke to her on the phone a few days ago." Shari held up the purse she was wrapping for her mother's Christmas present.

The woman sadly shook her head and again motioned to her house. "Please watch my kids," Shari whispered, hurrying out into the falling snow, her footsteps crushing the newly fallen flakes. She felt numb, but her hands were shaking when she dialed her parents' number.

"Who's this?" she asked when a man answered. Daddy never answered the phone.

"It's me, Shari, Grover Lewis," replied her father's cousin.

"What are you doing answering Mama's phone, Grover?"

"Shari, something's happened here...."

"Put Mama on!" she shouted. "I want to talk to Mama."

"That's impossible, Shari. Your mama's passed—"

She hung up. She didn't want to hear the end of that statement, or that word. She didn't go back to her trailer right away. She ran out of her neighbor's home and wandered around in the snow. She walked and let the cold air press against her, cooling her body that was fired so terribly by inner rage and the sudden onset of deep grief.

That night, Nat and Shari bundled up their kids and left for Mama's home. The trip was long and difficult. The driving snow made the roads slippery and made it hard to see. Husband and wife didn't talk along the way. Shari was left to her own painful thoughts.

She thought of the many questions she could have asked instead of just hanging up the phone. She knew so little—only that her mother was gone, dead. She couldn't get the feeling of the word, but she knew it would be more than a word in a few hours when they got to her parents' home.

"I wish I knew what she died from," she said to her husband several times, hoping that he would stop the car and make a phone call to inquire. She knew better than to ask, though. She couldn't bear to have him refuse that, too.

"You had Grover Lewis on the phone. All you had to do was ask him what she died from. But what did you do? Hung up the phone! That sure makes a lot of sense, now, don't it? You always do the stupidest thing possible. I really think you have some kind of special talent; you're always so stupid."

The way he laughed at her following his callous statement would have enraged her, except that instead it instantly brought her back to another scene that had taken place just one year earlier. His laughter had totally repulsed her then. When President Kennedy had just been shot and pronounced dead, and the nation—the entire world—mourned (if not for America's loss of its president, at least for a young widow and two little children), Nat had laughed heartily, primarily because the men he happened to be near at the time had laughed. Just like a gnat, he buzzed along with them. Then it had mattered. Now it was Mama, and Nat just didn't matter one way or another.

Shari wondered how she'd died, assuming it had been from a heart attack. She was so glad she had said "I love you" on the phone. She wondered whether Momma had heard it or had already hung up. And that dream. Shari remembered the dream and her friend's words:

"You'll never have more than you can bear."

When the children were awake, they sang Sunday school songs. The action ones were the most comforting for the kids. They could lose themselves in songs like "Peter, James, and John in the Sailboat," "Deep and Wide," and "Little Robin Red Breast." They also knew the words to some strengthening choruses, such as "I Know the Lord Will Make a Way for Me" and "At Calvary."

Shari was glad that Nat didn't know how much their singing meant to her, otherwise he would have put a stop to it. When the kids grew sleepy, Shari pretended to sleep too, while continuing to sing the words over and over, silently.

They arrived at Mama's at three in the morning to find hoards of people milling around the house. They looked like zombies with their blank stares and expressionless faces.

What are they doing here? Shari wondered. *Why are they in my mother's house at three in the morning, and why are they staring at me?*

She asked several people about her sister. "Where's Roberta?" No one seemed to know. Someone mumbled that she was spending the night with friends, but nobody knew with whom, or where.

When she asked about her mother, they looked at each other and back at her, saying nothing. All through the years, Mama and Shari had gone together to visit families in which a loved one had died. They always talked about the loved one. They talked about how fine they were, and they touched, hugged, and even cried with the mourners. Where were those people now? What was different here when Shari needed to talk about Mama and to be touched and hugged? She needed to cry. Didn't anyone remember how fine she was, and so recently, too?

Suddenly Ellis appeared. Shari asked him, "Where's Robbie?" She desperately wanted to see her. The sisters had always been close, and Shari wanted to be with her now so terribly.

"She's OK. She's OK. But we need to talk, Shari."

"Ellis, what happened to Mama? And why are all these people here acting so awful? Nobody will talk to me, and I'm hungry, Ellis. I never saw Mama's refrigerator so empty! I'm hungry and I want to see Robbie and I want to see Mama! Where is Mama? Why isn't she here?" She remembered how their other relatives had been placed in coffins, in a nice room of someone's home, and they were still a part of the family, as people came to visit with the family, and viewed them and talked about them and touched them. She had never come home before when Mama wasn't there and this was agonizing, excruciating!

"Now Shari, you've got to calm down, and we'll tell you everything. But let's go in the back where we can talk, OK? Come on."

Ellis and an aunt, their dad's sister, ushered Shari into the back room. This didn't seem like Ellis. But Daddy had watched his daughter go from person to person with her questions, and he had just stared. He saw Ellis motion her to the back, so she figured she was expected to go through this ritual back in her old room. It had been so pretty, and it still looked much like she'd left it only four years ago. She sat down on her old bed, which had become Mama's in her absence. She wasn't sure why Aunt Pearl was there, but she was willing to put up with anything to get some answers to this grisly riddle.

People are disappointments
They're cruel at times and hard
Some things they do we can't
Overlook or disregard.
It seems they're out to get us
And, sometimes they are,
That's when it's important
To know what we stand for.
It doesn't matter, good or bad
What we get from attention,
But the more important things,
Which we often fail to mention.

CHAPTER TWO

SHARI WAS AMAZED AT how such a pretty room, frequently the site for unwelcome news long ago, again seemed uncomfortably familiar. Seeing Ellis standing there, she had no trouble remembering what he was like years earlier when he would run into this room in terror, yet with a manly protectiveness, taking charge in the role the whole family knew too well.

"He's home!" Ellis would announce, pulling open the window while managing to grab a blanket or pillow before he jumped out first, then waited with arms outstretched for Shari to hand Robbie down to him.

Sisters and brother would hear Daddy's string of cuss words as he kicked the front door open. After helping young Robbie, Shari would be the last to scurry through the open window into the darkness. The girls would quietly follow Ellis into the warmth and safety of the night. Out there the three of them would huddle, crouched low in the weeds. They could hear the screaming, and they could see the beating their mama was taking, backlit against the windows.

Robbie would cling to her big sister, burying her face in her shoulder. Ellis would turn away from the house, pressing his hands against his ears. Only Shari watched, never taking her eyes away from the lit window and the silhouette of their daddy beating their mama. She didn't cry; she felt her mother's pain, but she didn't cry. Time was too valuable to waste with senseless tears.

Once Shari asked Mama why he beat her. Her mother sighed deeply and said, "It's because he drinks."

"Then why does he have to drink so much?"

Mama shrugged her heavy shoulders and frowned, "I don't know, honey. I don't know." Shari hugged her and asked why he had to kick the door so hard when he came in. Mama brought her arm around her daughter and hugged her closer.

"It's a good thing he does that," she said simply. "That gives you three enough time to get out of the house." She could always see a bright side, even in the midst of gloom. Shari always admired her for that.

In time, she stopped asking so many questions. She had grown old enough to understand something she could not yet explain; there was a logic to their existence that she figured was none of her business. She decided not to trouble Mama with her questions, her complaints, or her wish that her dad would stop beating her. For now, she just accepted what was.

These episodes had become almost routine. After a beating was over, the three children would slink back into the house. Shari always went to comfort Mama. She'd soothe her bruised skin, wash away the blood, and begin combing her hair back into place.

"It's OK now. Now he's gone," daughter would tell mother when she winced. Ellis would find sanctuary by himself in his upstairs retreat. He and Shari never once spoke to each other about their father's violent outbursts. But she and Mama seemed to share a silent communion of pain as Shari tended to her. What the young girl didn't know then was that she was absorbing a lot of guilt. She began to believe that it was their fault—her fault—that Mama suffered like this.

"I love you," Mama told her mature little girl over and over. She loved Shari and she loved her brother and sister. She loved them terribly. And it had to be this love that kept her with their daddy, kept her taking the beatings, the agony, the misery. Shari did her best to soothe Mama and tend to her bruises and wounds, yet deep inside she believed that there had to be a better way. One day they'd find it. There had to be a way for love to exist without fear or pain or guilt. There had to be.

Good times were when Daddy was away, when he was out of town with a load of lumber. Then the house was quiet and safe. Then the neighborhood kids would join Ellis and Shari on the hillside behind their house. They'd take a case of beer from under the staircase, and once on the hill, they would have contests, shaking the hot cans and popping them open to see whose beer sprayed highest into the air or farthest down the hill. Sometimes they'd devise targets and try to hit them with the fierce spit of beer bursting from the cans.

They were never afraid of taking the beer. No inventory was ever taken, and it was never missed. When the supply diminished, it was simply replenished. No questions asked.

But besides the cases of beer, there were the gallon jars of whiskey. These gallon jars were often poured down the drain in a never-ending and futile cycle. Mama knew she was fighting a losing battle. The problem was not with the whiskey; it was with the man. No matter how many gallons she emptied into the drain, there were always more by the weekend.

Then came the beatings. What was it that drove Daddy to work so hard all week long to provide a good life for his family, only to have him retreat into the horror of alcohol on the weekends? How could he care so deeply for them Monday through Thursday, only to torment them so horribly Friday through Sunday?

Once, back when Shari still supposed the problem was the liquor and not the man, she tasted the whiskey. Instead of discovering the luscious nectar she had expected, she learned that she couldn't even swallow the burning, foul liquid. For a time, she felt sorry for Daddy and believed she understood why he cried so much after he drank. She'd have cried too, if she had to drink that stuff. But he didn't have to drink it, did he?

And if he were really sorry about the way he broke all of Mama's dishes and things, or about the way he threw liquor all across the walls and floors, why did he keep drinking over and over again? Shari wondered if maybe it was just so that he could sleep. He always slept as soundly as a tiny baby when he'd finally fall asleep in total exhaustion. Shari remembered walking into the room one time with Mama and finding him lying on the floor, stark naked. He was sleeping so peacefully that Mama just covered him up with a blanket right where he lay.

One night, the family was a few miles from home when baby Robbie started crying because she needed milk. "I'll pull over and get her some milk," Daddy said. He stopped the car and went into a restaurant. They waited and waited. Mama tried to calm the baby, but with every passing minute, Robbie grew more and more agitated. When the baby was frantic, Shari climbed out of the car and went hunting for Daddy. She walked into the restaurant but couldn't find him anyplace. She went back out and spotted him sitting in a car full of people. After watching him for a minute, she tapped on the window. "Daddy, the baby's crying a lot now and we don't have any milk."

He got mad. "Dammit, go back to the car!" he snapped as he got out and followed his daughter. They finally bought the milk and went home.

People have troubles, all of us do
Some are imagined, but some are true.
You'll see it often hurts within
And seems almost to be a sin
To always have to stand aside
And watch their troubles go in stride.
Yes people have troubles, all of us do
We can't all help, but we can Be True.

CHAPTER THREE

SOME DRUNKS SLUMP DOWN and fall asleep before they even have the chance to do any harm. Daddy wasn't like that. He was a destructive drunk. He'd get violent and wreck anything and everything in his way— radios, bicycles, even the house itself. Mama and the children learned early not to cherish possessions too much. Even so, there was a red table-and-chair set that Shari loved. It was hers, and she used it whenever she played with dolls in her room. She should have known better than to get attached. One night, in a drunken rage, Daddy took that set and, piece by piece, threw it all down the long flight of stairs into the basement.

"No! No!" she screamed, pulling frantically on the pieces, trying to wrestle each away from him. But he didn't listen. He just stormed into her room, grabbed the table, and hurled it down with all his might into the basement. Next he grabbed a chair. Down it went. Next another chair, and another, until all four were smashed to pieces with the table against the concrete basement floor. No amount of screaming, pulling, or pleading could turn him away from his violent destructiveness.

Because of a rage-filled whim, Shari's prized little red table and chairs were no more. Defeated, she ran back to her room and sat on the edge of her bed. She stared at the spot where her set had been. Now there were only dolls strewn about the floor, the dolls that had fallen from the little red chairs. They looked so pathetic, so helpless on the floor. Shari started screaming at them. She hated helplessness. She hated that the peaceful refuge of her room had been brutally invaded by the anger of the outside world.

She came to understand that love was painful, that attachments were too easily torn away, and that peacefulness was only a fantasy that gave way quickly to angry, destructive reality. Shari was so tired of trying to sort out people and situations. She had grown weary of it. She was just six years old.

When she figured it wasn't the dolls' fault, she stopped screaming. They were silent only because, like Mama and her, they could do nothing but wait until he was done. Shari picked them up, soothed their skin, and tenderly combed their hair in place. She gently reassured them, "It's OK now. He's gone."

Six years old is pretty young to develop a philosophy for life, but that is exactly what occurred. Lying on her bed, her face pressed against her pillow, Shari told herself that life is difficult and that no one is to be trusted. Her experiences had already taught her that the only constant she would ever trust was disappointment. She would have to accept it. Disappointment she could cling to, and with that assurance, she lived.

It came as a complete shock to her when she discovered that some children found sanctuary in their own homes. For Shari and her brother and sister, sanctuary was outside, away from Daddy and the confines of the house. The world outside became their hiding place. In the dark, they hid behind trees and in weeds. Sometimes they stayed hidden for hours before sneaking back into the house. Even then, it never felt safe.

One night, Mama hung up the phone and urged them out of the house even before Daddy kicked open the door. "Go on, hide," she said. "And stay quiet!"

They knew the routine. They ran and hid in the high weeds behind the house. A short time later, Daddy came running through the weeds, chased by a handful of men who were yelling and cursing. The children nestled close and stayed down low, pressing against the warm earth. They felt their hearts pound as the sounds of heavy footsteps thundered toward them. Should they run? The posse veered in another direction right before reaching them. They breathed a sigh of relief.

Later they learned that the men chasing Daddy were the sheriff and his deputies. They were trying to catch Daddy for the disturbance he'd caused in town while he was drunk. It wasn't the first time. There was the time when he'd broken his hand by smashing it through a store window. His hand had finally healed, but it was left twisted and deformed. As a result, he could no longer use a typewriter. His deformed hand also rendered him unfit for military service, a fact that he never got over. It was a matter of pride to be able to serve and a grave rejection that he would never be able to.

Even after the men had rushed past the children, they stayed in the weeds. They were used to staying outside for long periods of time, waiting for the noise and movement to stop. It was only when things stayed quiet for some time that they would conclude that either he'd gone away or he'd fallen asleep, making their house safe again. Before that point, there was always the shattering of dishes and glass, or the heavy thud of furniture being lifted and tossed. When they'd finally return, they often found that the gallon jars of whiskey had been shattered against the walls and ceiling, leaving the dark, stinking liquid spilling down the walls and onto the furniture and floor.

Sometimes Daddy fired his gun. Their living room had bullet holes scattered throughout. Shari could vividly remember a time when he even fired the gun over the baby's crib—with the baby in it. "No, Daddy, don't!" she cried. He just jeered and pulled the trigger. Another time he fired several shots while they were all in the living room. Still holding the gun, he pinned Mama down on the couch. The children screamed at him while he threatened Mama. The scene was interrupted when the men from Daddy's planer mill (which was adjacent to their house) banged on the door. "Hey, you all OK in there?" A sudden silence engulfed the living room.

"Cecil," they called to Daddy, "what's going on in there?"

"Get the hell away from here!" he yelled back. "What I do in my own damned house is none of your business!"

"We just want to know if everything's all right." They peered through a window and saw that the family was all there but he was still holding the gun.

"Everything's fine!" he shouted back. "Get the hell back to work, or you don't have a job anymore!"

When they went away, Daddy grumbled about their "interference" in his private business. To him, his home was his private domain where he could "do anything I damn well please." Young Shari observed this—and more—and wondered. It was so confusing. When her brother started hunting a few years later and would nail the hides of rabbits, squirrels, and opossums to his wall upstairs, she wondered if their families had wished someone would have interfered?

"How come he always falls asleep like that?" she asked her brother, nudging him when they saw Daddy naked on the bed.

Ellis just shrugged, annoyed and embarrassed. He didn't talk much at home, and Shari didn't ask him about the large hole in one of Daddy's legs. She waited and asked Mama about that.

"He got that when he was running from the police one time," she said in an even voice. "He was running and he tripped. He fell on a stub that pierced up into his leg." She shook her head. "It never properly mended." Shari listened quietly, thoughtfully. The story of his life was tied up in Mama's words: "Never properly mended."

Of course, there were times when the kids came back to the house only to find he was still awake. Then it was like walking a tightrope, or trying to avoid hidden landmines. His "second bouts" were often worse than the first ones. He usually blocked the exit so they'd have nowhere to run. He was always angry at them for "running away and leaving" him.

"I'm your dad," he'd say in a voice mixed with self-pity, anger, and bewilderment. "Why are you always running away from me?"

It would do no good to answer, of course. That would infuriate him even more. They were safe only when he slept or left in the car. When he was gone, he generally stayed away most of the night. When he was sleeping, Mama and the kids sometimes packed a few things, like clothes, toys, and diapers, and left to a motel or a remote area in the woods for a "picnic." Mama would cover him with a blanket and then come out to tell the kids to gather their belongings.

"We're going on a picnic," she'd announce in a whisper. Their "picnics" would mean a safe area out from town. They'd bring their bathing suits, a few blankets, and some food. The kids would splash in the shallow water of the running stream, while Mama lay on the blankets, trying to gather enough strength to return.

Even now, years and years after those times, Shari cannot relax at picnics. The undercurrent of fear remains. It's as though picnics carry a hidden danger; while she's enjoying the warm sunshine and nice food, someone might come and "find her."

Back then, the family was well known at motels. They often checked in during the early morning hours when Mama managed to get out of the house with the car keys. The motel clerks neither asked questions nor seemed to notice when Mama was bleeding or her dress was torn. Shari wondered even then why some people can't seem to see the obvious. Not once did Daddy go after them at a motel, even though the car was parked in plain sight.

Mama and the children knew that the people in town didn't want to deal with their problems. Daddy had learned to respect that, so he kept their problems within their walls, never entering another man's property. As time went on, the family came to learn that there were ways of making the house "safe" and that these ways invariably had something to do with his not wanting to "lose control" in public. Thus, whenever Ellis or Shari brought friends over to spend the night, they knew that those nights would be safe.

Daddy was a physically powerful man. More than once, he picked up one end of the bed while the children slept on it and rolled them off over the edge. He did this with just one hand and hardly any effort. Shari could never decide whether he lived inside a monster's body or a monster lived inside him. His strength frightened her, but like everything else about him, it had another side. It was that very same strength that enabled him to carry heavy loads of lumber during the week, earning his living and providing for the family. His elder daughter couldn't figure him out.

She had seen him at work, his body drenched in sweat, and she knew that he had to love them to work so fiercely to keep them fed and clothed. But she had also seen him beat Mama and destroy their things. Many times she had seen him in a violent rage, but she had also seen him on his knees afterward, with tears streaming down his face while he swore, "Never again."

"I swear it," he'd say. "I won't ever drink again. Please, please. You've got to believe me."

And each time they almost did. Almost.

Her father's actions defined Shari's understanding of family. Her grandparents lived across the street from them, and they would let the grandkids hide in their garden from Daddy's rampages. Roberta came to hate the sight of the once-popular corn-silk dolls because they reminded her of cornstalks, which she'd hidden behind and even slept underneath for hours out in that garden at night while Daddy searched for them.

"We don't want trouble," Grandma would say. "He'll come looking for you here." He often checked their house but never their garden. These were Daddy's parents. He never vented his anger at them directly, and yet they hesitated to let their grandchildren in.

The same was true of another neighbor, Mama's first cousin married to Daddy's sister. Shari could remember one time when Mama had been badly beaten and was bleeding. She wanted a drink of water desperately, but she was too afraid to go back around her house because she knew that her husband was still there somewhere. So she and Shari crossed the street to her cousin's house. Shari knocked on the door, and when Mama's cousin answered, he looked at her in horror.

"Can I have a glass of water?" Mama asked.

He nodded and stepped back into the house, never inviting them in. When he came back with a glass of water, he smiled apologetically. "We don't want your problems in here," he said. Mama didn't argue. She wasn't even angry at his reaction. She just drank gratefully. Shari stood quietly by her side, but she was confused and angry. What did that mean, that they didn't want their problems? Shari didn't want their problems, either. Weren't these people family? Weren't Mama's problems, her problems, *their* problems too?

One time, a relative did show some real compassion. Shari's uncle, her father's brother who lived in Louisiana, happened to be driving past their house early one morning and spotted Mama staggering down the highway, bleeding from her most recent battering. "My God, Olive," he said, pulling over. "Are you all right?"

She shrugged. He leaned over and opened the passenger-side door. "Get in," he said. "I'm taking you to the doctor."

Shari never forgot this. She knew she'd always remember, always be grateful for his simple act of kindness. Her uncle could have been like the others, closing his eyes and heart to their problems, but he didn't. Of course, he didn't live in town, either, and perhaps that made the difference.

It was an old, white-haired family doctor who finally convinced Mama to leave.

"Olive," he told her, "your body can't take anymore."

"It has to," she replied, "for my children."

"Olive, I'm telling you, if you don't get away from Cecil, you won't live to see your children grown."

Mama stared at him. The doctor had patched her up many, many times, and he was not a man to speak without cause. "Are you just trying to scare me?" she asked.

He shook his head. "No, I'm trying to get you to see the truth. You love your kids, and the best thing you can do for them is to get away. Otherwise, they're going to be left without a mama to take care of them."

She looked at her daughter strangely. That rationale was the only rationale that could persuade Mama to leave. She stayed with Daddy so as not to lose her children. If staying turned out to be the cause of losing them, then she wasn't about to do it. Still, it wasn't that simple. How could she leave? All she knew was cleaning, cooking, washing, ironing, sewing, raising kids, and getting beaten.

"You have to find a way," the doctor said.

She lowered her eyes. Mama loved her children. She knew that she must listen to this doctor. He wasn't family, but perhaps he was a friend.

CHAPTER FOUR

THE DAY CAME WHEN Mama and the kids were moving out. Daddy sat quietly in his chair in the corner of the room, deep in thought. He glared at them while Mama collected their clothes and Shari held Roberta's hand and her piggy bank.

"Shari, you want to stay with me?" he asked, fixing his gaze on his older daughter.

She shook her head. "No, I want to go with Mama," she said firmly. She was brave in front of him that day for one simple and shameless reason: Her grandpa was there. Mama's father and brother stood by while she packed. And they had the gun. Daddy had no bravery toward men. It was a woman he was mean to. So this day, he was the one to sit still and be quiet. Grandpa could always back Daddy down.

Even so, Grandpa Deevens never knew the full extent of their problems. He didn't live nearby, and Mama would never tell him. She wasn't one to "worry" others. Besides, her parents had repeatedly warned her not to marry Daddy. Mama didn't want to share her troubles with them. She didn't want to hear, "you made your bed, now lie in it." So she chose silence.

Her two sisters had divorced and had returned to their parents' house with their babies. Mama was the eldest and felt a certain responsibility to make things work. She also felt that she should neither question nor complain, but just accept what was.

Three of them moved out that day: Shari, Roberta, and Mama. Ellis decided to stay in town. The fair had arrived that week, and Ellis had asked his Mama, "Who'll have more money, you or Daddy?"

"No doubt about it, we won't have much money. We'll be safe and have food and what we need. But we won't even have a car."

"I want to stay and go to the fair," Ellis stated. He remained in town, staying with another family most of the time.

Of course, Daddy always saw it as the day they left him, "they" being Mama and Shari. Roberta was only a baby; she had no say in the matter, and Ellis had at least stayed in town. No, it was just Mama and Shari who "turned" on him. It never occurred to him that they left with cause, that their self-preservation had something to do with it.

Although there was a definite sense of liberation in being free of him, it wasn't easy—not emotionally and not practically. They found an apartment in the city. Shari walked to school every day, but it was a lousy school, and she hated every last soul there, including the teacher. She didn't tell Mama that, though. No, she'd learned too well the art of protecting the ones you love. Instead, she told her that she liked the class and that her teacher was very nice. How could she tell her otherwise? They had finally left because Mama couldn't bear to take "anymore." Shari felt it wouldn't have been right for her to pile on "more."

It didn't matter, anyway. Shari had another skill to call upon, another skill she'd learned from Mama: perseverance. She could take it. She could make herself take it.

She missed her friends terribly, and she didn't make a single friend at her new school. She did, however, make a friend at the apartment. Sandra Seaver was a Catholic girl who lived alone with her mother. Together, the two girls would sit on the porch of their apartment building and eat seedless grapes. They understood that things were "serious." They were not deceived by girlish things.

Mama missed Ellis, and there was nothing Shari could do about that. Alone in the apartment with the baby, Mama's days were long. She missed not having a car, not having a house, not having a whole family. Finally the missing got too strong for her. They had only a few short weeks of freedom before they went back. At least Mama got some rest for her body, her nerves, and her soul.

Before they went back, Daddy's foreman visited. He assured and reassured them that Daddy wasn't drinking anymore, that the separation had sobered him up good. "God's healed him of his alcohol," the foreman told the hopeful family. Then he kneeled down in front of Shari.

"You know, Shari, your daddy loves you very much." He straightened up and looked at Mama. "Olive, Cecil wants you all back." He tipped his cap back on his head. "He's having trouble concentrating without you being around. He needs you back or else he'll lose his business for sure."

Mama looked at Shari. Neither of them could believe that Daddy wasn't drinking anymore. But both of them missed a lot about home. Mama missed Ellis and her house. Shari missed the house, too, and her friends and her own good school and her white rabbit.

After Daddy's foreman left, Mama had a serious talk with her daughter. "Shari, if he really has stopped drinking, we may have ourselves a good home life."

"Do you really believe he has?" Shari asked, betraying her own doubt.

Mama sighed. "I sure hope he has." She hugged her daughter. "You listen to me, now. Are you listening?"

"Yes, Mama."

"If he hasn't stopped, then there will probably be trouble. Maybe not now, maybe not for months or years. But if he does drink again, I know he'll kill me for sure."

Shari pulled away from her and looked into her eyes. She saw the certainty there.

"He always holds grudges, your daddy. He always blamed me for leaving, even when it was just for the night. I know he really blames me for leaving this time. And he'll blame you, too. So you remember what I'm about to tell you, OK?" Shari nodded.

"If he does kill me, you will be next, because you chose to leave with me. So if you ever come in and see that he's killed me, be very, very careful and get out. You hear me? Don't look back. Just get out because you would be next."

Certainly not the type of motherly advice a girl normally gets. Shari never forgot her mother's words. Never.

My Old Rocking Chair

As I sit in my old rocking chair
And think o'er the years of my life,
I see some old memories come dear
Memories of hardship and strife.
I think of my lawful companion,
Who left me so long ago, and feel perhaps I was cheated
Of memories I never shall know. But then,
There were those before me and those who will come
When I've gone, who'll hold not the slightest memory
Of the wonderful things I've known.
So when this Day of Thanks rolls 'round, and people kneel to
Pray,
I too, will be down, though I'm old and broken and gray,
And in my prayer I'll say,
"Lord, I thank Thee for things I know not, for things
That mine eyes cannot see;
Things that burn at my heart so hot that I know someday
Will be."
Then as my life is ending, for I think I'll feel it come,
I'll know I've seen the last time, the setting of the.
Sun. For I'll have served Your purpose, And Your
work for me......... Is done..

CHAPTER FIVE

BACK HOME AGAIN, THINGS did seem better. Daddy didn't get drunk on the weekends anymore. Oh, he was still angry about his wife and daughters leaving; he was quick to point that out.

"You left me here alone," he'd snarl. "You let the town see that you left me alone. You made me the joke of the town. What kind of woman leaves her husband alone?" Then he'd turn to Shari. "And you, you wanted to go with your mama instead of staying here in your own house with your daddy."

Sometimes his words were even more caustic. He'd tell Mama that he hated her guts. "I'll tell you what, Olive, when these kids are grown up, you're gonna get the hell out, too."

Shari watched Mama when he'd say these things. Even though to look at her, most people wouldn't see how she was affected, Shari could tell that she was.

"Don't worry about it, Shari," Mama would tell her daughter and give her a hug. "Anything's easier to take than his drinking. So long as he's not drinking, he's just talking. We just have to work harder to keep him happy, is all."

And she did, hurrying to run his errands, getting his meals ready on time, fixing him whatever it was he liked, having his place at the table set. No variations were ever allowed.

She'd occasionally mention her problems to her brothers, the children's Uncle Stan and Uncle Tim. Although Daddy wasn't drinking anymore, she confided in them, "Something's not right."

"Get off it, Olive," they chided her. "You've got it easy now. Who cares what he says? It's only words."

"That's right. Sticks and stones..."

"There's no use in complaining now that Cecil is only talking bad." End of story as far as her brothers were concerned.

But that wasn't it at all. What was "not right" was an understanding that Mama whispered to her daughter one night.

"See, Shari, I always thought your daddy was a good man and that the alcohol made him bad. But now he's not drinking, and he seems bad all the time. He doesn't hit me or wreck the house, but he's angry all the time, as though he wishes he could."

Shari mustered the courage to ask Daddy how he'd stopped drinking. She knew he had tried to stop before and couldn't, so what was different this time?

"I got on my knees and I told God; I told him, 'I can't quit drinking by myself. If I just see liquor, I have to have it. But if you, God, will take away the desire for drinking, then I promise I'll never play with it. I won't drink if you'll take away that have-to from me.'"

"What would happen if you did drink one beer?" his daughter quizzed him.

He looked at her seriously. "I figure he'd strike me dead if I did. But He done His part, I don't need the taste anymore, so I'll sure do my part and leave it alone."

A lot of things changed when he stopped drinking. He started reading detective magazines and murder mysteries all the time. He kept stacks and stacks of them all over the house, refusing to part with them even after he'd read them. He and Mama stopped sleeping in the same room, too. They never again shared a bed for the rest of their marriage.

Daddy even changed physically. He aged rapidly, almost overnight. He had trouble with his teeth and his eyes. He suffered strange, ill-defined problems. Mama worried about him, especially after his lumber business burned to the ground, sending $25,000 worth of uninsured lumber up in smoke. He became moody. He brooded for hours at a stretch. He no longer drank liquor, but he still needed an oral fix—coffee, cigarettes, cigars, candy, snacks. These all had to be delivered to him as he sat in his chair, in his corner, in front of the television.

In some ways, he seemed a broken figure, a pitiable man. Shari's feelings about him were ambivalent. She had no illusions about who he had been, but she couldn't help but feel sorry for him and found as many ways as she could to help him, whether by sweeping his office, making concrete tiles, or doing his billing and bookkeeping. She even learned to type so his billings would be neat. It would have been so easy just to condemn him for the ruckus, but it wasn't that simple. In some ways, he was a good man. He had an innocence about him, and he genuinely wished for understanding about a lot of things. The five of them even managed to enjoy many things as a family.

One of Shari's fondest memories was of the time they raised chickens—thousands of them. She loved to gather and crate the eggs. She loved being with the chicks and watching them grow. There was nothing about the whole process that she did not love—from the thousands of tiny yellow chicks stacked to the ceiling of their dining room in their vented boxes when they first arrived, to their growing, to their egg laying. Nobody in the family even minded being kept awake by their constant chirping all night long. They'd pat their fuzzy heads until daybreak, then the men would carry the crates to the big houses prepared for them.

But Daddy suddenly decided that they were getting out of the chicken business. His decision made no sense to Shari. Then again, Daddy was always almost impossible to figure out.

In his younger, drinking days, he occasionally went to his favorite church. When he went, the rest of the family went with him. Although there were other churches the kids liked better in town, there was something special about being able to attend church as a family. But whatever joy there was in being together was abruptly erased by the ushers when they denied Daddy the chance to participate in spiritual communion. Daddy had been drunk the night before, and they considered him unworthy to share in the Lord's supper. They passed the communion plate out of reach over his head.

Daddy never said a word to the ushers or the pastor, but he suffered a pain and humiliation that found a voice on the way home. It almost seemed like a cry for help. Shari knew he was contemplating spiritual matters, because he shared with her a theory he held.

"Listen up, Shari," he said to her as the two sat together on the porch.

"You know, like when Jesus was here on earth, I think He also visits all the other planets as well. He didn't just come to earth, because all the planets matter to Him."

Shari thought his theory was neat, and she enjoyed hearing Daddy tell it. Not that she followed it exactly, not then. Later, she wondered if Daddy had been trying to reach out to her somehow with his strange theory. Was he saying that he felt like an alien, even in his own community? Was he looking for reassurance that God loved him, too, that he mattered?

If only those ushers had realized that her daddy was reaching out for help and that he didn't understand about communion. Perhaps they "missed" other people as well, people like Daddy who were hurting and needed love and forgiveness. Instead, the ushers were nothing more than a reflection of the town's system of moral judgment. The irony in all this was that the head usher was himself a heavy drinker. But he had learned the real lesson about morality in that town: You can be a drinker, even a drunk, but you can't show it in public. Appearances were what mattered. Just like his town and his extended family, his church didn't want Daddy's problems, either.

After that slight, Daddy started attending another church, but eventually his belligerence got the better of Mama, and she refused to accompany him.

"You're a damned worthless fool," he would tell her as she ironed his shirt for services. "Nothing but a damned worthless fool."

Shari was proud of her Mama for not going to church with somebody who'd talk to her like that. But she went with Daddy, and she hoped with all her might that it helped.

Mama loved to attend what she called "real" church, particularly revivals where there was plenty of good preaching and singing. She made sure that the three kids were in vacation Bible school and that they attended church camps in the summers.

Baptist, Methodist, Church of Christ, Assembly of God, it made no difference to Shari. She loved all the camps and outings the same. Preaching, teaching, singing, and praying. These, along with the memorization of Scripture and the pledge to the flag were as much a part of her life as were her Saturday afternoon heroes, Roy Rogers and Gene Autry, who together, represented all that was good and wholesome in life.

While attending a two-week summer camp at age twelve, Shari sat in the upstairs window of her dormitory while all the other girls on the second floor were fast asleep. She enjoyed the solitude of looking out into the night at the stars and trees. Quite unexpectedly, one of the ministers came outdoors, and she recognized him as one of the favorites among all the camp kids.

"What are you doing up there?" he smiled and whispered loudly when he noticed Shari in the window.

"Thinking," she simply and spontaneously replied, enjoying the uniqueness of the moment.

"Thinking about what?" he whispered again.

Although her thoughts were an important part of her life, no one else had ever shown interest in them, so she was glad he asked.

"Of jumping," she immediately responded, knowing that would likely hold his attention and enjoying the twelve-year-old dramatic effect.

"Why don't you come down and tell me about it?" he continued, still respectfully and genuinely curious.

"OK," she replied, enough to confirm their agreement. As she hurried and quietly dressed, she knew she would have to clarify herself. But it seemed well worth the simple, unplanned response—to be invited down by this popular minister, while everyone else was oblivious to anything but their sleep.

When she arrived at the counselor's kitchen, he had hot chocolate made, and she knew that she was indeed privileged! More importantly, this had confirmed his trustworthiness. He was inviting her to talk, and she welcomed the invitation. It seemed to her that someone outside her own town of Clinton was less opposed to discussing her family.

She talked freely of how much she loved the camp, the kids, the counselors, the wiener roasts, the Bible study, and the music service at night around the campfire. She also talked freely about why she dreaded the camp ending and dreaded returning home.

He let her talk and he treated her fairly, impartially, as an equal with anyone else. He seemed concerned about her father's pain and about her mother's dilemma. He explained to her much that she had failed yet to understand about God's plan and Jesus' purpose. They prayed together for God's peace for her family. She knew that God loved her and that Jesus suffered a great deal of pain to demonstrate that love, but she couldn't help but feel a great deal of guilt for His sufferings. Still, this awareness of love and suffering helped her to understand that there was something "out there" worth striving for.

Other lessons were more difficult. The Ten Commandments instructed everyone to honor their mothers and fathers, and it was clearly the case in their town that "good" kids showed their parents both honor and respect. Shari, for the most part, complied with this instruction on the surface so that, for all appearances, she was the model daughter for the model parents. But beneath the careful facade, she was retreating deeper and deeper, expressing her more honest feelings in poems that she would read and reread, only to be confused by them. Yet her poems were her trusted friends, and they brought solace. She longed for love and for meaning, wanting desperately to believe that both existed. She wanted a life to be enjoyed and not just endured.

CHAPTER SIX

SHARI ENJOYED SCHOOL FOR many reasons. She loved reading and learning, so homework was almost always welcome. Certainly it was great to see her friends every day. In junior high, she developed a love for basketball and played first string throughout her remaining school years. As a senior, she won All-District honors at the state playoffs. But her complete lack of positive expectation convinced her that someone had made a mistake in calling her name, so she did not go down to receive the honors. Friends sitting by her urged her to go down and accept the award, saying, "Shari, that's your name," and "They're waiting on you. You gotta go down." Finally, they asked, "Why don't you want to go?"

Sitting high up in the bleachers, she replied, "It's simply a mistake, and I wouldn't think of going down there; it would be too embarrassing to get there only to hear them announce that it's a mistake. Just wait. You'll see."

Later, even her coach was curious. "Why didn't you ever respond to the call for recognition?" he asked. "I was looking forward to seeing you lined up with the others and representing our team. You did a real fine job and it's our honor to be selected All-District."

"I thought it was a mistake. I love playing basketball more than just about anything. But I thought it was a mistake."

Her class would be graduating at the turn of the decade, but ever aware of time's fleeting quality, she decided to accelerate her studies and graduate one year early. She was also, by then, dating a special young man whom she absolutely adored—almost as much as she adored his family. She spent more and more time with them and found herself responding to their love. She and Edd spoke of love and of marriage as they sat on the porch on moon-filled nights. Edd was a delight to be with, since he was funny, sociable, and very pleasant.

"I want you to come with me when I go to college," he said one night.

"To college?"

She had not thought of herself going to college. Much as she loved school, her only ambition was to marry Edd. She looked forward to working as a secretary and had top secretarial skills, and she didn't need to attend college for that. Uncle Stan had already invited her to be an executive secretary in his law office, and she couldn't imagine any job offer to top that. But she couldn't image life without Edd, either.

"Live away from home in a dormitory? Go to classes with you in the day and date you evenings and weekends? Sounds wonderful!"

She graduated high school at sixteen and did, in fact, join Edd at college that year. There she experienced one of the most glorious years of her life. Being so much in love, she almost forgot her earlier philosophy that the only thing to depend on in life is disappointment. She almost forgot that her understanding of love was inevitably and inextricably interwoven with pain and misery. Almost.

Her fears diminished. She felt she had found real sanctuary. Their talks were often about the future—their future. Edd was such a gentle man. He helped his father in the family business of raising cows, calling each one by name. He loved people, loved his family, and loved Shari. He loved life and God. He loved to laugh, and the two laughed together often.

The more she realized how perfect this was, the more she realized it would have a disappointing conclusion. Mama had told her many times that she had loved Daddy when she'd married him. Love would invariably turn sour. It could only endure if abandoned. Then it would be preserved forever. Thus, Shari put Edd through several tests, waiting for him to fail so that when she left, it would be permanent.

They often double-dated with their best friends, Ronnie and Molly. Ronnie had been Edd's best friend for years. Molly was a sophisticated, popular girl, but a dear friend. One evening, when the pair was alone, Shari asked Edd, "Is there anyone else you want to date before we get married? Anybody at all?"

Unguardedly, he laughed and answered, "Yeah, but that would be impossible."

"Really? Who?" She was quite shaken by the answer she'd gotten so quickly, but encouraged him to continue.

"Doesn't matter, I can't date her, ever."

"Of course you can. And you definitely must. Before we would get married, you ought to date anybody you want to, for sure! Who is it?"

"Like I told you, I can't date her—because she's marrying my best friend."

"Oh, you mean Molly?" she blurted out. This was a stunning new discovery. "But she's crazy about Ronnie."

"I know that. That's why I said it would be impossible. But you asked if there was anyone I wanted to date, and that's my answer."

Months later, after Molly and Ronnie were married, Edd and Shari were discussing their future. She inquired, "Where do you think we would want to live? I wouldn't want to stay in Clinton, but we could go to the city. There would be lots of jobs there for both of us, or better still, maybe we could go out of state and be different! What do you think about that?"

"Honey, I rather like Clinton myself. Or if we needed to move to the city to work for a while we could, of course. But I'd hope to return to Clinton in time and settle here. You've gotta be kidding about going out of state."

"But it would be fun. We could see places we've never seen and meet new people and experience new things. Surely you'd like to do that?"

"The main thing I'd like to do is stay close to our friends. I'd never consider moving far from Ronnie and Molly."

The subject subtly evolved into other things, and Shari was quickly realizing that the final exam was almost completed and that her darling Edd was failing. She sensed the loss would be excruciating after these three years of hopeful bliss. But disappointment was familiar, and she was almost eager to return to the familiar reality.

Worse than Shari's doubts about him were her doubts about herself. How could she ever make him happy? Love with him seemed too beautiful, too precious, too meaningful. How could she allow such love to be destroyed by marriage? So, without a word of warning or explanation, she turned her back on him. She traveled two thousand miles cross-country by plane and impetuously married someone she did not love—someone she had never formally dated, someone she did not even respect.

It had happened this way. Her eighteenth birthday was nearing and her summer job was ending when newlyweds Molly and Ronnie invited Shari to visit them in their temporary home in Missouri. It sounded like fun, and her folks were glad to give her this unusual birthday gift. She said goodbye to Edd as she left to visit their best friends for a few days before their next college year was to begin.

Toward the end of that visit, Shari confided in Molly that she already had plans in place to travel on to meet Nat. He lived in Washington State, but he was from their hometown and had been recently drafted into the army. Molly was stunned but did not try to persuade her otherwise. She just offered Shari her coat, which she would need in the cooler, northern state. When Ronnie carried her bags to the car, he gave Shari his angriest expression and no words whatsoever. Shari knew he thought she was deserting his friend. She also knew she could not tell him otherwise. Because Ronnie was a valued friend, that expression saddened her for years to follow.

Molly was also her friend, and in addition to double-dating, they occasionally went to shop in Little Rock since, unlike most kids at that time, Molly always had her own car. It was particularly fun to shop for school clothes. They'd usually first shop for Shari's clothes in the store her parents could afford. Trying on outfits and making selections with Molly's help was enjoyable, for she had good taste in clothes. Afterward, they went to the more extravagant shop to select Molly's clothes, which was an equally rewarding task. Then they'd have lunch in the city before departing for home.

But on one occasion, Molly also decided to purchase a movie camera. From the same shop, Shari bought a record album of her favorite songs from the movie South Pacific. When Shari got home and she and her mother looked over her "loot," Mama was pleased with the school clothes she'd bought and for Shari having stayed within their budgeted amount. Then she showed her the record album.

"How much did the album cost, Shari?" Mama asked.

"It was $5," she replied.

"How could you spend that much money on a record? I'm surprised at you, Shari. That was something you could have done without. Five dollars is entirely too much to spend for a record."

Instinctively, Shari knew she was right. She didn't even feel the need to point out that it wasn't just a record, it was the album from her favorite movie. She just agreed that it was unnecessary, and she felt badly about having bought it.

Later Mama returned to her room and asked, "Did Molly buy an album?"

"Yes. And a movie camera, projector, screen, and film," Shari answered.

Mama laughed softly. "Honey, I'm sorry I fussed at you. Actually, I'm very glad you got the South Pacific album. I liked that movie too, and we'll enjoy those pretty songs. I'm glad you got the album."

Although Shari hadn't fully comprehended it at the time, there was always an understood advantage that Molly had over the other kids. Her family was financially well-to-do compared with the budget-minded families. But she had another presumed advantage as well: she was being reared by her grandparents because her mother had died. That was a unique situation in their town and seemed to set her apart in a somewhat special class of admiration, pity, and mystery—something the other girls in town were unable to fathom. It was also something they couldn't compete with. Molly had a natural sophistication about her that made the girls like her and the boys prefer her. Although she was Shari's friend, those differences were always present.

Shari had another favorite friend with whom no such differences existed. Her name was Linda, and she knew how to make Shari laugh heartily and often over the most trivial things because of her superb wit. She was out with Linda one night, having a hamburger at the local hangout, when Nat had driven up. He was "the older guy" who hung around the malt shop and flirted with the girls and even with some of their mothers. He had a bad reputation in general and was known to allow his own mother to live in substandard conditions while he held lucrative employment out of town. But he was good-looking, drove a shiny car, dressed handsomely, and many of the girls in town wanted to date him.

Shari liked him because he preferred her over many of the other girls in town, particularly Molly. Although Molly was pretty and popular, she had difficulty being a good sport when given less than top billing, and she seldom got less than top billing—except in Nat's interest—among the high school kids.

Nat was very different from Edd. He was known to be a rabble-rouser. He sometimes got into fights with husbands of young women he dated, and occasionally he got arrested for minor offenses, even spending nights or weekends in the town's little jail. But he laughed about these incidents, and that made for exciting conversation among the teenagers. Most of the young crowd admired him for living such an exciting life.

So on that particular day he flirted, visited, and then finally asked Linda and Shari to do him a favor. "Hey, girls, that cop across the street is eyeing my car, and I think he's gonna stop me when I leave here, looking for liquor in my car. I've got a couple opened bottles, and I don't wanna be stopped and put in jail again. Will you girls take these bottles for me now? I'll get them from you later."

Shari squealed, "Heavens no! I don't want any liquor in my daddy's car."

Linda just laughed at the enticing idea. Certainly neither girl drank, nor had any intention of drinking. Nat knew that and was sincerely only asking the favor of them. He persisted.

"Aw, come on, girls. It wouldn't hurt to just lay these in your backseat, on the floorboard just to help me out tonight. Heck, you can throw 'em away if you want to. I'd rather waste 'em as to get arrested, and I know they plan to stop me. You girls have never been arrested, have you?" He knew they hadn't. Again they giggled and weakened. They told him they'd do it just this once and to never ask again.

He opened his door and passed the sack with two bottles into Shari's car. Linda grabbed them and jumped around a little as she placed them on the floor in the back of the car, laughing all the while. Then they watched Nat drive away. Sure enough, the policemen pulled out behind him, and the girls could hardly contain themselves as they sat there wondering whether the police had stopped Nat to check his car for liquor as he suspected they would. They admired how smart he obviously was to think of passing it to them first, fooling the cops when they did stop him.

Soon it was time for Shari to take Linda home and go home herself. But Linda urged, "We just have to drive by the jail and see if Nat's car is parked there, 'cause he would have come back to get his bottles if he could. He must be in jail for something else. We can't go home without finding out. Please, let's!"

Shari was easily persuaded and off they shot toward town, going just slightly out of their normal route home. They drove past the jail and were surprised to see no sign of Nat's car. Even more surprising and disappointing was that the jail, totally darkened, indicated that no one was locked up. They figured they'd have to find out later what had happened to Nat and proceeded to drive toward the lighted part of town when all of a sudden, lights shone on them! First it was car headlights, then red lights on top of the car. The officers had been sitting there in the dark and now were stopping them.

They never got in trouble, and these local officers knew that. They were scared, petrified even. An officer came to each of their windows, shining flashlights inside. Linda started crying with fright as Shari began jabbering, trying to get an explanation out. Being the driver, Shari felt like the responsible party.

"What are you girls doing back here in the dark this late at night?"

"Oh, we just wanted to see if anybody had been arrested before we went home," Shari explained, "and we're on our way home right now. Our folks expect us immediately, so can we leave now? We've just got to get home right away!"

"Well, sure girls, you have to get home and you will soon, but first we need you to step out of the car."

"But why? We just want to go home. Our folks are looking for us right now."

"This won't take but a minute. Each of you step out of the car."

By now, Linda was crying profusely, and Shari's heart was pounding so hard it felt like it could explode. Shari whimpered as she opened the door and stood beside the car. She called out to Linda, "Please don't cry, we'll be home in just a minute. Please don't cry, Linda. It'll be all right."

The officers found the bottles, admonished the two and told them they'd be in contact with their parents because this, they said, "Is a very serious incident. You girls are in deep trouble now."

Shari could barely drive. She was so nervous. But she managed to get Linda to her porch, who wailed loudly as she opened her door to exit. Shari then managed to get home and into bed, praying for a miracle to spare them of their pending scandalous doom.

The next week at school was pure torture, for Linda and Shari harbored a secret so painful that their guilt almost devoured them. They expected to be arrested and escorted from each class they attended. But the days and weeks mounted and eventually they saw Nat. He said the cops told him they figured he'd passed the bottles to them to save his own neck. He laughed when the girls told him of their ordeal. They later learned that their folks had in fact been notified, but they had all laughed about their "lesson."

There were things about Nat that Shari found compellingly familiar. She felt drawn to him almost irresistibly. Being older, he was bossy, and he liked to drink and curse. He would, of course in time, offer her a life almost completely like her mother's, yet Shari wasn't aware of that. She knew how serious his drinking was, but she naively thought she could change him. Yes, she knew she could change him, knew it with all her heart.

Shari's father and her attorney-uncle, Stan, had arranged to have Nat drafted into the army at age twenty-six just to keep him away from her. It would have meant a lot to Shari if her folks had given her permission to date him as she had asked on occasion, but they were adamant, as were most protective parents. When he was eventually stationed in Washington State, he wrote to Shari proclaiming, "I will never, never go back to Clinton to live. Never!"

This was music to her ears. Unlike Edd, who'd failed the test by wanting to stay in Clinton near Molly and Ronnie, Nat passed. She would be free, free at last. A new decade, a new life. A chance to be free.

CHAPTER SEVEN

SHARI AND NAT MARRIED. Edd heard about it from a fellow student while they were watching a school basketball game. He left the game and had a good, long cry. Not long afterwards, Edd married Molly's sister. They settled in Clinton and lived near Molly and Ronnie.

When Nat and Shari first married, they couldn't afford such "luxuries" as canisters and dish drainers. Shari's new husband welded these from iron scraps and presented them to his wife as gifts. They were absolutely beautiful, even as gigantic and heavy and crude as they were. Everything in their home was painted black or olive drab—the only colors of paint the army ever threw away. Once, when Nat brought home a real can opener for the cost of a quarter, Shari cried with joy. The beer openers had worked, but they sometimes cut her fingers.

Soon the couple learned that she was pregnant, and they were thrilled. They made plans to return home for a visit at Christmas to share the news, a Christmas that would mark four months since she'd left home. Four months had seemed like a long time until Shari contemplated a return visit. Husband and wife worried about how the visit would go. After all, there were family issues to reconcile, old boyfriends and girlfriends to confront, and many, many loose ends.

Thankfully, everything was as joyous and forgiving as the holiday season. Both Mama and Daddy had come a long way toward accepting their daughter's marriage. As Nat said years later, "They treated me like a king."

It felt good to be there—but only for a visit. Shari had not lost sight of the fact that she never wanted to live there again, even though she did miss

Mama and Roberta. She even felt a little guilty for being the one who got out. But the three never discussed it, and both mother and sister seemed proud and happy for her.

Shari's first year of marriage was wonderful, even without any material luxuries. She was happy. She was free from the past. She was experiencing new things and becoming an adult. By the end of their first year of marriage, their son was born. Shari was happy to be a mother, taking full advantage of the joys of motherhood. Through her infant son, she learned that love could be warm and soothing and caring and enjoyable. She often continued rocking him in her arms long after he'd fallen asleep, just to have him close, to absorb his innocent love. Aubrey, her son, was only two weeks old when Nat was discharged from the army.

"I want to go back home to show off Aubrey," Shari told her husband, smiling. "But only for a short time."

So once again they headed back to Arkansas. Shari was stunned by her father's offer of a new cottage he had just built. He meant well, and she was grateful, but the warning signs were appearing everywhere: old associates, jealousies, more and more frequent quarrels and accusations. And drinking.

Unfortunately for the nation—perhaps fortunately for Shari, though— the Cuban Missile Crisis occurred. For a short time, it appeared that the United States might enter war with Russia, which at that time was a superpower. As a result of their missiles in Cuba aimed at the U.S., President Kennedy formally announced American intentions to combatively remove them to secure the nation's safety. During that period of time, the U.S. and the world waited to see what Russia would do: Stand firm, or dismantle their missiles?

Meanwhile, U.S. Army Reserve units throughout the country were called into active duty in preparation for combat. Although the family had been discharged from the U.S. army, Nat had just begun serving his army-reserve duty, and his unit was deployed. Shari rejoiced as they packed again to leave Arkansas, convinced that living anywhere away from her hometown had to be better than living there.

They left town, yes, but to a life that bordered on destitution. They lived in Washington, DC, where they shared a single bed with little Aubrey. Shari was pregnant again, and she tried to be patient. There were no visits to the Smithsonian or to the White House or even to the parade to view President and Mrs. Kennedy. There was very little food to eat. Nat's assignment had been "unaccompanied," thus no allowance in pay for a family with him. He ate his meals on base and the few dollars they had went for little Aubrey's baby food.

As the year and Shari's second pregnancy progressed, whatever joy they'd once known was lost. Although they had left Arkansas behind, the ill feelings, mistrust, and disrespect that had taken root there in their lives flourished even in the nation's capital. Physical and verbal altercations became the norm, continuing even until their daughter was born—their breathtakingly beautiful, doll-like little girl. Shari would hold her in her arms and just stare at her.

"How can something so beautiful have come from a marriage so ugly and imperfect?" she'd ask her baby. The infant watched her mother with her beautiful eyes, seeming to communicate that she knew things that Shari could not even imagine.

It was, indeed, an ugly marriage. That realization forced Shari to question herself inwardly, while outwardly she continued to prepare for their inevitable return to Clinton. The additional year of army duty had ended, and Nat was again unwavering in his decision to return home. Even though she knew going home ran contrary to her better judgment, there just didn't seem to be any place else to turn.

They'd left only a year earlier but were returning this time with the fabric of their marriage ruined, with little or no hope and with two babies instead of one. She felt guilty in front of her family for having married so impulsively, and she could no longer pretend that her parents had been wrong. Even if she tried to hide it, the bruises on her face spoke volumes.

Shari was nineteen years old. Nineteen, and the phenomenon of youth had already passed her by. She had completely accepted her husband's assessment of her: "Ugly and stupid." Her world was shrinking. All she cared about were her two babies.

Her husband's philandering didn't bother her in the least. His absence from home was a relief. One morning, a lovely, well- manicured young woman came to their door and asked to speak to Shari.

"I'm so sorry," she said, lowering her eyes. "If I'd have known your husband was married, I'd never have been out with him last night."

Shari told her not to worry. She didn't care about that. What had concerned her more was how defenseless she had been to explain her own appearance or that of her house. The other woman was young and pretty. What could she know about a sleepless night with two babies suffering with fever, vomiting, and diarrhea? Shari was just a few years older than she was. Nonetheless, by the age of twenty, she was an old woman. She was weary and beaten. Her husband, as he repeatedly said, wished her dead.

"It would make my life so much easier," he often said with brutal candor. He had decided to be a preacher, as he had noticed the special attention that preachers in town received. But he felt that as a divorced man, he could never be accepted as a preacher. Only as a widower could he be fully free.

One time he repeated his wish while driving along the highway. Shari had reached the point where she just wanted to stop hearing those words. So she opened the car door and stepped out, as though entering an adjacent room.

Her next conscious moment was waking in a field some distance from the highway. She felt no pain and for a moment considered that maybe she had, in fact, died. Slowly, she dragged her body up to the highway. There sat the car, and there he was, leaning against it, arms folded in disgust. She made her way between the strands of a barb wire fence and trudged to the car. Neither of them spoke a word. She got in. He got in. He started the engine, and they drove on, while their two babies slept peacefully in the backseat.

CHAPTER EIGHT

THE ONLY ISSUE LEFT, the only issue that could seal Shari's fate for good or bad was simply: Does God exist? Does He exist for her? In May of her twenty-first year, she desperately needed to know why love was so painful. Where was God? With these questions burning in her heart, she brought her children with her and visited a church in Madison, Tennessee, a church where she was a stranger to everyone, a church where she could focus her attention on only the message and not on those in the pews around her. The evangelist stood in the pulpit, his Bible raised high as he spoke of the lady who had suffered for so long that she had literally begun to crawl among the feet of others.

"She asked only to touch the hem of Jesus' garment," he proclaimed. "Only the hem, and she knew she would be made whole.

"Busy as He was, with the multitude thronging about Him, the Lord not only noticed this woman but focused His loving attention on her. And you know what? She was healed. That's right, healed."

Shari listened intently, ignoring the tears filling her eyes. She felt both happiness for that woman and a powerful envy. Why did it have to be someone else from another time and place? Why couldn't that healed woman have been her?

The evangelist moved to the piano and began to sing "God Took Away My Yesterdays." As Shari listened to the words and melody, her soul wept. She wanted so very much to have many yesterdays erased. But it seemed totally impossible.

"I know you're hurting," the evangelist said when he was finished. "Jesus knows you're hurting. Won't you come forward? Won't you come forward and accept Jesus into your heart and be made whole?" He called for fathers to come forward to the altar, then mothers, and then young people. Shari wept into the sleeping child she held while her other child slept with his head on her lap.

"Young mother," he boomed, "are you capable of raising your children without God's help?"

She looked up at him. She knew, only too well, how incompetent she was. She had tried to live and could easily have died. She didn't know what else to do. She just didn't. She couldn't do it alone. At that moment a kindly gentleman, without a word, simply lifted Shari's daughter from her and motioned her toward the altar.

She expected nothing but more misery in return. She dropped to her knees at the altar and, covering her face with her hands, cried deeply. She cried because she felt that she was not worthy, that she was inept, that her children were so deserving and yet would receive only misery as their gift from her.

"Do you want your sins to be forgiven and heaven to be your home?" the young minister asked.

Yes, yes! She wanted it so badly! But she kept her face hidden behind her hands. She was sobbing now. She couldn't speak, only nod.

"Then believe!"

She may not have been good at many things, but she was good at following instructions, especially from loud men. She believed—and at that very instant, she understood why Jesus had come to Earth.

In their spiritual discussions, she and Daddy had never gotten that far. They'd always enjoyed Easter sunrise services, but they'd always wondered exactly what it all meant. But at that moment in church, even though she was a stranger among strangers, the answer came to her. She believed. And as she believed, she could feel— actually feel—a transformation occur within her. From the inside to the outside, a smile began to shine forth. Somehow she knew she would never again feel quite as ugly or worthless or stupid. Never again.

In that church, Shari found friends, real friends. They did not teach or preach, they simply lived before her a way of life that she desired, a way of peace. Shari wrote to Mama about these people. Three months later, she visited Mama and told her in person about the things she'd learned.

Mama smiled knowingly. She was not blind to the horror of her daughter's marriage, far from it. She was happy for Shari and for the children, that they'd found a church. "My own strength through all the difficult times has been my faith," she confided.

In the church, Shari met a lady who had recently lost her own daughter who had been, she explained, "About your age." She asked that Shari might become her little girl—"While you're so far away from your home and your own mother." And she did become much like a mother to her. Shari trusted her and loved her. She was the one Shari shared her awful dream with. "It was so vivid, so real," she told her friend. Too real.

"I was at my mother's funeral," she related her dream softly. "It was terrible. I... I didn't know what to do." She couldn't go on with the details. "If anything ever happened to my mother or my children, I couldn't stand it. I just couldn't!"

Her motherly friend touched her hand. "Honey," she said gently, "you never need to worry about that, because you'll never be given more than you're able to bear. You hear me? That's God's own word, so no need to doubt it."

The next day, Shari spoke to Mama on the phone, and they had such a pleasant conversation that she couldn't share her ugly dream with her. Instead they shared a form of Christmas via Mama's details of her preparations and their mutual anticipation.

She mentioned she was making the babies some pretty things. "And I even went to Conway to get a red Tonka truck for Aubrey," she added with delight.

"You drove all the way to Conway?" Her daughter was both surprised and pleased that she would do that for her little boy.

"Of course. You know how he likes red trucks. I just couldn't find one for him here that seemed just right, and I knew that in Conway there were more stores for better selections."

Then she talked about the matching pajamas and gown she was sewing for the kids and the red velvet dress for Cecelia. She continued talking about Christmas and the tree and the ornaments, emphasizing how nice it would be to, "Have the babies here, once again."

"In Mama's new room," Shari whispered to herself, smiling softly, remembering how wonderful Christmas always was at the house. This was one thing they could always count on. As she hung up the phone, she longed to be back home. She couldn't wait for Mama to hold her babies and for them to really visit like they loved to do.

Hearing Mama's voice again had helped to erase the morbid dream that had haunted Shari for days. Now she could turn her attention to the joyful trip home in anticipation of another special family day, which Christmas certainly would be.

EVEN ME

I was alone and scared. I feared each day to meet
The trials it would bring; the fervor of the heat
Of choices I must make and principles to claim
Were far too great a task for me to bear.
I sought to solve my problems all,
But in dismay each time would fall.
I knew that there must be a Greater Power
Somewhere.
My blindness lay in how and where to find
This One so strong. This One I knew deep down inside
Would shield me from all wrong.
I tried to pray and tried to say
The feelings of my heart. But how can any soul portray
What love does not impart?
I only knew that worse I grew and life more dark became.
I realized my unworthiness to even speak His name.
In desperation finally, I thought, O Lord, I'm through.
I want no part of this old world, but I can't get through
To You.
Then, suddenly around me, Believers came to plead,
To pray with me to God above And show Him
My great need For love to dwell within my soul
And Faith to make me whole.
I felt a hand of strong, strong faith, upon my low bowed
head, The word, "Believe," so simple, and yet so
different said.
I saw the darkness turn to light - I felt my soul washed clean.
I felt His love flow through my veins,
I knew what Born did mean.
My shameful tears were washed away, to never more appear
For always now I too, can say, "Jesus My Lord is near."
For through His mercy, by His blood, His own I'll ever be
I praise His name and thank Him still,
For saving, Even me.

May, 1964

CHAPTER NINE

THIS WAS INCONCEIVABLE. ONLY yesterday, Shari had looked forward to this trip back home. She had been wrapping presents, so eager to hug Mama and have her see how her beautiful grand-babies had grown. Now everything had changed. Mama was dead. Shari could hardly fathom one Christmas without Mama, but every Christmas? Every birthday? Every day? Forever?

The ride to Mama's house had been a painfully long one. They didn't get in until early in the morning. Nat dropped Shari off, then took the children to his sister's place where they could get some rest. He never returned to the house, but to his wife, it was just as well. She already had the awful feeling she was among enemies, and she didn't need another one around.

Shari sat in the back room, facing her brother Ellis and their father's sister, Aunt Pearl. She wanted a straight answer from somebody.

"What is it?" she pleaded. "Just tell me what's going on, for heaven's sake."

They told her that Mama hadn't died from a heart attack. She had died from a.38-caliber bullet to the back of her head. "It was suicide, Shari."

A bullet. Suicide. How could that happen? Shari tried to picture the scenario. Mama had fallen down, she figured, and could not get up. She was in excruciating pain and remembered her husband's small, loaded handgun in the desk drawer next to where she lay. She grabbed it and did what she had to in order to extinguish her unbearable pain. Somewhat like shooting a crippled horse to keep it from suffering. Only different. Very different.

Shari felt so cold and lonely, even hungry. Her assumption about Mama's death, which she shared with Ellis and Pearl, was abruptly dismissed. But they offered her no warmth, no nurturing support, no further answers. Shari asked for truthful facts — some explanation of the wild statement they'd just made about how Mama had died. Instead, Ellis' statements were curt and final, while Aunt Pearl concurred immediately, her eyes shifting. All of Shari's questions were ignored.

She finally insisted to be taken to see her, to be with her. Ellis drove his sister to a town forty miles away, where Mama lay very much alone, with Christmas less than one week away, the Christmas she and Shari had planned together so enthusiastically on the telephone mere hours ago.

Ellis dropped Shari off at the mortuary following a lengthy argument that had started when he claimed that Mama had killed herself because of something Robbie had done. Shari knew that was ridiculous and told him so. Ellis became very angry, demanding that she accept his explanation. Shari refused.

When they arrived at the mortuary at three in the morning, he simply let her out at the curb and kept driving. Shari was glad; she didn't want him to be with her. Anyone's presence there would have been an intrusion. She wanted to be with just Mama, alone. The front door of the mortuary was unlocked, but there was no one in sight. As she walked down long corridors, she saw little name plates next to the doors. She stopped when she found her mother's name. Mama was alone, and Shari had never, ever felt so alone in her life as she did at that moment.

Mother and daughter could always talk, just the two of them. After being in a houseful of relatives reluctant to talk, at last Shari found someone comforting to be with and oh, how she needed that!

Mama looked so very beautiful; Shari couldn't help but smile because she looked so pretty and peaceful, even angelic. She felt her shiny, black hair that had no hint of gray and traced the line of her high cheekbones. It helped to kiss her and tell her once again, "I love you Mama, let's talk."

She easily found the wound, behind her left ear. She did not ask why. She wanted only to know who. Gazing at her body, she noticed dark spots that marred her arms beneath the shawl she'd been wrapped in. Shari knew that Mama hated shawls and never owned one. When the mortician came in, introduced himself and asked if she needed anything, she looked directly at him. "Does a deceased person turn dark on their arms first?"

He frowned and then in the heavy, sorrow-filled voice his business demanded, he simply said, "Bruises, those are bruises." He didn't need to say anything more. Shari suddenly knew everything.

"Oh, Mama," she cried. "Oh, Mama." Then she chuckled softly through quiet tears. This seemed like a repetition of an earlier time.

"He can do anything, can't he, Mama?" But there was strength for her there in the room alone with her sweet mother, for she looked strong and confident and radiant.

Two days later at the church for her funeral, Mama still had not lost any of that radiance. She was finally free. But Shari was now drawn into the most ghastly of webs.

For two days, she wandered through the house — her childhood home — weaving through clutches of people who provided no comfort. All of them were her father's relatives. Her mother's relatives were nowhere to be found. And none of her father's relatives were asking any questions.

At some point, a young minister and his wife, friends of Shari, came to the house. They tried to speak with her privately. They moved from room to room, but they were never allowed privacy. Always, Shari's father appeared wherever they were, standing in the doorway, leaning to one side, his glassy eyes glaring. He controlled the house, the entrances and exits. An image of her childhood red table and chair crashing down the stairs to the basement flashed before her eyes. Mama had stood silently, helplessly, watching Daddy then, as young Shari had screamed while unsuccessfully trying to wrestle each piece away from him. Now she felt silently helpless too – no point in screaming or trying to resist.

Yes, he was in control, but he couldn't control her mind. Shari knew this was no suicide. Her mother's words from a decade earlier echoed through her thoughts. Mama had warned her daughter that he would kill her, and then she would have to watch out for herself. But only if he ever drank again. Had he drunk liquor again, after thirteen years?

She went through the motions of comforting Daddy. She knew she was being watched and was aware that much — including her very survival — depended on her ability to act the role that had been thrust upon her.

Roberta, her little sister, had just turned seventeen the day before. The remains of the birthday cake Mama had baked for her were still on the kitchen table. Robbie was having a horrible time. She didn't have the emotional strength to deal with the situation. Both she and her young husband were too distraught.

Shari kept thinking about her argument with Ellis on the way to the funeral parlor. He had been so content with, even adamant about, his pat little theory. How dare Ellis and Aunt Pearl say Mama killed herself because of Robbie! Mama was thrilled about Robbie, her boyfriend, and their engagement. If they had gotten married secretly, Mama would have loved it. If Robbie was pregnant, Mama would have been making baby clothes for more than just Shari's babies. How dare they say something so cruel and incredibly ridiculous!

Ironically, it had been Ellis and Shari, not Robbie, who had given their parents problems. Both had even run away from home. Ellis simply disappeared one summer, and the family later learned that he was living in Wisconsin where he'd gotten a job. Shari had run away to get married. Robbie was the only one of the three children who had never caused any problems of any kind. On the contrary, she was a tremendous help around the house. Something of a Ms. Fix-It, she had repaired all of Mama's broken-down appliances, her sewing machine, the lawn mower. *An interesting twist,* thought Shari, *to blame the most innocent, the most vulnerable.*

Shari tried to be a mother to Robbie, but she couldn't be what her little sister needed. She couldn't even be what she herself needed. On the morning of the funeral, Roberta locked herself in the bathroom. Shari's husband and brother stood outside the door, yelling at her angrily. "Get the hell out here!" Ellis shouted. "Dammit, what are you gonna do, stay in there all day and miss Mama's funeral?"

"What's going on?" Shari demanded as she walked into the scene.

"Stupid fool found the casing of the.38 shell," her brother replied. He turned back to the locked door. "Give it here, Roberta. Dammit, turn it over!"

"If she wants it, let her have it!" Shari said. "If it helps her, then you leave her alone!"

"Shut up," he snapped.

Shari turned to the locked door. "Robbie, honey, you keep that ol' shell if you want to. It's yours if you want it."

A short time later, she came out, but she was still inconsolable. And how could she not be? She had been living at home with Mama up to the last morning. Worse, she'd been made to believe that she was the cause of Mama's "killing herself," that her secret marriage and pregnancy had driven Mama to suicide. They'd made her a convenient scapegoat, but Shari knew it wasn't true. She just hadn't fully figured out who "they" were, and she didn't know what to do about it, because she was quickly becoming so scared of "them" herself.

She tried to remember what Mama had told her — to be very, very careful. So she tried to think only about her babies. She knew Mama would have wanted her to do that. But she also knew that someday, somehow she would show Roberta that whatever happened here, it had nothing to do with her.

"You're all crazy, the whole lot of you," Shari's husband stated with a disgusted laugh. Apparently they were too crazy for him to even bother showing his final respects. He dropped his wife off at the church and then drove back to Kentucky, with Christmas three days away.

Although Shari was relieved he was gone, since he had only added to her pain, she nevertheless felt her own aloneness, greatly. Shari welcomed the gesture when the governor himself escorted her from her mother's grave as the casket was lowered.

(Although the whole family knew that the governor was a close friend to Uncle Stan, he had been at Uncle Stan's house with Shari's aunts and uncles no doubt for another reason... to help Stan 'contain them' with the story they were given. "Everyone knows Cecil killed Olive, but the kids don't want their dad going to prison; so for their sake, we're keeping a lid on things, keeping it quiet, no big investigation that would lead to Cecil's conviction....").

The governor's presence at Mama's funeral helped to divert attention away from her, from who killed her, and from other probing questions. All eyes were on the governor. Some folks got to shake his hand.

Mama's funeral was turned into a political event.

Sure enough and all too soon, the governor was pulled away from Shari as they walked because a preacher, of all people, desperately needed the honor, at that specific moment, of meeting the governor. Then a relative from her father's side insisted she return to the gravesite, and she found herself alone again.

After the funeral, they entered a surreal existence. For three weeks Shari remained in the house with her children, Robbie, Robbie's husband, Ellis, and Daddy. Of course, Daddy expected his meals to be as regular as clockwork. He *never spoke a word* about Mama's death—as if nothing had happened—nor did anyone else. Although it was the Christmas holidays and everyone was home, none of Shari's schoolmates called or visited. She figured they must believe Ellis' theory and were ashamed of Mama, or ashamed of Shari, or both. Her former school principal did stop by, and she appreciated that greatly.

Shari and her babies slept in Mama's room. Often she'd awaken in the middle of the night and look up to find Daddy standing, silent in the doorway, watching. Wanting both to divert his thoughts — whatever they were — and to get him away from her babies, she would jump up and go cook him something to eat. He always followed her and sat at the table as she cooked. Then he ate quietly. They seldom talked, and when they did, it was never about Mama. No mention of Mama, in her home, with her things everywhere.

Aunt Pearl harshly criticized Shari for questioning the simple explanation of suicide the relatives had given. She told Shari it was her fault, not only hers but her sister's and brother's, too. She said they were horrible children who had driven her to suicide. The accusation was painful, and on some level, Shari did feel guilty. She was the one who had upset Mama by running away and marrying the town outcast. Yet Mama had accepted it so well. And why were the velvet garments she was making Shari's children for Christmas still on the sewing machine if she hated her daughter for running away and marrying a bum four years earlier?

She thought back to an event Mama had shared with her about that 'jolt' Shari gave them when she got married and went to live way off in Washington. Mama had immediately put her picture and an article about the wedding in the County Paper for all to see. Right away, she said, one lady in town stopped her.

"Olive, I happen to be familiar with Washington state law and I know they have a three-day waiting period there before anyone can get married.

Your article gave Shari's wedding date as September 6, near Labor Day, and I know she didn't actually get married then, because the courthouse would be closed."

"And your point in stopping me is...?" Mama asked.

"Well, I wanted you to know Shari didn't really get married so soon after she went to Washington as she told you she did."

Mama replied without hesitating. "Oh, so you're suggesting that Shari was living in sin a few days before she married? Is this what you're going to all this trouble for?"

"Well, you need to know that she lied to you."

"What really interests me, Carey, is that you of all people would stop me for such a silly reason, when the whole town knows that your daughter was five months pregnant when she walked down the aisle in her white gown."

The woman left abruptly.

Shari had her marriage certificate with her when she and her new husband first visited her parents, but Mama wasn't interested in it one way or another. She loathed such pettiness. She only wanted her daughter to be happy. Don't all mothers want that for their children?

Yes, Shari figured she was guilty, but certainly not of offending Mama, she realized as her aunt rambled on. She was guilty of asking questions. She questioned the only version anyone ever uttered about Mama's death. She knew her mother too well to accept their contrived story. She had her letters, and she had just spoken with her. She saw the bruises on her arms. Daddy's people never asked a question. They were prosecutor, judge, and jury. Their verdict was direct, to the point, and final: Suicide. It was as though that one word was sufficient and settled everything.

Shari was told later that Daddy had made the pronouncement of suicide to the very first people who had arrived at the house the afternoon she died, and he had instructed the mortician to embalm her immediately. He had people clean the house. He had a repairman come fix the stove that had been knocked loose from the wall the day Mama died sometime after Robbie and her girlfriend had left for school in the morning. No one asked any questions. There were no investigators, no officials.

No one but Shari.

People treated her as though she was the criminal, simply because she wanted to know what *really* happened to her mother. After leaving Daddy's house, which is how she came to regard the place after Mama died, she and her babies returned to their trailer park in Kentucky. Away from home again, she became consumed with her memories, fears, and nagging guilt — so much so that she grew negligent. One day, her children were napping in the back of the trailer home, and Shari had fallen asleep on the couch in front. She was awakened by a pounding on the front door. She went to the door, opened it, and a man rushed past her and went directly to the wall furnace.

"This is about to explode!" he screamed, having seen the heavy black smoke hurtling out the chimney. "Get out!"

Shari grabbed her babies and ran out, leaving him to regulate the furnace and prevent a real disaster. She never knew who this man was, and after he left, she never saw him again. She could think of him only as an angel sent by God to protect her and her children. She liked angels.

After that, she worked hard to pay attention to the world around her, even as her inner thoughts and memories swirled faster and faster. Mama was always with her. So were Shari's questions: What really happened that awful day? And why? Were her questions and suspicions outrageous? Was she wrong to want to know what had happened? To need, desperately need, to know? Why had all relatives, all classmates, all lifelong friends, rejected her?

About a month after they'd returned to Kentucky, her father along with her sister and her husband came to visit. When Daddy and Shari were alone in one of the rooms, he abruptly shifted the conversation. "We had a long kiss," he said, waving his hand and arm dramatically. "A long, long kiss on that last day. Our teeth got in the way and we laughed about it." He lowered his eyes to hers. "We laughed."

Shari stared at him. Daddy was anything but dramatic, and to see this performance shocked her. She knew he was lying. Or else, at that moment he did not know who she was, because if he did, he'd have known that she knew better. She knew that for Mama and Daddy, romance was nonexistent and had been for years and years. Even common courtesy was nonexistent. More to the point, Shari had been told that Mama's false teeth had come out of her mouth because of the impact of the.38 — not from some kiss she'd shared with her husband. Did this torment amuse him?

She felt a tremor run through her body. "We'd better get back to the others," she said, suddenly frightened to be with this man, this man whom she had always feared but had never before seen as such a stranger.

In the pit of her being, she also felt fear for Roberta. Shari knew that she and her husband would be returning with him to that house, his house. She also knew that she would not be returning to school. Yes, her dear little sister had broken the rules. Married girls were not allowed in school, and she had gotten married. Their hometown was 'proper,'... rule conscious... "right and wrong" oriented. So concerned with appearances. No one seemed to be overly concerned about wife beating, or even murder. Those rules, broken in one's own home, apparently were made to be broken. But none of the rules could be broken in public. And now Roberta would be in that house with him... every day.

"I'm worried for you," Shari confided in her sister. "Something's wrong with Daddy. Please be careful — very, very careful." Robbie told her that she was having a lot of morning sickness and that sometimes in the bathroom as she vomited, Daddy would be cursing her. Once she had checked into a motel room in near hysteria, needing to be out of that house. Daddy tracked her down at the motel and told her to kill herself, too. Shari found it difficult to bear. At a time when her little sister needed most to be with her friends and stay busy, she was separated from them and stuck in a nightmare — at the death scene, with the killer.

Yet there were times when Shari felt guilty to assume something so horrible about Daddy when there wasn't proof. She told her father, "It may have been someone passing the house who came in to rob it and wound up killing Mama. We need to find out." She wanted to know for sure so she wouldn't be guilty of playing judge and jury herself, as these people had done with Mama. But there would be no proof if there were no investigation and no questions, would there? She felt sure she couldn't live with that situation. That would be more than she could bear: to never know and never try to find out.

She remembered her friend's words: "There will never be more than you're able to bear" (1 Cor. 10:13). And she remembered Jesus' words too: "You shall know the truth and the truth shall set you free" (John 8:32).

"Oh, Jesus," she prayed, "how I want that truth and how I want to be free." Dr. Martin Luther King, Jr., had made famous the phrase, "Free at last, free at last, thank God Almighty, I'm free at last." Shari realized that was becoming her life's purpose — to find that truth that would make her free at last.

When her visitors left, the telephone calls started again. The jeering, mocking telephone calls. They'd begun the evening after Mama's funeral. Always a female voice. "Can I speak with Olive?" she'd ask.

"Who's calling please?" Shari would reply.

"I'd like to speak with Olive, with Olive, with your mama."

The first couple of calls, she had tried to explain that Mama was dead and that the family had just come from her funeral.

"Your mother, your mother. I want to speak to your mother." Shari would hang up in despair. When the calls continued, she had the telephone company put a trace on them, and the calls stopped. But they started again a little later, reaching her at her home in Kentucky. And there were also the mysterious "cousins" whom Daddy began visiting often, cousins who had become suddenly so important to him, but whom even his own mother did not know. Everything started to get more and more strange, really a continuation of the bizarre events that had begun during those weeks Shari stayed in Clinton after Mama's death.

One morning, during Daddy's visit, he was standing by the kitchen stove about to pour a cup of coffee when he made reference to the car mistakenly as "the murder." He paused, "I mean, the motor," he corrected. And he grinned, broadly.

There were also the footprints, the large, heavy footprints Shari would find on Mama's grave when she would visit, footprints with cigar ashes sprinkled around them. So many questions, yet she had no way of addressing them, no way of searching for answers.

CHAPTER TEN

A FEW MONTHS LATER, Shari, her husband, and their children relocated to a small town in Arkansas. She watched the newspaper for any upcoming event at which the governor would be present, because she greatly desired to speak with him. She had only to approach his aides, say, "Stan Deeven's niece wants to speak with him," and she would be permitted. She remembered the numerous times during her teenage years when she took her school friends to his office in the capitol building so that they could meet him or even have their pictures taken with him. Her own senior graduation invitations had been typed on his typewriter, which typed in gold cursive. These had been special privileges, because her Uncle Stan had friends in high places. Now, she desired to see this particular friend in a high position for another, distinctive reason.

One day, she realized her wish! Shari read the article naming an event at which Governor Faubus would be present, and it was not too far away for her to attend with her children. She carefully planned ahead for this date, telling no one of her intentions. There, after his public speech, she had an opportunity to speak with him privately. She explained to him how disturbing it was to her that months were now passing and no investigation had taken place.

"I know that by law a person is supposed to be innocent until proven guilty, yet someone said my mother committed suicide. No investigation at all has occurred, and there is ample proof to the contrary. This is tormenting for me to live with," she explained.

Indeed, every time she heard the word suicide or saw the stares of contempt on the faces of the people who had supposedly been her friends, she longed for Mama to be free of that unfair label. She told the governor, "The coroner told my sister and me that it was definitely not suicide, that he knew she did not use such a gun to shoot herself in the head from such an angle, because he knew of her arthritic condition. He told us emphatically, Governor, that she was definitely not depressed in any way and that this was no suicide, but actually it was the most blatant murder he had ever seen. He even pointed out to us that if she had wanted to die, she easily could have killed herself with her insulin needle."

The governor just shook his head.

"So why did it go down as suicide?" she asked.

"Since the local sheriff chose not to investigate, the only way I could have the state investigate it is if you accuse someone.... directly," the governor said.

She had to accuse her own father! The thought was overwhelming.

He continued, "Since there was no evidence of suicide, the death certificate can never state suicide, but can only read 'assumed suicide.'"

That was little consolation to Shari. "Can I accuse my father?" she blurted out. "Can I?"

The governor went on to inform her as to the consequences should her father be investigated and convicted, saying, "He would be given a term of seven years and would be released in three years. Are you willing to assume this responsibility — for the responsibility would be fully on you?"

Her mother had been killed, and she was the only one asking questions. Now she was being told that the responsibility would be all hers. What sense did that make? Fair or unfair, she nonetheless felt like a coward, because she knew she wasn't willing to take that responsibility, not with two small children who needed her.

Meanwhile, her sister's baby was stillborn, and after the delivery Robbie's life was seriously in jeopardy. That became the higher priority. Shari rushed to the hospital to see her and beg her to live. She prayed to God and to Mama. "Let this little girl live! Let something make sense and let somebody survive!" Robbie's will to live had sunk very low because of her own inner torment. She had been a convenient target for the calculating thinkers to blame for their mother's 'suicide.' All these intervening months, Shari knew the baby she carried had little chance.

She breathed a sigh of relief when Robbie and her husband Chuck finally left Daddy's "house of horror" and found their own little apartment. It was a cute apartment, very private and hopefully a refuge of sorts from the hell Robbie had been experiencing the past months. While her sister recovered in the hospital, Shari tried to fix up the apartment with bright, pretty decorations for her homecoming. She returned frequently to the hospital to try to encourage her.

After Robbie had been informed that her baby was stillborn, she made one request of Shari. Wild horses could not have prevented her from granting her sister's wish. Robbie wanted to be sure her baby was OK. "Shari, they won't let me see him. They're going to bury him and I'll never know if he's OK or not. Will you go to see him, please?"

Shari assured her that she would, in fact, see that child of hers. She rushed from the hospital to the mortuary to view him (the same mortuary where, less than a year ago, she had spent the early morning hours with Mama). *If I have to dig him up, I will see that baby,* she thought. At first the funeral parlor personnel tried to prevent her from seeing him, saying, "It isn't proper; he isn't dressed yet." They soon found they had no choice, however, and directed Shari to his room.

There lay a beautiful baby boy. She cried at seeing her first nephew, who would join his grandmother in heaven rather than enter the family's hell on earth. Sad as it was, she wondered whether he was better off. Now her sister could rest in the assurance that her firstborn was OK as they buried him to rest a few feet away from Mama's recent grave.

Weeks and then months went by. Shari continued to ponder the governor's proposition. Could she openly accuse her father of murder? Was this the only way to acquire the courtesy and dignity of an investigation into her mother's death? The rippling effect of that deprivation was so great and grew greater with each passing day. Yet Mama's own words from years earlier came back to warn her: "Be very careful, or you could be next."

My mother lives in heaven now, but she's not alone up there
For all the saints of glory now meet her every care.
She walks and talks with Jesus, the way 'twas meant to be
And often I am sure I feel them both smile down on me.
Ah, yes, saints miss their children, left down here on this
earth
And Jesus understands it well, for they gave us our birth.
But in all His great wisdom, of things mighty and small
He worked it out in His perfect plan, for comfort to us all.
He knew there would be children left
And mothers left as well,
When He would call some loved ones home,
To ever with Him dwell.
But for each child in heaven now, there is a mother, too
And for you mothers left alone, on earth because your
child Is gone, there's someone needing You.

CHAPTER ELEVEN

LATER THAT YEAR, NAT and Shari were informed that Aubrey had a serious speech problem and would be unable to start school because the teachers could not understand him when he spoke. Because she could understand him, Shari had never realized that his speech impediment was serious. She made inquiries into speech therapy, only to learn that no speech therapy would be available in their state for at least two years.

Her good friend, Dixie, however, informed her of a program in Nashville, Tennessee. She asked her friend to enroll her son immediately. Excitedly, she told her husband the good news, that there was an opportunity for the imperative treatment in Nashville. But he said they couldn't relocate. Why? Because he did not wish to relocate. Having lived in Nashville recently, they well knew that his construction work was plentiful and he could resume his former position at any time. Again, she heard priorities arranging themselves. Her husband stayed firm on the matter, saying, "End of discussion." Aubrey's need for speech therapy meant absolutely nothing to Nat.

When he left for work the next day, she packed their car and drove the two children to Nashville, where they stayed with Dixie and her family and put the children in speech therapy. The speech instructor explained that the problem was partly emotional and that she was overly protective of her children. Little wonder! Her fears were spilling over onto them.

The doctors clipped Aubrey's tongue, freeing him from a tongue-tied condition, and he responded well to the therapy. Cecelia spoke his language also, but she had just learned it from him, because they were so close. Nevertheless she, too, had to relearn the English language. Shari was grateful for the speech center. Eventually, her husband reluctantly transferred his job and joined his family in Nashville.

It turned out to be a wonderful year, being back among good friends and in their own good church. There, Shari's questions and suspicions were welcomed and discussed respectfully. She found long-delayed comfort. But it was also there that Aubrey, now five years old and in kindergarten, fainted for the first time. It was seemingly insignificant at the time. A little girl had pulled a tooth, it bled, and he fainted. Yet he continued to faint on similar occasions until he moved into adulthood. Little did Shari know then that mother and son both were carrying emotional baggage from their "bloody nightmare years." As an infant, Aubrey had watched his father beat his mother, heard her screams and saw the blood. Being too young to have a clearly defined separate identity, he was incorporating his mother's fearful experience. Later, the mere sight of blood reactivated that intense fear, though he had no conscious memory of the events themselves. Fainting is an unconscious way to avoid re-experiencing the painful, emotional intensity. When a person uses this emotional defense, the system simply 'shuts down.'

Around that same time, Robbie and Shari visited Aunt Faye, their mother's sister who lived alone in her apartment in Little Rock. Her attitude was not like that of the other relatives. She spoke openly, clearly suffering with the young women in grief for their mom, her sister. "I loved Olive, and I love her kids," she spoke tearfully but with conviction. "I told Stan and the others that I'd never go to your dad's house, because I have no use for him whatsoever. Nor would I ever go to you kids and start anything. But you girls are welcome at my house anytime, and I'm glad to tell you anything I know about your mother."

She was consoling in that she didn't shush them up. Heavyset and pretty, she looked something like Mama. She had always had a fabulous sense of humor, and together they had laughed a lot. Her black hair had grayed and was now beautifully salt-and-pepper. They all marveled that Mama had never had a gray hair her entire lifetime, although her lifetime had been limited to her fiftieth birthday. "I spent Thanksgiving Day with Olive, and the tension at that dinner table could be cut with a knife," Aunt Faye said.

"Olive and I drove down to look at the lake, where we could be sure Cecil wouldn't sneak around and try to listen. Girls, we made our plans that day, and it meant a lot to both of us. You see, your folks were just about to be divorced, because Olive had had her fill of your dad. He was making more and more demands on her and talking meaner all the time. She'd said now that Robbie was about to be settled with a good husband, she had no more reason to put up with Cecil and didn't intend to. She was looking forward to telling you about her plans during Christmas, Shari."

"I know," Shari replied. "She hinted some over the phone the last time we talked, but I thought Daddy might have come in, when she turned the conversation back to Christmas."

Aunt Faye shook her head. "Yeah, he sure ruled everything in that house, even the conversations. But that was about to end. The last time he told her that she would have to clear out — like he loved to do, as you know — she surprised him. She told him she certainly was clearing out and would take her half with her when she went. She referred to Rev. Billy Graham's perspective in telling Cecil, 'I've lived with you thirty years, we've raised three children in this marriage, and what we own is equally shared.'

"Yeah, Olive told 'ol Cecil that she had sure earned her half. She told me that he turned as white as the cook stove she was standing by when he heard that."

The trio talked about a lot of things — old times, Shari's babies, Aunt Faye's grandson, and Robbie's loss and sadness. The sisters returned for more visits with Aunt Faye, because they loved her and because they were welcome at her house, and because she would talk with them as no other relative would.

"Your mom and I were going to share my apartment and we would have had a blast," she said, her voice drifting off. "Stan would get her a job at the capitol building too, and we'd walk there together. We had laughed about the fact that she could drive and sew, whereas I can't do either, so we knew it would be fun being together." Aunt Faye really loved Mama.

Shari remembered her coming to their house through the years when Mama would have to be hospitalized. Her first two babies had died – she'd had miscarriages – and the surviving three siblings had been born Caesarean. So much damage was done to her stomach from pregnancy complications that she'd endured numerous surgeries, but Daddy's beatings had exacerbated the natural problems until the doctors had to 'pack' her stomach, years ago. Mama equated this packing, to 'screen wire.'

"My stomach is held together by screen wire," she had said. She couldn't buy store bought dresses anymore because of the resulting disproportion. She had a lady in town make them for her. As Shari got older, whenever she wanted to buy her mother a pretty dress, she just bought her the pretty yardage with matching thread and matching purse and she'd have it made.

Aunt Faye well knew what Daddy's beatings had done to Mama, so when she came to cook their meals, clean house and take care of the kids while Mama was in the hospital, she also protected Mama from Daddy until she fully recovered and regained her strength. Yes, she knew Daddy, and it was no wonder that she cared so little for him. Shari still remembered how her aunt would stand up to him, cuss back and hold the broom like it was a baseball bat, threatening, "You try and hit her again and I'll kill you, Cecil," while Mama was bedridden, recuperating from surgery. She had done more than just cook meals for them by the time Mama came home from the hospital.

"But Faye, why didn't they arrest Daddy?" the nieces asked. "We wouldn't have cared if he'd gone to prison, and he should have. Why in the world did it go down as suicide?"

"Girls, your Uncle Stan felt it was best for you kids not to lose your daddy, too. He said it wouldn't bring Olive back, and you kids had lost one parent, no use in making you lose both. I would rather that he'd gone to prison myself, though, and with Stan the warden there, maybe it wouldn't be a pleasant stay for him."

Shari was groping for answers. "Do you think Stan just didn't want to see Daddy in his prison every day?" she pressed.

"I don't know. All I do know is that Stan said, 'For the kids' sake, we won't press the issue and arrest Cecil, for the kids' sake.'" Everyone clearly knew that local law was regulated by Uncle Stan via his proximity to the governor.

But that wasn't a good enough answer for Shari. "But Faye, it isn't helping; it's hurting. I've begged Stan to investigate it and bring out the truth. I've begged the governor. How can it be for our sakes when what we need is the truth brought out?"

Aunt Faye shrugged. "Well, Stan just told us this is the decision and we were to abide by it. I told him I wouldn't go to y'all, but if you came to me, as you're doing, that I'd tell you anything you wanted to know. You're my sister's girls, and I loved her and I love you. If it were turned around, she would do the same for my child." There it was: Aunt Faye was living the Golden Rule. Had everyone else forgotten it?

Yes, it was good to be back. Their visits with Aunt Faye brought them closer to Mama again — and closer to normalcy, being able to talk freely.

But Uncle Stan and his wife, Begonia, kept telling Shari not to talk to Faye because it would worry her, just as they didn't want her to mention Mama to them, because it would worry them.

"But Stan, Faye says she doesn't mind talking about Mama because she loved her and loves us and we all like to talk about her," she protested.

They never really listened to what she was saying, though. And when Aunt Faye, in her mid-forties, suddenly fell over dead one night alone in her apartment, Shari got the blame. "Just as we told you, you caused her to die. You talked to her and worried her until she had a heart attack and died. Now don't talk to anyone else or you'll cause them to die too!"

They had been right after all, and now her guilt was that much worse. And she missed Faye terribly, and there was no longer anyone to talk with about her mother. The guilt and grief were a heavy combination as she went to Aunt Faye's funeral under the glares of contempt from so many people who were supposed to be family.

Today I feel the loss - Oh God, how great the cost
Of being real and choosing still to live amidst reproach.
My heart dictates two statutes, Lord, to go and do Thy will
Despite all obstacles that come, despite all else, prevail.
Yet also Lord, my spirit tires, my body aches as well
And deep within my heart a wish to be accepted, still
The frowns I know whence cometh, the icy attitudes...
Chiding all my words and deeds, confused distrust exudes
My flesh is weak I'm finding Lord, and growing weaker, yet
My spirit thrives and ever strives to never dare forget
From Whom cometh my strength, from Whom cometh all good
And Who allows all life's events, though by me, not understood.
So please, take all my weariness of spirit and of flesh Please
take my discouragement of things present and past. And give
me rest at last, Dear Lord, there's none outside of Thee,
The peace You give no man can take, Bestow Thy peace on me.

CHAPTER TWELVE

EVERYONE REJOICED WHEN, ONE year later, Roberta gave birth to little Ken. She and her young husband, Chuck, were certainly deserving of good things and had waited for so long; maybe now their turn had finally come.

Meanwhile, Shari continued to consider Governor Faubus' proposition that she could perhaps be granted the investigation into Mama's death if she would assume full responsibility for demanding it by accusing someone of murder. She also enrolled part-time at the University of Arkansas. She was hoping that this new endeavor would somehow make her tough decision easier. Maybe in school she would find answers to her mounting questions, and those answers might bring some comfort.

She remembered how much she had loved school from elementary throughout high school and even during the brief one year of college. School seemed friendly. School also promised a better life than what she had, if she could succeed at it, and she needed to succeed at something. Nat was away from home most of the time, and she never really knew what his life and activities consisted of. She'd carefully saved her money, and when she had collected thirty dollars, she approached the college dean, inquiring whether this would be sufficient to enroll. The meeting itself was somewhat embarrassing, because he asked her age. When she answered, he noted, "We're the same age, yet I am dean of a college and you are trying to enroll on thirty dollars." She knew she looked drab, in clothes and persona, but neither seemed to matter at that moment.

Her nerves were taut from the frightful melee of trying to avoid her dad and the fear he could invoke in her with so little effort on his part. The phone often woke her in the middle of the night. Dad would say, "I'm coming down to get you and the kids." She didn't know what he meant by that phrase, but it was extremely frightening.

She'd say, "Now, Daddy, it's late and the kids are little and are sleeping. Let's wait till morning or till this weekend and we'll visit then."

Sometimes he'd say he wasn't far away, and she wondered just how near he might be. Shari would keep the lights off so that it would be possible to look outside without being seen. Once, in near hysteria, she telephoned a teacher from the college she had started to attend. "Is there anything to do besides wait and pray?" She didn't get the answer she was searching for, but with all of the mental, emotional, physical, and spiritual exhaustion, she did eventually get to sleep... that night. Sleep was rare and usually disturbed. She often had dreams of Alfred Hitchcock, to which she would awaken in a fit of both laughter and tears; subconsciously she was seeing her entire family as characters in one of his hideous dramas. Through it all she kept asking: "Where does it end? And where did it all really begin?"

It was not unusual for her to spend several hours a week in the library, her children remaining occupied in a corner or on a pillow, while she read and researched any related topic that might bring some small measure of peace. It all seemed so wrong, so unfair, so cruel. Somebody should have done something so that, in death, her mother could at least have the dignity she deserved. But no one was doing anything. It seemed over and forgotten for everyone. Except for her.

Mama had been "convicted" without a trial. The official conclusion of suicide went completely unchallenged. It was as if she had been lynched in broad daylight and the vigilantes were making it an extended joke by calling it a suicide. To make a ruling on a suspicious death without any sort of a formal inquiry was barbaric. To decisively call it suicide in the absence of any facts was unconscionable.

For Shari, there was another serious question at stake. How was she to treat her father? And was she already convicting him in her mind, before he was proven guilty? That would be equally barbarous and cruel. Maybe so, but she felt surrounded. She viewed her hometown as being ruled by a pack of barbarians. They didn't even care if she and her sister suffered terribly—as long as they suffered in silence. It was just like the town's unwritten rule for Daddy's drunkenness and his beatings of Mama: Do it in private, out of public view, and everything will be just fine. The public never wanted to be bothered with their problems.

But if her brother Ellis and the rest of the town were willing to close their eyes, she and her sister weren't. Not because they were so noble, but because they simply couldn't let a lie pass for the truth. And because they loved their Mama too much. The facts seemed to show quite clearly that their mother had been murdered. What kind of children would they be if they just stayed silent and let a murderer walk free? Something simply had to be done! But what? How can a grieving daughter persuade the powerful men to do their jobs?

She looked at her two small children, so beautiful, healthy, innocent, young, and unknowing. She vividly recalled how Mama had taken so much pain herself because she loved her children. And remembering Mama's warnings of her own possible death, she certainly didn't want to invite her sudden destiny. Shari wanted to stay alive to rear her children, too. She could not accuse anyone — not openly, publicly. She could only wonder and suspect.

During the ensuing weeks, Shari's husband became good friends with her father. Her fear of both of them escalated. Her husband began leaving horrid little notes in their kitchen and bedroom drawers: "Shari disappointed her mother," they'd read, referring to her marrying at eighteen. Her guilt increased tremendously, and Nat knew it.

The visits with her father were as scary as his late-night calls, which continued, making every evening a dreaded event. Shari's paranoia mounted. When she walked past an uncovered window, she could sense a bullet striking her before she could get the shade down. She still was not allowed to mention her mother's name, neither at her father's house, nor at her own home. When she forgot at home, her husband would become violently abusive. She never forgot at her dad's house.

Sometimes she woke up in the middle of the night, hysterical. Her husband's cruel, hard slap across her face would bring her back to reality — the nightmare that she was actually living. Often her husband would point his index finger to his head and say, "Pow, pow," laughing as she ran from the room crying. So much went on in Shari's mind and emotions and outwardly in her marriage; her whole being ached for peace. But there was no normalcy, only craziness. She knew she was wearing down.

Though she had been strongly conditioned that divorce was never an option and had witnessed her mother's almost superhuman example of endurance, Shari felt that some things were truly understood only by God. That made her happy. He understood her, and He would give her peace, "The peace that would pass all understanding." (Phil. 4:7).

Thou knowest how to find a way
Through things I cannot see
Thou knowest all the answers
Though to me, no answers be.

CHAPTER THIRTEEN

NAT TOOK A JOB out of state, which meant he was seldom home. Aubrey, Cecelia, and Shari found relief in seeing him infrequently. When he was home, he often used his belt on all three. Sometimes he forced them to attend a church that would let him preach, which they detested. Service there lasted all day long and late into the night. The kids usually went to sleep. Shari would sit and read the songs in the hymnal for hours, tuning out the self-appointed "preachers."

Despite the respite they now had from Nat, all was not well on the home front. The broken-down trailer they lived in became tougher and tougher to tolerate. It was located several miles out of town, and they had no running water, no telephone, and no car.

Trying to make a better life for herself and her children, Shari got a part-time job close to the university as a grocery checker. After walking Aubrey to his first-grade class, Shari and Cecelia walked a mile to catch the bus that stopped first at the kindergarten and then at the university campus. Things were beginning to look hopeful at last.

But this optimism was short-lived. Shari's father became hospitalized in Little Rock, and she'd stop by and visit him whenever she could, despite her already full schedule. She arrived at the hospital one afternoon and was immediately confronted by her dad's new wife, who jumped up and began yelling at her heatedly.

"Shari, I hate you! Do you hear me? I hate you, I despise you, and I wish you were dead!" She was a loud, tactless woman, and on this particular day she was unusually loud, even though Daddy was dying only a few feet away. Shari found herself numb and bewildered.

The woman went on. "Nat was here and said that you think Cecil killed your mother!" That statement was neither false nor new to anyone; during the three years since Mama's death, many people had wondered if Cecil was the one who pulled the trigger. Regardless of the agony and mixed emotions, though, this was still her father. Shari had always cared for him, even though she feared him. Lately, she mostly feared him. But with him so near death, her guard went down and her heart softened. She felt he was not prepared to die, at least not until he'd tell the truth about Mama's death. This was her hope.

As her father's health deteriorated, Shari felt sad that things hadn't gone the way she had hoped. She'd watched Daddy bring his new wife, this unwelcome stranger, to live in Mama's house, to use her things, to sweep the floor where her blood had been spilled. Shari was heartbroken to learn that his second wife was selling, giving away, and throwing away bits of Mama's belongings rather than allowing Mama's own children to have them. She refused to let Roberta have Mama's sewing machine or deep freeze.

But the biggest heartache had come when Daddy told Shari that they had burned her children's baby clothes, which she and Mama had packed so carefully in a cedar chest to keep safe. Hardly anything brought Shari comfort. Her Uncle Darren, Daddy's brother, helped ease the pain when he neatly summed up her father's new marriage: "He needed a cook, so he married a woman."

As Shari stood in that hospital room, putting up with her "stepmother" and watching her father slowly dying, she knew too well that her own marriage was quickly crumbling. Their utilities had been disconnected for nonpayment, even though her husband earned good pay. Nat ridiculed Shari for being a "college girl," laughed at their insufferable living conditions, and swore he would "break" her. With no running water, Shari and the kids were reduced to using a bucket for a bathroom, which she carried to the nearby pond.

Worst of all, Shari resented her husband for eating the food that she had either earned or borrowed or begged for. Every day was a distressing challenge. But knowing she could not afford to fail, with God's strength she wouldn't. She often reminded herself, "God's grace is sufficient," and "He will not allow more than we are able to bear" (2 Cor. 12:9; 1 Cor. 10:13). Sometimes, though, she nudged Him to please be sure He was not miscalculating her capacity.

As her "stepmother" repeated her vehement words, something gave way. Shari realized that one of the two, either she or her husband, would be rearing the children alone. Doing so together, in any form, was impossible. She was thankful that they were not yet old enough to fear the social stigma that divorce might impart. She left Daddy's room with a new resolve. She had enough strength to walk into a phone booth and dial, praying that her friend Janet would answer her telephone. She knew she needed help. Janet came to the hospital, found Shari still in the phone booth, and brought her back to reality.

The two had met at the university. Shari would pass by a coffee shop and smell the enticing coffee and freshly baked donuts but was too scared and backward to enter, and she certainly wouldn't have spent her dimes on the coffee and donuts. But that changed when Janet introduced herself and a friendship quickly developed. She treated Shari like a normal person until she finally came to feel near normal herself and even began to enjoy the coffee shop with her. Janet had become a real friend and had shared her family's Thanksgiving dinner in her home with the three of them— Aubrey, Cecelia, and Shari. Janet was the trusted person whom she could telephone from her refuge in the phone booth that day.

The pair walked over to the hospital coffee shop. "I can't. I can't. I can't stay married to him, Janet. I can't!" Shari wailed repeatedly as though in a furious argument with someone.

"Of course you can't, and you mustn't. You have to get out of this ludicrous marriage as soon as possible!" Such dynamic words coming from such a petite woman. She wasn't even five feet tall, yet she had a firmness of confidence and a head full of sense that Shari had come to respect so greatly. She was the one who had gotten her the grocery-checking job and had even personally trained her when no one else would have had the patience. Shari looked at Janet's face and realized she was not adverse to her own realization. She understood completely, and it mattered. She mattered. This was the truth. Janet valued the truth and what needed to be done, and she believed that Shari mattered and that her pain mattered. All of that was virtually brand new to her, though certainly welcomed.

She calmed down and thanked Janet for coming, and together they walked to the hospital lobby to get the children. They drove to a cafeteria they liked but seldom patronized. Though Shari's heart ached and she felt eighty years old inside, they relaxed, smiled, and enjoyed their meal. Finally, rather nonchalantly, Shari told her children, "Kids, I'm going to divorce Daddy."

Cecelia responded first, her big, blue eyes aglow as she tossed her long brown hair to one side. "Oh, I know what that means, because Susie's parents are divorced, and they live in different houses. Daddy doesn't live with us much anyway, so it won't be very different."

Then Aubrey, quite seriously met his mother's eye. "Can I keep going to my school?" he asked.

Neither hell nor high water could prevent that, she told herself. She answered Aubrey simply, "Of course you can. You can be certain that you won't change schools."

Then brother and sister went on to talk excitedly about more important things, and Shari inwardly rejoiced that God was performing such a miracle in their lives. How sweetly and neatly God wrapped up a frightfully disturbing decision she had to disclose to them.

The next several months were awful as Shari waited for the divorce to be finalized. Nat contested it and fought for custody of the children. Sleep became rare, and nightmares were filled with torture chambers. Shari spent many nights figuring money and bills to manage another week in school or to enable Aubrey and Cecelia to live normal lives. Thank God, they sensed her trials and helped her immensely by being understanding. And they didn't seem to suffer, whereas they could easily have been scarred and damaged for life.

Friends were precious during this time. Shirley, a classmate, was a nurse by profession, as well as by nature. She well understood their plight and was close at hand to share the horrid times and the beautiful. When Shari had not slept for several nights and her nerves were stretched brittle, Shirley would appear unexpectedly at their trailer.

"I took the day off and thought I'd spend it with you kids," she'd say to them. "So let's get busy doing something fun. As for you, Mom, here are my keys. Take my car, and go over to my house. There's food in the fridge and you can watch TV or sleep or use my phone. But you get the day off too, so get." And the whole time Shirley was smiling warmly, and the kids were already making suggestions because they enjoyed her so.

There, in the privacy of her friend's home, Shari could scream and cry without alarming anyone, and she would find some measure of relief. Then she would eat freely, watch television, or just sleep for a spell. Afterward her soul, body, and perspective were rested, and she could return home to join the fun times with her kids. Later on, Shirley also accompanied Shari to her father's funeral, which was anything but a sad event. They enjoyed strawberry shortcake afterward. Only a genuine friend would be able to celebrate that kind of occasion in such a way.

The divorce incurred several delays because Shari was unable to speak up in the courtroom. The sight of so many male authority figures was overwhelmingly frightening. Her husband introduced himself as a "minister of the gospel" to the court and portrayed a distorted picture of their family situation. She was unable to dispute his attempt to deceive the court, because to do so required that she speak. There was so much to say, but she had been warned against speaking out for so long that even when it mattered so greatly, she could not get the words out.

When the members of her church heard of her court plight, the pastor wrote the court a letter on Shari's behalf, attesting to the poverty in which she and the kids lived. The church had assisted them with food, babysitting, and emotional support. Shari retains that letter to this day.

Others also helped. The lady from whom they rented trailer space agreed to come to court to testify that they were alone and without a car. Then Janet came down the aisle, fully ready to spill the whole sordid story. But to their surprise, it wasn't even necessary. On that very day, the judge simply said to Nat, "This court does not care if you are a minister of the gospel or an Indian chief." He granted the divorce, giving Shari custody of the children.

With the final signing of the paper, the air became clean and sweet. The court ordered the three moved closer to town, and they were thrilled to find themselves settled into a nice apartment near their schools. They still had no car but now they could easily walk everywhere—to the kids' school, to Shari's classes, to her job, to the stores, to the donut shop! Life was great. They had carpeting, a dishwasher, electricity, and heat. And whatever they may have lacked, they never noticed. For days, Aubrey and Cecelia walked from room to room, grinning. Shari promised God in her heart that she'd never stop thanking Him.

When they sold that horrid house-trailer, they bought lots of good things to eat. Greatest of all, they bought a small house one block from the kids' school. With the little cash they had, they carefully invested in carpet, a used car, stove, refrigerator, and living room set. They couldn't stop marveling about their "new" house, though actually it was quite old. But it was theirs, and it was home. They were happy there. Friends came, and good times were enjoyed at last. God was there and they loved it.

It came as a simple relief when Shari's father died. She knew that with him were buried many answers that she ached for, but also buried with him was much pain. She had loved him as a child loves her father, for the good that was in him. But she had never reached him and had so wished to. There were indeed some good memories: He could and did walk on his hands for the kids when they were little, and he could figure math at a glance, as no one else's father could do.

But somewhere along the way, this normal, decent Dad faded out and gave way to a stranger—perhaps somewhere between the pages of his many murder-mystery magazines. Maybe even earlier. Maybe the bitter alcohol had absorbed what personality he'd had, until absent of alcohol, none was left.

The last moments Shari shared with Daddy were in the hospital just prior to his death. He looked at her as she walked through the entrance to his room. He lay very much alone. Their eyes locked and suddenly, as though hypnotized, she could go no farther. Although she wanted desperately to go to him, she stood stationary, neither of them speaking. So much to say, but no words. Still, so much seemed to be conveyed.

One thing caught her attention when she viewed him in his coffin: He was incredibly small. Whereas he had previously weighed 180 pounds, at his death he weighed only 97 pounds. There seemed to be some kind of symbolism in that. He had always seemed monstrously powerful. She never really knew what he died from medically, and she supposed it never really mattered. She experienced no grief, for he had already been dead for so long that it was only appropriate that his body admit the fact. Shari's grief for him began back in December of 1964, when seemingly, both her parents died. The only difference was that his body walked around, while her mother's lay still. Mama was strengthening in her radiance, while he evoked terror with his eyes.

Daddy suffered a unique experience as he drew his last breaths, however, for Robbie was there with him when he died. Shari was glad he didn't die alone. Robbie explained, "For several minutes he opened his mouth wide, making hideous grunting sounds, as though he were trying to speak, but no words were discernible. I leaned down close to him, trying to understand, but they weren't words, Shari, they were just sounds. His eyes were wide open and looked terrified, as though he were looking at Mama, or maybe at the devil himself. It was awful."

"I'm sorry you had to see all that, Robbie, but you were helpful to him I'm sure. For him, seeing and speaking had come too late, I guess."

Whatever he may have been seeing, experiencing, or trying to say, Shari can't help but wonder whether his life and death were those of the loneliest man she ever knew. On separate occasions, his own brothers told her, "Cecil had no friends."

The saddest thing about her father's entire life was that he never learned to ask. He maintained his aloneness as an entity unto himself. What if his church had invited him to ask, seek, and knock, rather than rejecting him? What if his children could have understood and had invited him to ask, seek, knock? Shari would never know, of course. Perhaps it was already too late; perhaps it had been too late for him for a long time. Hopefully he left this planet to enter another planet where, as he theorized, Jesus has yet to visit and invitations are more freely given. Perhaps there, her daddy will learn how to ask, seek, knock. Many would say such thoughts are unscriptural, and perhaps they are; Shari's just glad that God knows the heart as no man can and that only God can measure the extent of psychotic loneliness.

She ended her speculations with the reassuring thought that it's good some things are known only to God. And in the seconds that transpire as one draws his last breath, all things are possible with God.

CHAPTER FOURTEEN

AFTER BEING AWAY FROM school for eight years, Shari dove into anthropology, sociology, and psychology—the "people" subjects. She longed to really know and fully understand people. Shari found the experience of formal education at the University of Arkansas to be exhilarating.

Her friends were the best part; they opened up a new world for her. There was Shari's Japanese boyfriend, her beautiful Iranian girlfriend (whose husband, daughter, and son shared both her first and last names), and a precious couple from Thailand. They were so playful that Shari easily forgot that he was a surgeon and professor of medicine and that his wife had a master's degree in social work. The couple often spent hours sitting on the floor playing with her children.

Dr. Gilbert Butler was her favorite professor, and she felt it was his compassionate nature that allowed her to pass his impossible courses. He later became a dear friend to her children also, and that family friendship reached a new level when the three learned he had a brain tumor. They continued to visit him, bringing him strawberry pie and joining him on the floor as he played his gospel records. He had been so brilliant, yet in those last days as he lay dying, unable to stand because the pain would be excruciating, he knew only who his visitors were and that they were there with him. He always smiled whenever they said, "Gil, we love you."

The pride Aubrey, Cecelia and Shari felt on her college graduation day was almost palpable. They could hardly contain it. They suspected life would never be quite as dismal as it had recently been. Shari's new degree led to a new job. She found the experience of teaching social studies to junior high kids truly thrilling. She brought history and government to life by giving her students roles to act out. Class was often held outdoors on bleachers, speakers were invited into the classroom, and field trips were taken, all of which helped make these courses vital and interesting for her pupils.

Shari was asked to sponsor the Christian Council, a voluntary club held during lunch hour. At first the club met in a classroom, but eventually only the gymnasium could contain the enormous group. These kids certainly were interested in drugs—but from a constructive point of view. They wanted to help others stay away from drugs. Seven busloads of students and their chaperones went to see the movie "The Cross and the Switchblade," about a New York City gang leader's powerful conversion. After watching this, the kids wanted to support Teen Challenge, an organization that provides faith-based solutions to the problems of alcohol and drug addiction. They solicited day-old donuts from nearby shops, which they then sold each morning before school, giving the profits to Teen Challenge. Shari was proud to be able to help such an enthusiastic, service-oriented bunch of teens.

She never thought she'd give up teaching for any other profession. But two years later, she received an advanced degree in social work, Shari decided to change careers. She had always admired people in this field, and besides, it felt familiar because it dealt with people hurting and needing assistance. In graduate school, she began to understand for the first time her own strengths and weaknesses. She realized that there is a fork in the road for everyone. At least at some point in life, everybody has to decide what to focus on: their weaknesses or their strengths. The choice each person makes ultimately defines his or her character.

Her newfound knowledge was freeing. Nobody had ever taught her these things before. She'd lived her entire life in survival mode. As she discovered how much she needed people to learn from, she saw that learning was reciprocal. It was a wonderful feeling to be useful and acceptable as a person. This encouragement was what had led to her desire to enter social work. She hoped that her concern for individuals and their dignity would genuinely make a difference in people's lives.

She remembered back in high school how she and the other students had taken aptitude tests to determine their proficiency. Her results revealed a social work aptitude, but not being acquainted with the term, she thought it meant "social butterfly," the kind that flits from one cocktail party to the next. Because of this simple misunderstanding, she had dismissed the assessment.

"Shari, it's your turn now," her high school principal had called to her from the door of his office, wanting to discuss the results of her aptitude test. "I'm very, very sorry, Mr. Brook, but I don't have time to speak with you now," she replied and dashed away from his office. Every time he approached her to discuss that test, she made up an excuse until he apparently forgot it, which was exactly what she wanted. After all, Shari had taken care of his children in the church nursery. What would he think about her supposed "cocktail party" inclination? It was both amusing and refreshing to learn the real meaning of "social work," even after so many years.

School illuminated the upheavals that had pockmarked Shari's life from the very beginning, starting with the dreadful experiences of running and hiding in the night as a child, and moving into running and hiding in various ways as an adult. The saddest part was that running away always seemed necessary for survival, whereas survival itself often seemed less than essential. When Shari graduated with top honors, her teachers recommended her as a most-qualified social worker, although they hardly understood why she was so competent in relating to people who were in painful straits.

For her internship she was placed, ironically, at the state psychiatric hospital to work as a professional. Earlier in her classes, she had first heard the term therapy and wished she could indulge in it, but certainly couldn't afford it. As she became a therapist to her patients, she found great pleasure in giving them what she had wished for: plenty of time, patience with their difficulty in articulation, smiles of acceptance (even when the patients weren't pleasant to be near), and most importantly, attentive listening.

Shari asked many questions so that she could fully understand them, and they were never offended. Rather, they seemed honored to be heard and respected. Fairly soon into their treatment, she needed less and less time with patients because articulation became easier, and when Shari needed to frown it wasn't interpreted as non-acceptance. Thus, the people there became more pleasant to be near, more interesting to listen to, and more intriguingly unique as human beings, really worth getting to know and understand.

Her work with the hurting became like a soothing ointment for her own pain, in the sense that love and understanding were reciprocated. The language of the psychotic was clearly communicated to her through his artwork, because his world was vivid and real—similar to her own private world—and thus easily understood. During her internship, even a psychopath was healed, because she never doubted (as did the more seasoned professionals) that he could be healed.

Shari highly treasured the chance to be near psychiatrists. So many times had she longed for such a visit with one who could understand. She seized opportunities to ask her own questions, making it seem as though they pertained to her clients. She always carried a file with her for her "supervisory consults."

More puzzle pieces emerged as Shari participated in group therapy—another requirement for her graduate work. During group therapy, one of the psychiatrists, Dr. Catherine Baxter, flatly stated, "You have a murderous parent inside your head." For Shari, concentrating and focusing had at that time become so difficult, as she constantly bore the heavy, dark questioning cloud that overshadowed all else: What went on that day, and why did no one care, and how, oh God, could she correct it?

During one group meeting, Dr. Baxter spoke to Shari, but she seemed miles away. Shari could hear the doctor talking but could not decipher her words. She could see her, but she could neither focus on her clearly nor respond to her. When Shari realized Dr. Baxter was kneeling beside her chair and holding her hand as she talked, speaking slowly as if to a child, then she understood. She had knelt to be lower than Shari was. As she looked down instead of up, there was no threat and no fear. Looking down, Shari could see horizontally and could respond as though to another human being, an equal. She had spent her whole life looking up from a fearfully intimidated position. Dr. Baxter noted, "You should be a mental patient, a prison inmate, or dead."

Since Shari was just beginning to grasp concepts that were still new to her, she didn't understand that the doctor was pointing out she was making it, despite the odds against her. Misinterpreting her statement, she heartily attempted to carry out Dr. Baxter's "prediction" by applying for work in a mental ward and a prison ward, half expecting sudden and tragic death to be imminent.

The term 'death imagery' hadn't been introduced yet at that level of her schoolwork, but in retrospect, it was the appropriate term because of her constant struggle with thoughts of death. These thoughts even invaded her dreams. Since she didn't want to alarm her children, her nights were often spent in the opposite end of their house, with a washcloth stuffed inside her mouth so that she could scream and cry making the least possible noise.

But "pretended normalcy" sufficed for the most part, as Shari strove to blend in with the "fully functioning adults" in both her school and professional work setting. She learned to keep quiet and to look interested in what others said, to smile when others smiled, to nod when others nodded, and to keep busy making notes or lists. This helped her maintain a protective yet acceptable distance. Not to succeed in this endeavor obviously would have resulted in her exposure and most likely, her expulsion. She never forgot for a moment that Aubrey and Cecelia were her first priority, and they were not responsible for the family's problems and must not suffer as a result of them (or at least, as little as possible).

Shari's ex-husband never ceased to torment them during her two-year master's program. He'd call on the phone and relay vulgar, curse-filled, threatening messages whenever he felt like it, or he'd go to the restaurant where her Japanese boyfriend worked, threatening that he would never permit a "stupid foreigner to raise my kids. I'll kill you first."

He also invaded their home whenever he felt like it. On one occasion, as the police checked the broken frame of Shari's kicked-in door, they advised her, "Get yourself a gun, lady, and next time you see him coming, use it." Her phone was torn from the wall, and she had been beaten. By this time, she and Nat had been divorced for two years.

But instead of buying a gun, Shari had a better idea. With her newly earned master's degree, she felt that she and her kids deserved the luxury of separating themselves from the difficult life they had tolerated for so long. Shari took Aubrey and Cecelia for a luxurious vacation in Hawaii, after which she interviewed for a state job in California with the correctional system. Her new title would be "correctional social worker." Long had she wished to "correct" what was done to and within her own family, so she felt it would be an honor to do so for other families.

Extremely excited, the three packed their pregnant cat and a tidbit of gear into a new, flashy car and headed west. "If the early pioneers could do it, we can do it! California or bust," the kids quipped. Nevertheless, it was a difficult move for them as they separated from their close friends and activities: Cecelia from her softball team and Aubrey from his boys' club. They also left behind their church, their very own first ever home, and of course, their school. This time, Aubrey was giving up his school. This time, he knew it needed to be done, and this time, he didn't even ask otherwise. Both children knew that the family was prioritizing and that new privileges weren't without a price. They had already discovered and loved the Serenity Prayer, knowing well that they could not change everything, but they could change some things, and seeking the wisdom to distinguish, they set about the task.

The three of them had a delightful trip. Shari was cheered by the thought that God never forgets the pleasures that His children need and deserve, and that He simply wants them to have. She and her children saw scenic wonders, met lovely people, and had fun being together on their long trip. Finally, they arrived at the outskirts of Los Angeles.

Shari's only contact was a minister in the church of their affiliation. He assured them there'd be no problem in finding immediate housing and offered his services. Many lay people of his church also began searching for an apartment for the family. Shari's wish was to live near the church so that she and the children could be actively involved in its many functions. All efforts failed, however, and no shelter was located after a week of frantic searching. Then, quite unexpectedly, a wonderful thing happened on the last hour of the last day that they were permitted to stay in their motel. Because they had a cat, they couldn't stay even an hour longer.

A clerk at the post office asked Shari whether they'd found a home yet. As soon as he heard that they hadn't, he wrote down an address and suggested that they look into it.

The apartment complex was decorated Hawaiian-style, which Shari and the children loved immediately since they'd just been to Hawaii. Both cats and kids were allowed, and the apartment was absolutely lovely. There was only one vacancy left. The landlady was from Shari's home state, so they felt like friends the moment they met. The family got the apartment.

"I moved to California with my two children many years ago, so no way could I refuse you three," said the landlady. That explained why the other applicants had been turned away. Nice couples could go elsewhere more easily than nice, single parent families could. Shari and the kids sure felt thankful to be "chosen."

Their only disappointment was not being able to locate an apartment near the church they'd planned to attend, for they loved being near the church grounds and didn't want to miss any activities. But when they woke up that first morning in their new home, they noticed a church and even a Christian school immediately next door. They rushed outside to check and were thrilled to learn that this was a church of their affiliation and also a church school for the first six grades. Again, it was almost perfect.

"Oh, if only this school included the seventh grade as well, then maybe we could both go, huh, Mom? But I guess it would cost a lot anyway, and I wouldn't even want to go if Aubrey couldn't. But it sure is almost ideal, isn't it?" Cecelia went on. She enjoyed helping with major decisions, but never wanted more than "her share," being always considerate of Aubrey.

Aubrey just grinned and looked longingly at the idea of it all. It was a look Shari had seen only a few times before. When she had pawned her solitaire diamond a few years earlier, she had received all of forty dollars for it, and that seemed like a lot of money to them. But as they left the pawnshop with their two twenty dollar bills, Shari noticed her kids looking at a pizza parlor. They didn't say a word, but their look said it all. Shari suggested they celebrate their success with pizza. What a pleasant surprise for the kids. In the end, they enjoyed that pizza much more than Shari had ever enjoyed that stupid ring.

They visited the church next door, became family immediately, and thanked God when it was soon announced that the seventh grade was added to the church school for the ensuing year. Shari had a short drive to her job, and she figured that, too, was part of a perfect plan for their lives. But when she reported to her new job, she felt an overwhelming fear that stemmed from intermingling with multitudes of dangerous juvenile criminal offenders. This fear was even further compounded by her inner feelings of sudden attraction to a youth counselor there. Her reaction to this double fear took the form of earlier patterns and scripts: Shari wanted to flee. Completely distraught, she gave notice to terminate the job after only one week.

She found another job in the mental hospital nearby. It seemed the psychiatrist's prophesy was being fulfilled. Once again, Shari turned to prayer: *Dear God, with Your help I can— I must—break old feelings of fear and compulsions to run away. I'm so tired of running away. Please show me,*

Lord, how to, "be still and know" that You are God. Then she cautiously withdrew her resignation and remained on the job to face... whatever.

She soon grew close to the youth counselor. And although she came from the South and spoke with a southern accent, she came to realize that she was not in the least bothered to be attracted to this handsome African-American. Occasionally a thought ran through her mind: *If Ellis or Uncle Stan knew, how angry they'd be, since they're so bigoted.* But they couldn't know, as they were far away. This man's inner self contrasted sharply with his outer image of heavy gambling and drinking. He even informed Shari that he had killed a man. She simply replied, "At least you were man enough to kill a man, not a woman."

He grinned and took the time to understand her story as well and to help her recognize why she, too, was actually prejudiced. Her prejudice was against her own race, however—against the white man who seemingly tried to dominate everything and everybody. He amusingly referred to Shari as the "little white warrior."

Although she well knew he could be dangerous, she trusted him. She met him where he was in his discouragement with his life, his desire for a better one, and his inability to discover it on his own. Shari was touched as she watched and listened to him sing the Lord's Prayer at a gathering. He had many questions, as though he were approaching a foreign land, even though his mother was a strong Christian. He questioned why he had been unable to trust or hold on to his mother's values. With sad longing, he recalled who he'd been years earlier, before he had deteriorated to his present condition.

To camouflage a broken heart and spirit, however, he bragged openly about his vices and blamed other people along his way.

"You accept responsibility for your own successes and for your own failures!" Shari finally yelled at him one day.

"Isn't this a bit out of character for you, Babe?" he jabbed.

"I don't care what color or circumstances, a man ought to accept responsibility for what he himself does or what he himself does not do, but this blaming somebody else? It irks me to death!"

"Yeah, I can see that. You know who the first cowardly man was?"

She didn't know and figured he might be changing the subject. She wasn't quite ready to do that. She was onto something, and she wasn't ready to show any leniency, at least not yet.

"In the Garden of Eden, Adam blamed Eve for his own stupidity, and I guess we've been doin' it ever since. Women come in handy in that way, you know," he said with a chuckle.

"That's it, that's it!" Shari remembered how her mother had been blamed for her own death, and how her seventeen-year-old sister had been blamed for driving her to it. Then Shari was blamed for Aunt Faye's death and even blamed, in advance, for anyone else who might die if she so much as talked to them. It all seemed so clear at that moment.

"I'm the one who put me in prison!" she blurted out. "Women blame women, too.

He laughed loudly. "Honey, you're on a roll again, and I wouldn't interfere for all the money in the world. When you get it all put together, let me in on it, OK? But meanwhile, give those poor white jerks a break. If they live long enough, they might come around. Course, I'm first to admit they'd hafta live a long time."

He was still horsing around as Shari jaunted down to her office at the end of the hall. But she felt she'd already accomplished more important work than whatever waited for her inside her office.

When a friend from graduate school came to visit her, Shari was pleased to introduce them. Right away, she saw that they were attracted to each other. When they began laughing at her soft drink preference over hard liquor, Shari lost her own interest in both these people. When her friend wanted to see all of Los Angeles, Shari just wanted to go home, and did. By the time her friend returned the next morning, Shari had her bags packed and promptly took her to the airport, extending no further invitation.

As for her conflicted counselor, she met him at the local bar just to match him, drink for drink, with his hard liquor. It was a foolish gesture on her part, and she knew it, but it seemed important at the time.

"You see, I can drink. I just choose not to," she said.

"And I apologize for the things we said about it. I take full responsibility for acting a fool the other night." He looked sincere and Shari hoped he was.

"That's good. Maybe you have the makings of a real man. Someone will be glad to get you."

CHAPTER FIFTEEN

ONE EVENING IN SHARI'S church congregation, a kind man approached her and her children with a dinner invitation. Over a hearty spaghetti meal, the trio soon learned that John, too, was a native Arkansan. Shari and John were delighted to discover that they'd attended the same college and even knew some of the same people. A meaningful friendship developed that would last for years. His children were the same ages as Cecelia and Aubrey, and all the kids struck up immediate friendships. Soon the seven of them were spending fun-filled days exploring the vast city of Los Angeles.

When John discovered that the family was paying the kids' tuition at the private school by working as the church's janitorial crew, he was aghast.

"Honey," he said, "it takes a man to lift that equipment and do that kind of work."

"Are you suggesting that we aren't doing a good job of it?" Shari replied, wanting a straight answer. She was proud of the job they were doing. Every morning they awoke early to start cleaning before daybreak. When they were done, the kids went to school and Shari went to her fulltime job. Then after the last evening program at church, Shari and her children began the night cleaning, usually finishing by midnight. They truly considered themselves a "crew." Each one had specific jobs to do, and the three learned to do their jobs as quickly and efficiently as possible. Their incentives were more free time at home and, of course, money for tuition. With Christmas approaching, they were tremendously grateful to be employed.

But with the Christmas programs and rehearsals scheduled on a nightly basis, they had their work cut out for them. Every night they had to clean the entire church and two-story school, including the restrooms, of course, which were in awful shape by the end of the day. To spare her kids, Shari took on the bathrooms herself. But she didn't have enough time to get them cleaned in that small window between school being out and the evening programs starting. That's when a co-worker and dear friend, Jan, stepped in.

She had agreed to come help Shari through the Christmas season. Jan was an African-American social worker. Shari couldn't help but notice that the popular phrase at the time, "Black is beautiful," was quite true with her. Even more beautiful was her personality.

One night at the church, the toilets overflowed and all the dressed-up folks were waiting on Shari and Jan to finish the cleaning and move their heavy gear aside. Jan leaned on her mop and just started laughing heartily.

"Hey kid, you laugh on your own time, not on mine," Shari joked. "Cut this out or you won't get your fancy paycheck." Which was twenty dollars a night, all she could afford to pay her friend for her gracious help. Jan straightened up, tried to dry the tears of laughter from her eyes, looked at the dressed-up people waiting impatiently, and said, "Shari, if my momma could see me now, she'd kill you, girl. I mean, kill you dead!"

Her laughter was contagious. By now, Shari was laughing, too. "How do you mean?" she asked.

"Well, my momma scrubbed toilets for white folks so that she could send her little girl to school. She sent me six years to college, for a master's-level education to be sure I'd never have to do what she did. And you have me in here, scrubbing the white folks' toilets! I mean it, if she could see this, she'd kill you dead."

They finished as quickly as they could that evening, doing a less than efficient job, and stepped aside to let the impatient crowd in. They hoped everyone would forgive them. It was, after all, the Christmas season of goodwill and cheer.

It had taken John a while to discover the hectic routine his new friend had been keeping day after day. "Why did you even ask Jan to help you when you know I'd be glad to?"

Until that moment, Shari had no idea that he'd "be glad to," but now that he mentioned it, she decided to take him up on his offer. John came aboard, refusing payment. Shari was able to save more money, and Jan, who declared it would be a long time before she'd tell her momma about scrubbing toilets for a friend in need, got a well-deserved break.

Shari and John talked often of marriage, and all of their kids kept thinking that for sure it would happen. The pair went house hunting and even picked out furniture together. But when it came time to set a date, Shari had second thoughts.

"I think the world of you," she shared with John. "You're a wonderful person, and you've been extremely kind to us in showing us around so much. It's even nice to have an escort, and someone to sit with in church. Can't we just keep it this speed?"

"There's something you're not telling me, isn't there, Shari?"

"There's no one else, if that's what you mean," she quickly reassured. He was right, though, there was something she'd been hiding. "Maybe there is something you don't understand. You see, as wonderful as you are, there are a few things that disqualify you from a permanent place in our lives."

She cringed as those words left her mouth. His expression made her heart ache, and she really wished she'd chosen less candid words. John asked her to elaborate.

"I could never marry a white man from Arkansas."

His mouth opened wide as if to argue. "Sweetheart, wait a doggone minute here. It's not my fault where I happen to have been born, or that I happen to be Caucasian. For crying out loud, how in the world can you hold that against me?"

"It isn't fair, is it?" Shari could only muster in sad shame.

"Well, this is something we can work on."

"Oh no, it isn't, because it's something you can't change, and every time I look at you I'm reminded of the dominating, white, male Arkansans."

"But do you find me dominating?" he asked defensively. He seemed to be holding back tears.

"Not really, but I wouldn't trust you, and I'd never give you the chance by marrying you."

Inwardly, Shari wished she had taken the time to learn to play some of the "games people play." Her blatant honesty was destroying their friendship and hurting him so much. But she had spent so many years keeping quiet. It felt good to finally speak up, to share her true feelings. Despite everything, she knew she was doing what needed to be done.

She also knew that the good times with John wouldn't likely last much longer. Both of them recognized that her entire being literally cringed at the dominating controls of the white man. The nightmarish scenes from Shari's childhood and those from her marriage had indelibly portrayed the Caucasian man as totally devoid of love, trust, gentleness, goodness, understanding, warmth, patience, and integrity. As she thought back to her days teaching school, she felt that in the American history courses she had identified with other minorities in great fear of the "mighty pale face."

John had helped her in ways he may never realize. He helped Shari realize that one day, she'd need to be healed. Some of her distorted perspectives had to change. Not yet, though. She was at a different point in her process of reconciling her feelings with her past. Inwardly she desired not a romantic knight in shining, white armor, but a wise person—a shrink in the shining, white armor of truth—to help her with her deepest questions. Until he or she arrived, Shari understood no alternatives but to remain alone in her protective cocoon, which sheltered her from further pain but denied her the blissful freedom of flying.

God has been good to me all through the years
I really can't complain -
He gave me a love when I was so young,
Such a love but a boy, not a man.
I ran when I wanted so much to be still
And I ran and I ran and I ran
So tired I became and adept at the game,
That I played and played and played.
Yet, still God was good to me all through the years
I really can't complain.
Ah, one little thing, just one minor thing,
I'm very disheartened o'er,
He gave me a love when I was adult -
Such a love, such a man, but what for?
Yes God has been good to me all through the years,
I really can't complain.

CHAPTER SIXTEEN

IN SHARI'S WORK IN the correctional setting, it became vividly clear to her how impersonally people interact with each other. People are ever attempting to classify, categorize, and label others according to particular traits and stereotypes. Shari began to wonder: What purpose are such divisions intended to serve? Do they not instead hinder, inhibit and even obstruct actual understanding, cooperation, and relating among people? When do we care about the essence of a person, and how can we begin to see beyond the label and the container—or do we even wish to?

She remembered that her mother was only in her early to mid-forties when the famed Central High School integration resistance made headlines throughout the world. Mama herself had attended school at Central High and was sad that it had to carry such negative fame. But her concern went much deeper than that. One of her real concerns was, "Those poor little elementary school Black children never get to see their yards in the daytime in the winter months, for they're loaded on buses before daylight, and they return home on buses after dark. There's something wrong with that when there are good schools nearby. That ought not be."

Mama sometimes saw the buses pass by the house in the early morning as she walked to the front of the yard to get the newspaper. "That's just not right," was her conclusion. She was a native Southerner, so why did she question the labeling that was done in the decisions that put African-American children on buses back in those days? Was she quietly disloyal to her own locale, or did her concern indicate something bigger—a mentality that perceives and appreciates people for who they truly are, for their very essence?

A prison setting is a telling place to observe the categorization process, and Shari, for one, was pleased with some of the categories, believing them to be essential for everyone's safety. But she didn't understand other forms of labeling, and she sought to understand the value systems behind them. When she first began her job, the wards (as the inmates were called) felt a need to classify her, and they did just that. The white wards called her "sister" because of her skin color. The black wards countered, "She sounds like us, so she's *our* sister."

The Mexican wards felt left out. So they came up with a solution: "We'll teach you to speak Spanish, then you'll be our sister, too."

"You've got a deal," Shari agreed. "I'd love to learn to speak Spanish. You're on."

"If we do a good job by you, will you speak good for us at our board hearing and recommend early parole?" they asked, grinning.

"Yes, I'll speak good for you at your board hearing. Yes, I will." They were fully satisfied with the deal.

Shari learned quite a lot of Spanish from them, but when later, in a formal Spanish class, she related with great pride what she'd learned, she was practically expelled from the class. The teacher cried, "I will not have you use those words in my classroom! That is gutter talk! Street talk! Gang talk!" Even when Shari explained where she'd learned her Spanish, the teacher was not very understanding. Shari learned to confine her Spanish to within the prison walls.

Her wards had felt the need to classify her just as her job required her to classify them. Shari came to realize she was guilty of classifying the Caucasian race as a stereotype. To transcend that, she needed to take the time to examine their essence individually and avoid the stereotyping. But of course, that would require a lot of time and interaction, a lot of talking and questioning.

Was it really worth it, when she could sum up the whole group and be done with them? Especially when she could sum them up, be done with them, and basically just discount and negate them? This way would keep them down (inferior) while seemingly elevating herself (superior). Similarly, she could avoid the burdensome responsibility of taking the time, organizing her thoughts, and investing effort towards making more accurate assessments on an individual basis. She could maintain her anger at them, "the villains," by projecting blame without giving them the chance to defend or redeem themselves. Thus, she would win by default.

Deep down, Shari knew that to be responsible means to be fair. When practicing prejudice, though, neither is possible. Yet it seemed to her that this was how the bulk of human interaction was conducted: with the least amount of personal exposure, the least amount of effort, and the least amount of responsibility invested. *How in thunder,* she wondered, *did we arrive here when we all need human interaction that allows our vulnerabilities, our exposure, our responsibility, and mutual support? Aren't humans more alike than different?* Shari pondered these questions as she made it a point to look each ward, client, or patient in the eye and ask personal questions about their home life, family, and interests.

The response Shari got was exhilarating to her. Some people gushed at the personal attention. Others practically ran away from her in mid-sentence. What made the difference? It certainly wasn't related to color, nor did it have anything to do with the prisoner's offense. Status, gender, education, age—none of these accounted for it. All of the categories were crossed. She knew there was a valuable truth to be found here. She mused, *Is prejudice the value system from which we operate when we just haven't learned to relate otherwise? When we're too lazy to learn?*

She reasoned that certainly it was impossible to get close to everyone we come in contact with. But just as in the military a soldier recognizes another soldier with a salute, in civilian life a person can recognize and identify with the humanness of another by a smile, eye contact, an unspoken exchange of, "I see you, and I'm glad we're both alive."

When she visited New York City to attend meetings, Shari was excited about the opportunity to catch a Broadway play. She quickly checked into her room and dashed out to find the metro, the city's extensive subway system, to get to the evening showing of *Evita*. Having never ridden the metro before, she didn't know where it was, nor did she know how to get to her destination.

She got directions along the way, and to her relief she arrived just in time. When the play ended, however, it was almost midnight. She found herself sitting in a subway train a very long way from her hotel, the train growing emptier and scarier at every stop.

She noticed a group of young men at the far end of the train. They reminded her of the wards she worked with. Were they gang kids? She wasn't sure. But they definitely had that look about them. She wondered how to handle this awkward, and maybe even dangerous, situation. She decided not to ignore them; with them and her being the only ones left on the train, she didn't want to be misinterpreted as rude and aloof. She also decided that she wouldn't smile at them, so as to not be mistaken as flirting. And she decided that she wasn't about to appear scared—even though she was—and look like a waiting victim.

After coaching herself, she turned towards them, nodded respectfully, and then turned her eyes toward the entrance of the train, praying every second that she'd been successful at conveying a sense of mutual respect. She made it back to her hotel room without incident.

The desolate late-night New York streets made her ponder the plight of the human race again. It seemed to her that the withholding of basic respect and warmth in an impersonal environment had done great damage to humanity. She remembered studying a condition in which babies who were seldom touched died. These babies were adequately bathed, fed, and tended to, yet death resulted because they needed something more: human warmth. Even though adults don't die physically without human warmth, perhaps they die in spirit, self-esteem and hope when they are ignored as valuable human beings.

Thinking of those teenagers on the subway, Shari wondered if they would evolve into juvenile delinquents, perhaps resorting to the loyalty of a gang, which does recognize, dignify, and value their presence. Many will choose gang behavior for the sake of identity. Maybe God let her respectful gaze delay that choice for those teens—at least for that evening.

When her New York meetings were over and she began making her way back home, her thoughts again centered on teens when four nice-looking young adults boarded her airport bus. They reminded Shari of her own violent wards, who didn't look that different from these men.

When she first started doing social work, she had been surprised to learn that most criminals have a self-concept of victim and want to get revenge, get even, or get back when they commit their crimes. They transfer their own status from "victims" to "villains," from the powerless to the powerful, believing that these are the only two possible positions in life. If anything, they're victims of *dualistic thinking.*

Shari had learned that many feel they missed important aspects of childhood due to their one-parent home, loss of both parents, bad or negligent parents, poverty, or in some cases by being a minority. Consequently, they feel ill-prepared for life as an adult and are scared. Feeling deprived, they rationalize a shortcut—a taking of something. Getting caught even suggests some restoration of that missed element: personal attention. Sure it's negative attention, but any attention is preferable to being ignored.

The four teens in front of her on the bus were so polite, without any of the anger her wards harbored. She wondered, *Is rehabilitation still possible at this point for the wards?* Yes, if a "new" authority person can fill the void by giving each young man time, attention, and respectful direction. Humans need and respond to role models. Humans need "heroes," because every person instinctively knows he or she needs help in order to handle adulthood.

Shari felt an ache in her soul for some of the young, direction-less boys for whom no positive role model will ever appear, unfortunately reinforcing their earlier identity as victim. She could clearly see how their rationale would become, "Crime is not only justified, but under my circumstances, necessary." In their eyes, the solution was to emerge into adult figures similar to those they resented, the ones who create victims via victimization. By turning into their "enemies," these young men feel vindicated, no longer one of the inferior, powerless have-nots. Now they are the superior, powerful haves. This is their understanding of what it means to 'achieve.'

A week later back in Shari's office, she was attacked by one such youth. He had just arrived at the center for raping an elderly woman. Shari frantically activated the panic alarm installed in her office—every office had one in the event of such an occurrence. But the immediate assistance she was supposed to get never came.

The young man finally left on his own, leaving Shari unharmed. Later, a "shank," a homemade knife made from a toothbrush and a razor blade, was found in his room. Did he have this weapon with him when he had attacked Shari? Nobody knew for sure. But one thing was certain: Nobody had come when Shari pressed the panic button. There were men on salary whose job it was to respond to such emergencies. But no one came. No one.

Years later, a female school teacher was stomped to death at another facility. Shari wondered, *Did no one come? Is that how it happened?*

Shari began to question the authority figures at her facility. Why had no assistance arrived in response to her distress call? At first there were no answers. Finally, she was told directly that there weed no concern for her safety. Her superiors made absolutely no move to rectify the dangerous situation, even after she approached every level of administration. Even the superintendent jokingly stated, "If a social worker gets hurt or killed, our agency would get more money because the state always moves after the fact." Shari wasn't laughing.

There was prejudice everywhere. In her line of work, it seemed directed at social workers. Specifically, female social workers. Those in charge had the ability to control the situation, and they did, in fact, call the shots. But not in a way that was fair or responsible. They controlled every situation based on their own prejudice. Some openly defied the rules of the agency, while others protected these rule-breakers, fully cognizant of the seriousness of their defiance, all because they shared the same prejudice.

Shari filed grievances because it was the only procedure available when general apathy prevailed. Knowing that would be a slow process, she desired to speak with the governor, feeling that if he were aware of such a situation, he would surely intervene. One day she actually met him on the streets of Sacramento. Thankfully, Governor Brown did intervene.

Shery remembered the tragedy of the previous year's Christmas vacation. Her friend Jan, who was the other social worker on her unit, had turned in formal instructions to have a particular young, physically small, minority youth moved to another unit immediately. She felt he was in danger where he was and belonged in the unit that housed younger wards. He had been inadvertently placed on an older unit, and he was terrified. Both Shari and Jan were told it would be done, pronto.

The social workers returned from Christmas vacation and were shocked to discover that the young man had been found dead. He had never been moved out of the older, more aggressive unit.

"It's just one less mouth to feed, no great loss," was the response they received from the counselors who had failed to heed Jan's instructions to move him. When both women inquired further up the chain of command, they were met with nonchalance. They soon learned that the ward was very poor and had very little family. Other than Jan and Shari, nobody at the facility had any interest in him.

By the time the situation had escalated to the newspapers, plenty of feathers had been ruffled. Shari would never again return to her earlier days of naiveté. She watched as reprisals came in many forms. When she left for home at the end of the day, she was forced to walk through a corridor of fifty naked youths because the counselors had decided to have them shower early so the wards "could get an early start watching television." This instantly brought Shari back to another place and time, when she'd heard a similar statement: "For the kids' sake." She wondered what these tactics shared in common, knowing that they shared something significant.

Shari had often felt honored and privileged to work in a prison because her admired Uncle Stan had also worked in corrections. She felt he'd be pleased, and she was glad to follow in his footsteps. Shari began to wonder, though, whether he learned these same tactics from his prison days?

On one occasion, as she waited in the main administration building for her ward's parole hearing, one of the male administrators scoffed at her loudly in reference to the situation. When she responded, he became angry and grabbed her by the shoulders. This hurt her physically, but more than that, it hurt emotionally, for it occurred in plain sight of several fellow employees. The others acted as though they hadn't seen a thing. Shari told the administrator loudly and in no uncertain terms, "Don't you ever put your hands on me again!"

Oddly enough, this man died the very next day. The on-the-job harassment eased, at least temporarily, as everyone was so stunned at his sudden death. A few personnel considered whether it might be an omen. In jest, they alerted others that they better "Lay off Shari... or else."

Deciding to capitalize on the events, Shari and her friend John came up with an idea. They mailed a telegram to her superintendent that read, "MENE, MENE, TEKEL, UPHARSIN." In the Bible, this is the mysterious riddle written in Aramaic by a hand on a wall at Belshazzar's feast. The words mean, "You have been weighed in the balance and found wanting. Your kingdom will be divided (Dan. 5:27)." Then they mailed a second telegram to the superintendent's assistant that read, "Chapter 5, verses 25-28. Bible." Both telegrams were unsigned.

Soon thereafter, the superintendent was transferred to another facility. John and Shari often wondered whether he associated his transfer as prophetic.

In addition to John and Jan, two other people comprised Shari's support system. They were the Catholic chaplain and the training officer at the facility. These were wise men who clearly understood the situation for what it was, understood why the system operated in this manner, and were honestly concerned for Shari's safety. When she felt lonely or devastated, she was always welcome to visit either of these gentlemen to find renewed strength. Sometimes they'd discuss the most recent occurrence, which she would find enlightening. Sometimes they made her laugh, and that always helped.

When she could no longer laugh, she knew that she absolutely had to leave. Despite the relief periods and the attempt at humor, there was no denying the reality of potential danger in her situation. Shari tried to assess the larger picture within which this particular realm fit. She was reprimanded frequently for infractions that had not occurred but became her responsibility to disprove, formally, in writing and by obtaining necessary signatures from significant personnel. "Guilty until proven innocent" tolled an all too familiar ring.

Every time, Shari was able to prove that she had not committed the infraction she'd been accused of. But the whole process was extremely time-consuming and draining. Consequently, her workload increased, and her designated time to complete it decreased. Shari likened her dilemma to the Hebrews in Egypt who were ordered to make the previous quota of bricks at a much faster pace, without the previously furnished straw. Various levels of personnel became her "superiors," and they began giving contradicting orders.

Meanwhile, Jan had had enough. She took the common sense approach: She resigned and moved away. Shari missed her friend terribly. She felt torn: What should she do? As much as Shari valued perseverance and wanted to make things work, she realized that perseverance was not synonymous with stupidity.

One night, as she went in to do some catch-up work at the office, she was informed, "The policy's been changed, and you have to go to the unit."

"State policy dictates that we never, ever go down to the living unit at night," she replied. "You know that. Go ahead and send someone for the wards I need to interview. You know this is policy."

"Sorry. We're told to inform you that policy's been changed and you're to go down to the unit."

'Down to the unit' meant walking across a dark football field that lay between the young men's living unit and the administration building. Calmly, Shari opened the door and started walking in the opposite direction. She didn't have her car with her; the kids, who were now driving, had dropped her off. So she went across the street to a store and phoned John to come pick her up.

The next day, however, reality returned, reminding Shari that she had to formally resign or show up at work again. The family's livelihood depended entirely on that job. She phoned in sick, which truly was the case. Her body literally broke out in large welts every time she considered resuming her work. She and the kids had a talk, and they all agreed that she would not be returning to the facility, despite whatever consequences they'd soon face.

Although my life is not just the life
That I might choose if I could
I thank my God that in this world of strife
He has made my life this good.
I do have my wealth in my family and health
And more I must confess
So a lifetime ambition already I've felt
In this short span of true happiness

CHAPTER SEVENTEEN

DECIDING TO LIVE LIFE outside prison walls requires a great deal of adjustment. Deciding to seize life, rather than just exist or react to life, is even more complicated. When a person has spent his or her entire lifetime coping and perceiving situations a certain way, it can never be simple to make a total transition. It is a slow, painful, and arduous process.

For Shari, it was nothing short of sheer bliss when she signed those resignation papers. It didn't matter that suddenly there were no more benefits or paychecks. It didn't matter that "the system" thought they'd won. Shari figured she was winning much more than she was losing, and perhaps they had lost much more than she'd lost.

During that first week out of work, Shari found the much-needed rest absolutely delightful. It was a luxury to cook, clean house, read, write, sleep, meditate, and reflect. Part of her peace of mind came from knowing that her family was going to make it. Their home was in escrow, scheduled to close any day. Their newly purchased house, already vacant and waiting for the three to move in, was scheduled to close sequentially. At last, all the bills that had added up to thousands of dollars would finally be paid.

Shari would have a few weeks to find a new job in their new area. She and her kids relished the thought of their relocation, and a shorter commute to school. Between their new school and the job she'd just left, they'd been averaging a hundred miles a day. The wear-and-tear from weeks of this long commute had started to take its toll.

With her income gone, their finances and future appeared shaky, but with their escrow closure just around the corner, weeks of waiting were behind them. They were full of plans and excitement as they packed for their upcoming move.

It was not going to be that simple, though. In the midst of their preparations, the phone rang. "Your buyer doesn't qualify after all. Both escrows are suspended."

"What do you mean, doesn't qualify?" Shari protested. "He's well qualified and has been approved for almost three months now."

It made no difference. The deal fell through. Shari was stunned. She wasn't prepared for such bad news. No job, no income, and now she'd just lost her five-hundred-dollar down payment for the house she had planned to purchase. To make matters worse, Shari was two months behind on the mortgage, and other bills were also overdue.

Shari felt a cold panic start to set in. How were she and her teenagers going to manage? So much had suddenly gone wrong, where to even begin? What to manage first? The old, faithful guilt inclination threatened to rule again. She beat herself up. How could she have been so stupid? Deep down, she knew she couldn't let guilt consume her. She'd been blindsided. There was no way to have foreseen the deal crumble.

Her guilt succumbed to fear. For the first time in four years, she had no money and no medical insurance. She talked with Cecelia and Aubrey about this new concern, since both of her children had made recent visits to the doctor for minor illnesses. Considering Shari was a professional social worker, they thought it ironic that they were at the point of needing immediate welfare. Without it, their house could go into foreclosure. They didn't even have money for food.

Shari had never asked for welfare before, even when the family was in dire poverty back in Arkansas. How could she bring herself to do that now, with a master's degree and home ownership? For the first time ever, she wished they didn't have a swimming pool. It seemed such an expensive luxury. There was simply no way to pay the bills and no way for Shari to immediately return to work.

Although she would have liked to just take a pill, go to sleep, and not think about it, she knew that wasn't the answer. The problem would still be there in the morning. So instead she took a deep breath, phoned her ex-husband, and told him their plight.

"I knew you had no business going out to California in the first place," he scoffed. "You can't afford to live out there, and you don't belong there. If you stay, things will only get worse for you, so you ought to bring the kids and move back here."

Shari decided to try Uncle Stan next. She called him, told him about their situation, and asked, "Would you buy all or part of my property back there?" She hoped he would. He had, after all, bought Shari's share of her mother's two acres near the lake when she'd needed money for school.

"No, honey, I just have all the property I need and wouldn't be interested in that."

"Well, perhaps a loan, and I'd put up the property for collateral?"

"No, dear. That wouldn't be the thing to do. I try not to get involved with things like that. I made loans to your mom and dad years ago and they always paid it back. But your situation is a little different. You went out there of your own accord. You have your education, so I'm sure you can make it. I pulled myself up by my own bootstraps, and I've got confidence in you. You can too. Tough times just help us all to grow up."

She politely thanked him and hung up. She'd stomached about all the sideline coaching she could take. Her next thought was her brother Ellis. But she remembered that he had borrowed two hundred dollars from Shari and her then-husband a decade earlier and never paid it back. When she needed a refrigerator and asked for help getting it, he refused. She decided to skip calling Ellis and save the price of another long-distance call. Instead she called her church and explained her plight. Their response was similar to what she'd already heard. They suggested that her financial difficulties might be stemming from her own misdeeds.

Regardless of how stupid she'd felt before many times, she had to put that behind her. Shari knew she could not lose their home to foreclosure or risk losing healthcare for her children. She swallowed her pride, what little she had left. But it wasn't easy walking into that welfare office. She'd never forget the look of astonishment mixed with suspicion when she told the eligibility worker of her previous employment, salary, and education, and even her swimming pool. Their present circumstances did seem to qualify them, though. The eligibility worker visited their home and reviewed Shari's employment termination papers. She gave the family cards for immediate medical services.

Although Shari was deeply embarrassed, her two teenagers actually found the ordeal amusing. They noted that their situation truly was appropriate for aid. For many long years, Shari had supported it for others; now it was her turn to get support. Her kids offered other realistic suggestions with such calmness that Shari absorbed their peacefulness, which she greatly needed.

Aubrey and Cecelia came up with solutions. They could take their lunches ("brown bag it," they said) to school. They could remain in their present school, or they could transfer back to their area. They could simply re-list the house for sale and remain hands off and emotionally detached through the process, letting the real estate agent do the work.

A picture began to emerge. They were losing the house they thought they were buying and weren't selling the one they thought they were selling. Shari had no job, no money, and a mountain of bills. But they could handle it. Cecelia and Aubrey agreed that their mom probably wouldn't be hanged or even jailed for having to postpone all their payments. Together, they'd find a solution. They'd make it work. After all, they'd been through much worse in the past.

Aubrey's primary concern was that they were driving on a bald tire. Shari assured him that the first money they received would go for the car and groceries. In the meantime, they'd just drive cautiously and budget carefully.

A few days later, Cecelia became seriously ill from a reaction to penicillin. She was rushed to the hospital where several doctors worked frantically to save her life. Had the family not obtained the state medical card, they might have postponed the hospital admittance, unaware of the true severity of the situation. They were thankful that they'd been willing to go on welfare when that, too, needed to be done. They were also thankful, a few short weeks later, to return their state medical cards and go off welfare. Throughout everything, they learned valuable truths about life, principles that apply equally across all circumstances.

One night, in a group-discussion class that Shari attended, the conversation centered on how difficult it was for people to shift from a management position to one of receptivity. That summarized her own recent experiences precisely. She had been trying to manage. As head of the household, it was her responsibility. Yet despite all her efforts and ingenuity, it was an impossible task. When Cecelia's life was spared, they were glad that they'd failed the task and had instead submitted to "forced receptivity."

As the discussion continued, once more her thoughts wandered back to her mother and her "assumed suicide," as the original death certificate read. Because of the nature of the circumstances, it must have been a deliberate and premeditated event. Considering the large gun from some unknown source that had been cleaned, oiled, and fully loaded with new.38 shells, some time and preparation had obviously been spent. Some calculated management had occurred.

Shari's mother, like Aunt Bea in the fictional town of Mayberry, had never worked outside her home. Her entire life had consisted of raising her children, cleaning the family's large house, cooking three full meals a day, sewing, and shopping. Her management was limited to her services for others. She responded to what needed to be done. Her life was in service, never control.

With Christmas approaching, Mama already had accumulated numerous flowers to make her holiday poinsettia arrangements. Shari managed to salvage the red velvet jumper her mother had been making for Cecelia, in addition to the matching gown and pajamas for her and Aubrey. To Shari, these unfinished garments attempted to show where the grandmother's attention was during that time, that awful time.

Years before, when the doctors informed Mama that she had sugar diabetes, she was heartbroken. But because life to her was so valuable, she diligently injected insulin into her own body on a daily basis. This daily routine took place at 5:00 A.M., prior to preparing breakfast. She knew well that an excessive amount of insulin or no injection at all could be fatal. Her attentiveness resulted in no mishap for over a decade. She had taken her injection on that day, too, the day she died.

So she had taken her insulin to stay alive (routine for many years), cooked breakfast as usual, then obtained this huge, mysterious gun, cleaned, oiled, and loaded it with the new shells she'd secretly bought and kept hidden? Yeah, right.

Even Mama's doctor had reported to Roberta and Shari the arthritic condition of her hands, which would have prevented her from being able to grip a pistol. Shari had often wondered why she would have placed the barrel of such a gun toward the back of her head when the heart or temple would suffice. One further item: a small, flat handgun was always loaded and easily accessible to the entire family had there ever been a need for such. This gun was always kept in Daddy's desk in the dining room of their home. Why was this known gun not used?

Had they been able to determine the owner or even the origin of that.38, its story would clear away all the mystery. But the owner of the.38 was, for the time being, invisible. When Uncle Stan called in the forensic experts to administer the paraffin tests (to determine powder burns on the victim's hands), they were unable to administer the tests because Mama's hands had already been washed. Who had washed her hands after she was dead, and why? Shari wondered whether Mama got blamed for that, too.

And why was no investigation done? Uncle Stan—Mama's brother—called in those forensic experts when he was first notified. As an attorney, Uncle Stan knew exactly what to do for investigation purposes. True to form, in keeping with his character and his profession, he immediately began the investigation process.

He had also earlier (over the phone when he was told that his sister was fatally shot) made the immediate statement, "The SOB killed her!" in reference to Shari's dad. It was common knowledge in their town that Uncle Stan had left the prison grounds (where he lived) with his gun "to kill Cecil!" he'd said. He was stopped on the way by the state police. Thereafter, he was totally subdued. Whatever could those state police have told him that would affect him in that way and stop the investigation he'd started? Why had he decided to protect Daddy?

The term "politics" had been suggested to Shari from time to time, but she couldn't understand the implications. The gun had been passed around to the early arrivers by the local resident who worked as a state policeman, "to handle and observe" (gawk at). Consequently, no fingerprint check was ever done. But then, why was the fingerprint process so blatantly defied when officers are certainly trained otherwise?

One year after her mother's death, Shari was numbly searching for some indication of what had really happened when she discovered a detective magazine in the back of her father's desk, behind and underneath the desk drawers. The feature story was titled "Lady Killer." Although Shari's husband took the magazine and disposed of it, in spite of her pleadings to the contrary, she could never forget that story. The lady had been shot in the head with a.38. She had then been placed in front of the stove so that the process of rigor mortis would be interrupted by heat from the stove; thus, time of actual death could not be determined. Shari's mother was found in front of the stove also. Her "time of death" was listed at 2:00 P.M. But if the heat had precluded accuracy, then what time had she really died?

Shari often wondered where all of Daddy's detective magazines had disappeared to, for they were missing when she first returned after her mother's death. Yet that one magazine was saved, even hidden. Why? Was it his secret map to Treasure Island? Was it his trophy of success? And why couldn't Shari keep it and show it to the authorities? Why had someone hung large religious pictures in different locations in their house since Shari's last visit a few months earlier? What purpose were they supposed to serve?

At any rate, until or unless an investigation revealed the true account of what happened to Mama, Shari stored away both stories. She had either premeditated, sneaked around with those new shells and hidden gun, and killed herself, or she had been murdered. Both versions haunted Shari's dreams for years to come. No matter where she was—at work or school or anywhere else—both versions played out disturbing scenes in her head. Time made no difference at all. Their intensity never lessened.

Shari knew one was truth and the other, a lie. Her search for the truth was like seeking an oasis in the desert. She prayed her oasis would someday come along. Shari prayed, *Please God, don't let it be a mirage.* She detested being judgmental and drawing conclusions based on anything other than fact. She believed in innocent till proved guilty. She wanted to stop the thoughts and suspicions regarding her father, since he had not been proven guilty either. Yet her mother was dead, formally labeled "guilty" without any proof!

Thirteen years later, sitting in a class with other inquiring minds, Shari was discovering the most poignant evidence of all that would silence forever the contention of a suicide on that day. After thirteen years, Mama could finally rest in peace, and Shari could begin to rest (at least somewhat) in life. The preparation of a pistol is a calculated, managerial action. Her mother had, for fifty years, been of the extreme opposite character: receptive, not proactive.

She had endured numerous operations, numerous beatings, even near deaths at the hands of another. She had been for years scorned by Daddy for being herself, for being diabetic, and for taking her "damned shots," as he called them. She had been degraded and diminished in her marriage.

Yet she had found a way to keep moving forward, day by day, by choosing to live. Life for her was more arduous than for many people, yet she had chosen to live. Had she at any time chosen to die, she could easily have done that, more easily than for most others, in that she had only to skip her shot or inject too much, and no one would have known it was suicide. In her needle and medication lay the power of life and death, and she had chosen life, a choice that prevailed for years. For her fifty years on this earth, each day she chose life.

It is indeed a fundamental law of the universe—dictated by no man and reversible for no man—that the hardest thing for any human being to accomplish is to change one's mode-of-being in the world. If one is predisposed for years to be receptive, he or she can hardly become a controller suddenly or easily. If one is conditioned to be a controller, it is likewise extremely difficult to cease being a controller and become receptive. It is possible, but extremely difficult and at best, gradual. The longer one is conditioned to his or her mode-of-being, the more difficult such a transition would become.

If a controller becomes depressed to a point of despondency (which, by the way, is hardly an overnight event) capable of suicide, the chosen mode for suicide would be consistent with the mode-of-being in the world—hence, with the person's overall perspective of calculated, controlled action. If a receptive person becomes despondent to the point of suicide, his or her chosen mode for suicide would also be consistent with the mode-of-being in the world—with the person's overall perspective of giving in and letting be. Had Shari's mom really wanted to commit suicide, she would have taken the needle route. Yet the gun that they were all aware of, lying nearby for years—the small, available, easy-to handle, fully loaded gun—was not the one used in her death. Does impulsiveness take the time to discretely purchase new .38 shells, clean the gun barrel, and oil the cylinder of a mysteriously obtained gun? No. That is calculated, controlled.

In fact, suicide itself is indicative of a controlling nature, much as can be recognized in the similar act of homicide, for suicide and homicide are not that different. State law describes suicide as "a heinous act." Both suicide and homicide require the personal initiative of ordering a death. No rationale is sufficient to truly distinguish between the two, since both are murder. Both acts leave a rippling effect on the family of the victims.

The person who consciously elects to take a life (his own or someone else's) is saying in essence, "I want what I want, and the effect on others as a result of my having my way is insignificant to me." Suicide and homicide require a selfish, self-centered, self-serving person. It also requires an assumption of superiority to God himself. For death is a decision that recognizably belongs to God. So a person who elects to judge a person (himself or another) and condemn that person to death, fails to recognize either the existence of God or the omnipotence of God.

Premeditated suicide and premeditated murder are calculated, controlling acts that require calculating, controlling people to administer them. These are people who refuse to reach out for assistance, to admit they need help, to ask. These people are 'non receptive.' These are people who take what they want. This is indicative of gross immaturity and irresponsibility in addition to a controlling rather than a responsive nature. "Doing what needs to be done" is not valued. The combination of obtaining, cleaning, oiling, purchasing shells, loading, and using a gun would likely indicate someone interested in and experienced with guns.

The smile that parted Shari's mouth into an open "Ah ha!" felt most invigorating to her. She looked around the group. They were still discussing the mode-of-being in the world, and they hadn't even noticed that she was in a private world at the time. But then, they wouldn't mind, because they had come to this group because they wanted to learn. They were receptive, responsive. She so much preferred this type of person!

Shari began to compare herself to her mother. She had been unconsciously and finally consciously striving to break free of various cobwebs, or prisons, that hampered her full development. Shari remembered her divorce at twenty-six, how difficult it had been, how awesome was the task of becoming a student again after eight years, and how strenuous simple survival had been with full-time school, work, and the rearing of two children alone.

She thought about her mother's life and the hardships she had endured. As her thirtieth anniversary approached, Mama had told her daughter that her marriage "has been a thirty-year sentence." And she was making sensible plans, even sharing them with her siblings, to do what needed to be done: get a divorce, move to the city, and live with her sister. Mama deserved freedom after such a sentence, certainly not an ugly, Mafia-style execution. But most definitely she deserved the dignity of representation, of the truth being told on her behalf. First the truth had to be found, for the calculators and controllers had meticulously attempted to bury it beyond retrieval.

In her heart Shari knew that Mama had been warmly received into life everlasting, and that she'd know her mother again in total liberation. If Mama could see Shari and her children now, if she'd been aware of the torment that followed her death as they wondered how she left, she can at last know that they're released from that agonizing inner turmoil. Yes, Mama, *we do miss you and love you and look beyond this life, toward that heavenly meeting place where never enters strife. No, no more strife.*

As the class ended, Shari practically floated out, feet barely touching the ground, so thankful that Mama and she had just been exonerated. Exhibit A had just been entered, indisputable. The mode-of-being produced the verdict "not guilty." They were exonerated simultaneously because they didn't know how to be controllers. In that arena, they failed. Thank God!

CHAPTER EIGHTEEN

WHEN HER OWN ENERGY reserves reached depletion, mangled portions of Shari's story unveiled themselves to her therapist at the Garden Grove Community Church Counseling Center. It certainly wasn't a pretty story, and she fully expected rejection or at least reprimand. Consumed with guilt over so long a time, she expected to be burdened with additional guilt. Instead, Shari was shown the compassion that Jesus showed when He walked with people, in human form, unable to be critical toward people who were writhing in the pain of their own blindness. "Consider the lilies," she was told (Matt. 6:28). And she wondered how she could be more valuable than a beautiful, radiant, white, fragrant lily? Yet Jesus Himself said it, so she dared not question and found it to be a soothing acceptance to just believe it.

That was the beginning of the discovery of truth that sets humankind free. She learned to trust in man for the extent of a counseling session, and to recognize that some men, even Caucasian men, are directed and used by God, according to their commitment to Him. After several such sessions, the process continued into her home life, work life and innermost dialogue. The awareness was steadfast that living water had been discovered and that she was thirsty after her lifetime of desert travel. She would awaken in the night with thoughts, new realizations, emanating from her brain and heart. For a season, the compulsion literally to vomit was so strong that she feared she might create a ghastly scene at any moment, wherever she happened to be.

In the middle of the night, the struggle mounted until Shari was wrestling with the angel of her very soul for her soul's release from emotional blockage. There is no bondage greater than that of distorted thinking, false assumptions, illusions, devastating misnomers that restrict, limit, strangle. "Yes, yes. I will, I will," she said many times in the middle of the night and would, in fact, get pencil and paper to roughly record the thoughts that were swiftly emerging to the point of waking her.

More realities appeared in place of false notions. Then there was peace and sleep. The next day and evening consisted of more and similar notes, things that must be written down, ugly as they were, in order to become tangible and thus disposable, freeing her mind and energy for constructive activity. Unexpectedly, an intense need arose to return to the counselor, who would permit the ugly ordeal of emotional vomiting once and forevermore. A twenty-mile trip was necessary, and with no appointment this day, there was only a remote chance of catching the counselor before the workday ended. It had grown dark by the time Shari drove into the sprawling parking lot. With her eyes dimmed (as occurred regularly in her struggles for inner vision), she observed a blurred figure a distance away and called out his name loudly.

He stopped, surprised and curious, possibly almost amused at her unkempt appearance. She asked to speak with him without an appointment. He was silent; his workday was completed, family waiting. *What right do I have to impose?* she wondered.

Yet for the first time in her life, she chose to impose herself. It seemed urgently important. Perhaps she was as valuable as that lily, but she needed help to find out. And she must find out. He allowed her to read the pages of garbage that her mind had released in the night. He allowed her to talk and to confess before him her sins. Yet again, he passed no judgment; he simply understood and allowed the process to transpire. When the major work was revealed and he accepted the verbal, written garbage to dispose of, she knew it was a permanent disposal. Both were astounded to hear water falling from the ceiling, a most unusual event, particularly on the fourth floor of a thirteen-story tower! It seemingly confirmed the breakthrough— her breakthrough. (Undoubtedly, as simple as an overflowed sink from the fifth floor?).

When Shari thinks of the seasons, she especially thanks God for His beautiful timing. Her process had begun shortly before Easter, and she knew that a death and burial of the old, confused, weary, fearful, guilt-ridden desert traveler had occurred. What a relief! And resurrection followed and could and must continue. Awakening is so delightful that one is enticed to climb higher on the ladder of elucidation. She knew that the season was appropriate, and she was that Easter lily!

Shortly thereafter, Shari heard Dr. Robert H. Schuller speak about the unfinished works of Michelangelo—marble statues that had been begun but after the artist's death, remained locked forever in blocks of stone. She knew she desired total freedom, so much confinement had she already experienced. She wanted all the truth available for all the freedom that could be attained; she didn't want to be locked away, unfinished.

One thing that she really desired was her state license for clinical practice. Because her own journey had been so gradual and difficult, she longed to assist others in theirs. When a moment of strong apprehension caused her to doubt that she could pass the state exams, her counselor reminded her of Psalm 84:11: "No good thing doth He withhold from him that walketh uprightly."

She passed the exams and received her license—and the glory was given to God. Exuberance overwhelmed her as she held that license to help others see clearly and be liberated from bondage! Along with Dr. Martin Luther King, Jr., she shouted, "Free at last! Free at last! Thank God Almighty, I'm free at last!"

By Independence Day, she had accepted freedom as a glorious way of life; the "revolutionary war" was indeed ended and she had been declared victorious. Freedom seemed to mean a never-ending assault against barricades. Through the years, many had presented themselves as normal and inevitable. It soon became apparent that anything serving as a barricade was detrimentally deceptive. People too often accept these barriers against real progress, real living, and abundant life, because they simply never realize the possibility of living without them.

Thanksgiving Day was truly monumental for Aubrey, Cecelia, and Shari. They attended the Harvest of Hope Dinner, presented by Dr. Schuller's Garden Grove Community Church. They were honored to present their small check to the ministry that lovingly releases people from false illusions of bondage and "puts strong wings on weary hearts."

As they left the banquet, Shari mentioned that she'd love to meet Dr. Schuller. There were so many people between them, however, that Shari and her children didn't even attempt to. The next morning, they arrived for the Thanksgiving Day service and were surprised to see him standing nearby, talking to some people. Shari wished, oh, how she wished. When he concluded his conversation, it was time for him to enter the sanctuary and begin services. As he turned to go inside, Shari thought, *Surely someday*.

Then, unexpectedly, he turned around, walked back to Shari and her kids, asked their names, and warmly visited, as though there were no service waiting on him at all. They felt very important at that moment. He even asked if they lived in the area. When the family explained that they wanted to, he prayed then and there that their desire become a reality. Shari's teenage children were awed by his awareness of their deep need to meet and speak with him, although there was no time and many others were waiting for him. The three noticed his eyes, deep and encompassing, much like (Shari expects) were Moses' and even Jesus', because of His awareness of people's needs and because of His own great vision. That Thanksgiving Day confirmed for them the truth of God's promise: "Delight yourself in the Lord, and He'll give you the desire of your heart" (Ps. 37:4).

Then, quite unexpectedly, Shari's sister telephoned her. Visits with her had been possible only when she and the children were able to return to Arkansas. But, of course, cross-country travel was expensive, and Shari never shared their struggles with Robbie, for she had her own share and by comparison, hers must be worse. But she'd wished they could visit more often.

"Will you be coming back here for Christmas, Shari?" her sister asked.

Regretfully, Shari replied, "No, we won't be able to make it this year."

She hardly wanted to give Robbie the bulk of their why-nots, but would leave it at that. Then a strange thing happened. It sounded like Robbie was very sad that they weren't coming. The last holiday spent together had been years ago, when they agonizingly unwrapped the pile of gifts under the tree, hoping they would somehow reveal a clue. But prior to that, their Christmases as a family growing up were joyous times together. The tone of her sister's voice kept echoing in Shari's mind, and at her children's unselfish prodding, she agreed to travel to Arkansas prior to the holiday just to visit with Roberta. She felt a strange enthusiasm for returning, vastly different from ever before.

The trip was full of apprehension, and as the plane hovered over Little Rock, Shari fully lost control of her emotions. As she looked into the waiting lounge, she saw so many people at so many windows. Yet in one window stood a lone person—her sister! She began crying hard and it seemed that years of fear and guilt, sadness, doubt, distance and longing erupted from her system.

Finally the other passengers began moving and she knew that this time she and Robbie would have a wonderful visit. When she entered the terminal, there was her sister, crying too, questioning her own emotions. Shari was overjoyed to see her. She looked absolutely beautiful! Years from the past flashed across her memory. Shari had always adored her baby sister since the day she was born. She cried with her for awhile until both eventually calmed down.

They visited relatives they hadn't seen in years. Uncle Timmy proudly related their ancestral heritage, back to the Choctaw Indians. He noted Shari's black hair and her sister's dark eyes and other features. Minutes turned into hours as they carried their adventuresome study right into the attic. Timmy was their mother's baby brother, and he related the good times they'd experienced growing up. Some stories Shari had heard before, but they were refreshing to hear again, and she observed his likeness to Mama as he spoke. Her mind recalled much love as she looked around the house where her grandparents had lived. Both of them had been remarkably loving people, poor only in money, but wealthy in love.

Friends and relatives continued to drop in to visit them— uninvited, unannounced—because the welcome mat was always out. There was always coffee or tea, biscuits left over from breakfast, and lots of reminiscing, funny stories and warm laughter. No one could relate an event or a conversation like Shari's grandfather could. People would simply be crying from the intensity of their laughter before he would finish. He would exaggerate to add color to the tale; he knew it, and everybody knew it, and it worked. He drew people away from their serious concerns and let them take a timeout to laugh and enjoy each other's presence. He realized there was time enough to be serious, but that laughter was needed, like good medicine.

Grandma looked much like Shari's mother, also short, stout, and devoted to others. It could rightly be said that she adored Grandpa. They were a good match and reared their six kids on love. Without exception, Shari can emphatically say that her dearest early memories were those around her grandparents down at their old home place. Sitting on the floor near the fireplace till late at night, listening to Grandpa tell funny stories to Shari, her brother, and their cousins was an experience that no Disneyland could surpass. Sometimes they popped popcorn and sometimes not, but there was always a lot of fun and a lot of love. Grandpa called all the girls "Daughter," and somehow they always knew which one of them he meant. His temperament was easily regulated by his wife's soothing remark, "Now, Herman." And, oh, how he loved and responded to her, "Dovie."

Mama had talked often about her initial announcement to her parents of her intention to marry Daddy. Her folks had been supportive of him as a person, saying, "Oh, Olive, he's a good boy, a fine young man, and we think the world of him. But, Honey, he's so different from us. He's just been raised differently!"

"Now, Mama, he's just kind of shy around a lot of folks and doesn't talk much. But he likes to be with all of you. He's just not the talkative type. We've all been so noisy, I thought it might be nice having somebody quieter, for a change."

"It's just that everybody knows the Lewises, and they're real strict about things. They don't know how to laugh. I've noticed that when Cecil is here, too, he don't really seem to see what we laugh at as funny. That's OK, of course, but I'd hate to think of you not being able to relax and have a good time with people."

"Oh, he likes our friends and he likes good times, too. I just admire him so much. You know, he's worked at his daddy's sawmill since he was twelve years old. That's pretty decent, I think. I know we'd make a good living. We're even thinking of going to Washington State and picking apples when the harvest time's there."

"For sure he's a fine boy, and he does work hard. Actually, most folks wondered why he did. His folks are pretty well-to-do and I don't see his brothers working like he does."

"I think it'd be great fun to go to Washington State in the apple orchards. Can you imagine all the way to Washington! Cecil said we could save enough to build or buy us a little house later on."

"Folks say that Mr. Lewis is real strict at mealtime and that nobody can talk while they're at the table. Have you seen that? And they say he drinks a lot too."

"Well, I've not been there at mealtime, but I'm sure they can talk if they want to. Now that'd be silly, wouldn't it?"

Shari had been told through the years by both her parents that neither affection nor other emotions were demonstrated in her father's childhood home, except when Grandpa Lewis got mad, and he could blow his temper. Many times she'd asked Daddy about his family and he wouldn't tell her anything. He just seemed to not like his brothers or sisters. Sometimes when Shari queried about them, he just got irritated, so she knew to change the subject. Daddy talked about his sister Ethel who'd died when she was just a little kid, but he couldn't remember what it was that happened to her. She was the one he'd liked, though.

He once related his first day at school in first grade; for that was the day he'd whacked another kid over the head with his lunch pail when the other child had ridiculed him. Later in high school, on a dare from his peers, he'd broken the ice and went swimming in a frozen pond, in January. Then similarly, he and another student in school had drunk the chemical mixture that had been prepared in science class. This was also in reaction to their peers' enticement and in demonstration of their bravery. Shari wondered if maybe he liked being the center of their attention too? She didn't think he got much attention unless he did something outlandish like that.

But he never talked of friendships that were meaningful to him, as Mama often did. And he shared no good memory of home. That's not to say none occurred, but Shari asked him often, and he'd just look at her strangely, as though there were none there. Daddy did talk about his high school graduation.

"I had typhoid fever my senior year and missed school most of the whole year. So I had to graduate a year late. Then after I missed my own graduation, my dad refused to get me a new suit for the ceremony. All the other boys' dads managed to get them suits, but not my dad. And everybody knew he could afford it easier than most."

"Why not?" Shari pressed. "Was he mad at you for getting typhoid fever, like you wanted to be sick a whole year and miss everything?"

"I don't know. I never did know what he was thinking. But there was another man in town that got me one. He said he got his boy one and he'd get me a suit too."

Shari was grateful to that man, although she never met him. His name was Hensey Lackett. "That was nice of him." She felt grateful to that other dad who was sensitive to her dad's feelings, even way back then.

"Yeah, it was. But it was humiliating, too. I was already older than the other kids and missing my own group. But I didn't even want to go if I was going to be the oddball in the bunch."

"I don't blame you. But I'm glad you did go, because I like your picture, the graduation picture; it's real handsome."

He grinned. "I had hair then."

"You got hair now, just like little curly bacon strips when you comb them over to one side.

"Yeah."

Shari knew Daddy felt his folks didn't like him much, and Mama said it was true that they did make an obvious distinction between him and the other kids. She told Shari about his class ring, and it was like the suit. They couldn't be nice to Daddy, and that must have worried him a lot. When it was time to order class rings, the other students got to order theirs, but he couldn't have one. Then years later, after he was married and had kids, his mother brought him a ring, the kind that's supposed to be engraved. His wasn't engraved with anything; it was just blank. Mama said she figured they felt guilty all those years, as they bought all the other kids their rings. But Daddy just tossed it in the cabinet. He never wore it. He didn't like blank rings, Shari figured.

Daddy had really wanted to go to college, for he loved math and was exceptionally intelligent in that area. He enrolled at the Church College, but after two weeks, his dad decided not to send the tuition so he had to come home. He always regretted going to college for only two weeks. Mama said he had wished for a copy of his birth certificate and didn't feel like his birthday was really his birthday, nor was he certain as to where he was born. Then when Uncle Stan worked for the Vital Statistics Bureau, he had a birth certificate made up for Daddy. But Grandma got really mad about it, saying, "It is none of your business, Stan Deevens!"

It always seemed to Shari as though Daddy's problems began before he was born or early after, and she could probably guess why, considering he was the firstborn. Back then, people didn't have babies "early" if they were uppity folks. It's a pity that the little baby gets the blame when that's the case. Shari told Mama she thought it probably was the case. But she just said, "Oh, you can't be sure of that. It could have been anything." Shari figured her Mama felt sorry for him being the black sheep of his family, though—especially when her own family had been close and fun-loving.

But no individual worked harder at making a living, and an honest one at that, than did Shari's dad. He just never quite earned his parents' approval, and he never stopped trying. He owned his own home and business and had arranged for a pond to be dug on his land, which he stocked with fish. He was pleased with this, his achievement. Yet he would learn from time to time that his own father had claimed ownership. Daddy owned the planer mill, and Grandpa the sawmill. Sometimes Grandpa wanted to store some of his lumber under Daddy's big shed to protect it from the weather. Daddy was glad to let him, because he was glad to do the favor for his own dad.

Yet when Shari's dad's planer mill burned to the ground on New Year's Day in the early fifties and he suffered a total washout of $25,000 uninsured equipment, his father demanded reimbursement for the lumber that he had stored. Daddy, it seemed, always owed—as though he never needed or deserved to receive. He always wondered when he saw his younger brothers and sisters assisted in various ways (college, homes, loans, gifts) why he was treated so differently.

That's one reason he didn't seem to like his brothers and sisters. Then, too, he'd mention seeing them, "Hauling Poppy's Coca Colas off to their house whenever they feel like it." That also bothered him, because he tried always to keep his folks supplied with Cokes, as he had a Coke machine at his office. So he took them up to their house by the case.

Mama always regretted that they had settled so close to his parents, across the street. She said it would have been better if they had lived far away from all of them. But Daddy had wanted to live close by. The day the planer burned was New Year's Day, and they were having lunch in their pretty dining room with the good dishes when Uncle Stan ran in.

"Cecil come quick, the planer's on fire!" he yelled.

When Daddy saw the fire, he frantically ran under the shed, grabbed a bound bundle of lumber under each arm and ran back out to safety, salvaging the metal bound lumber. Normally, three men were required to lift one of those bundles of lumber. Yet in his panic he ran with two bundles, alone. Shari often wondered whether he didn't use physical, mental, and emotional energy in advance—as a credit card. But then later on when he needed that energy, his supply was depleted.

He had a tough time adjusting to his loss. He had known only the lumber business since he was twelve years old. Now in his early forties, he felt totally inept at learning anything new. Mama tried to dissuade him from going into debt to replace the lost equipment, because the changing times indicated that the small business was soon to become obsolete as credit cards and large supply stores were quickly appearing on the scene. "We won't be able to compete with the credit-card business, with our cash-and-carry, one-man ownership," she pointed out to him.

He suffered a lot of depression, crying bouts, and excruciating fear. He finally did replace the equipment, but later regretted having done so because it sat unused, rusting. He would stand for hours in the hot weather, spraying the stacks of overly dried lumber with a water hose to keep them from warping. The one and only area he had confidence in had been his business. Now it had been totally destroyed. He had tried to build it back, at great cost, but the equipment sat idle, like a stagnant pond.

Here his own identity lay. His foundation was gone. Shari wonders now whether he was affected more deeply than any of them realized at the time from that loss and from the monetary insecurity he felt with no one to turn to.

He did turn to someone else for security, Shari thought, on one other occasion. He told her himself: "I got on my knees and prayed to God to take away that desire to drink." He prayed hard and long and he told her all about it. He said he couldn't quit drinking on his own, but if God would take away the desire, he would promise never to drink again. As far as anyone knew, he never did drink again after that day, and he sure gave God the credit. Shari never could understand how, years later, he could so calmly and confidently contend, "There is no God. When you're dead, you're just dead, and that's all there is to it."

Mama always defended him up until the drinking ceased, saying that he was "a really good man," and that it was "just that liquor that was so bad." However, it soon became evident that all of the blame didn't belong to the alcohol. She tried hard to shield the truth of their relationship, particularly from her kids. But it was too obvious to be missed, and to a few trusted others, she confided.

In one of the last letters Shari received from her, Mama was recognizing the futility of their marriage of thirty years. She had stopped crying and worrying, becoming realistic and hopeful for the first time in a long time. She was discovering that life existed outside of servitude. No longer was she shaken with the ever-present threat that she must hit the road ("get the hell out," as he liked to put it) when the kids were grown. She had begun to agree and to look forward to taking her half of their assets and doing exactly that.

Her last child, Robbie ("My baby," Mama liked to say) was the only one remaining at home. By then, she was a senior in high school, making good grades. She had been engaged for a while and had just gotten secretly married. Mama had cooked Robbie a birthday cake and had let her invite a girlfriend over for the night. All was well and natural.

The following morning, the girls left for school as usual, not knowing that would be the last they would see of Mama alive. Only God Himself fully understands what that daughter experienced when she got off the school bus to find cars and people filling the lawn. She ran toward the porch but was stopped by Daddy, telling her, "She's gone." Then Robbie was physically restrained from entering her own home for hours.

Their dad's cousin Grover was, at that time, considered a powerful political figure in the town. He personally and forcefully escorted Robbie across the street and barricaded her in an aunt's house. The aunt herself was hysterical, they said, for she and Mama had been high school friends. In bewildered shock, Shari's sister looked out the window as they loaded up and left with their mother. She was not allowed to see her, to make decisions for herself, to ask questions, to give answers, or talk to anyone. From the beginning, there was only forceful control—totally devoid of compassion, inquiry, or comfort. When at last the bulk of the spectators had dispersed, she was allowed to return home.

"Shari, nobody would talk to me. I knew it was Mama that they took away because there was a sheet over her and you could tell it was her large stomach. I kept asking people, 'But what happened?' and they just stared at me.

"You could tell there was something wrong with the floor. There was a big wet spot, and it was kind of white where the wax had come off in washing it. I asked them, 'What's wrong with the floor? Why does it look like that?'

"'That's where they washed up the blood,' was all they would say.

"'Blood? Well, what happened? Did she fall on her scissors?' I asked them."

Robbie knew she sewed a lot—every day—and the sewing machine was near the wet spot. She was trying to get it to make sense.

"But nobody would answer anything else. My head was spinning by then, and I thought it was about to explode, so I wanted to get away from those staring people and try to think. I went upstairs where it'd be quiet and sat down on the bed. Shari, I put my head down, kind of holding my chin with my hand, like this," she demonstrated, "and then I thought, Well what's a wet spot doing up here, like the one downstairs? She couldn't fall on her scissors both places."

"Robbie," Shari said, not even clear herself about any questions to ask, but wondering why somebody didn't go upstairs with her to try to help her. "What were the people doing in the house then, while you were upstairs?"

"Well, somebody was working on the bathroom heater."

"What was wrong with the bathroom heater?"

"You know, I don't know. It was OK when we left for school that morning. But I heard them saying it was broke and the repairman was working on it."

"What could be wrong with the bathroom heater?" And why was it so important at a time like that?

"So many things were weird. I couldn't think; I was just sick to my stomach."

"Well, sure you were. Gosh, I wish I had been here with you. That was so awful for you, and you were all alone. You'd think someone would have gone upstairs with you."

It had been one day after her seventeenth birthday; had her mother discovered she was married? That she was pregnant? And if so, so what? Their mother was probably stronger than any woman in town. She'd proved that already.

At the time in her life when Robbie was entitled to be the happiest, she was inwardly beginning to rage with hysteria. No one was able to help; no one was trying to help. No one was interested in helping. There was another agenda, and it wasn't about the victim or the victim's grieving youngest child.

What was the agenda? It's commonly known that the truly guilty can easily shirk guilt, whereas the truly innocent will readily accept guilt. That is obviously what began occurring there at that house, and very quickly. Robbie's young husband, Chuck, tried to help her, but he was also assuming guilt because he was also innocent and non-controlling. Her friends would be able to comfort her only indirectly and temporarily because a gulf had quickly formed, separating her from everyone.

Shari thinks Robbie was plagued with suicidal thoughts for a long time (she knows she herself was, feeling so guilty and undeserving to live) because the guilt was actually handed to her. Only by the grace of God did she survive the terror that she alone experienced. It is little wonder that her first baby was born dead.

Years later, Robbie was able to recognize, at least in part, that she had been extremely convenient for certain people of a particular nature to project blame onto for the death of their mother. At first, these people blamed Mama directly for her own death, then Robbie, indirectly. In this way, these certain people could protect their own status quo. For them, Christmas would be happy as usual that year, as would the Christmases to follow. For Shari and Robbie and a few others, though, they would forever be a nightmare.

One thing was certain: they were by nature more in resemblance to their mother, because they had no control. They just responded reflexively to those who did assume full control. They were told what to do, and they acted and reacted exactly as robots for, Shari believes, two reasons. They were in a state of numbness, unable to think for themselves. Also, they assumed guilt because they had not been perfect to their mother. Obedience, even too late and to the wrong people, seemed to atone somewhat for their imperfections as her children. In retrospect, Shari wonders how anyone could have purposely attributed guilt to them at such a time. But they did, and both daughters accepted it.

Months later, when Shari was terribly distraught, her mother's brother noted that they were normal kids. "Your mother wasn't perfect either. She did just like all kids do as they're growing up. She gave her mom and dad some headaches. But parents expect that of their kids, and they remember how it was when they were coming up. It's normal, and they get through it."

"But she didn't want me to marry who I did," Shari told him.

"Neither did her mom and dad want her to marry who she did. But she did anyway, and they kept right on loving her all the same. I know because they were my mom and dad, too. Your folks keep right on loving you just the same."

Although Shari's visit with Robbie was brief, it seemed to make up for many years of wrenching separation. It was truly heartwarming for her to visit with her sister again.

Now it seemed clear to them that they weren't so bad after all, considering everything. So for the first time in more than a decade, Shari was able to walk the streets of her hometown without guilt. When she visited her uncle's new office, she felt as if she were looking through her mother's eyes and, to her wonderment, told him that Mama definitely would have approved of his pretty new office. He told Shari that life was like a huge library, housing hordes of books: "A good library has some novels, some mysteries, some comedies, some tragedies, some love stories. But each person can choose the bulk of the ones he collects over the years."

In many ways, Shari had patterned her own life after this uncle. Her first year of college was at his alma mater. She taught school. She worked in a prison and then counseled people as he had done in his work through the years. But he was close to the governor of the state and to all the state offices and officials. Shari had tremendous difficulty understanding why an investigation was denied to such a man's sister and why he was so helpless in this matter and so powerful in other similar matters?

When Shari was with him, he asked her not to talk about anything that would make him cry. His wife, Begonia, cautioned her privately not to talk about anything that might injure his health. After all, she had talked to her aunt about her mother's death, and she had died. Perhaps if she talked to

Uncle Stan, he might cry or even have a heart attack and die, also. She had experienced sufficient guilt and had no desire to invite in any more.

I can do all things through Christ who strengthens me,
I can do naught but waste precious time, without Him.
In my stumbling, faltering way,
He sees, and He understands
And with His infinite Love, He lifts me up again
And redirects my Path.
I will think well of myself today
And in so doing, will think well of others.
Tomorrow's need is not important today -
My days must be lived one at a time
And each one in God's care.
It is a beautiful world and I am a beautiful person.
I love my God and I love my neighbor as myself.

CHAPTER NINETEEN

WHEN SHARI'S SHRINK IN shining white armor finally appeared, he came in the form of an employer. *At last I'll have the answers I've been searching for,* she thought. His name was Dr. Lex, and he was a highly qualified and prominent psychiatrist who soon became Shari's trusted friend. The first and most assuring qualification was his love for God. He spoke of Jesus' redemptive work on the cross as though it occurred yesterday. And, of course, in a most profound way, it had. He also spoke as though it occurred for each client with whom he spoke. Again, of course, it did. He intimately knew Christ as the one and only mediator perfect enough to take the sins of others upon Himself, which no one else was qualified to do.

Shari had been well aware of these truths of God, at least for the thirteen years past. Yet there had also been some confusion, some conflict, some exhausting competition. She wondered, *Is it possible to know truths and yet to forget or repress them so deeply that we settle for living with lies?* Perhaps. But why would anyone choose to do that especially when the result would be mental torment for so many long years? By that point in her life, many questions like that had invaded her thoughts. But they were no longer threatening. To the contrary, these questions now promised fulfillment, answers, understanding, peace, rest, and release.

But there was no time to press the psychiatrist for explanations because his time was valuable and tightly scheduled with needy patients. Having waited so many years, she figured a little longer wouldn't hurt, as she built her own practice from the one-day allotment to full-time. But growth is slow—maybe patience demands that all meaningful rewards must come about in such fashion. She remembered the ten lepers who were quickly healed, nine of them leaving without expressing gratitude. Shari wanted to be as that tenth leper—grateful, so if more waiting was required, so be it.

Yet as more time passed, it seemed that the wait itself served as preparation for what would be later revealed. In speaking with clients, it was apparent that a useful depth of understanding could be attained only gradually. And what good is truth without understanding? In retrospect, she realized that very few of the facts she had learned in school could be retained over the years unless they were accompanied by understanding. So this must be a clue. If God be God, then surely His ways and His thoughts are much higher than ours; our time limits can't be dictated to Him, nor can a way and means by which to do His perfect work. The control is His. Yes, Shari could wait a while longer, however long was needed. Meanwhile, it was comforting for her to edge ever closer to those longed-for answers.

The depth of Dr. Lex's spiritual wisdom—combined with psychological understanding based on study, experience, and commitment demonstrated regularly in staffing sessions with peers—was a marvel indeed. His was truly a beneficial presence to all of the clients and employees who came his way. One day in their staffing session, he expounded on the alcoholic syndrome. Shari questioned him about the dynamics of an alcoholic who would regularly get drunk and extremely violent. She described her childhood experiences of her father's drunken, violent episodes as though she were reporting the experiences of a present client. She chose to ask questions of this group of experts from a neutral position, wanting to obtain objective facts—truth.

She held no preference as to which to believe—murder or suicide—for it was not a matter of preference. One was true and one simply was not true. Both did not happen (except hypothetically in Shari's mind thousands of times over). It was either murder or it was suicide. She needed to know which it was and did not want her own emotions to enter in and contaminate a non-biased exploration of the facts. Dr. Lex responded with simple psychological terms and explanations.

"Such a young man, a heavy smoker given to excessive coffee drinking and eating, was emotionally deprived at an early age in his home, resulting in what is technically termed an oral fixation," he said. "Upon reaching adulthood, sufficient damage was incurred through emotional deprivation—lack of parental love felt—that a great amount of infantile rage against the parents now existed, but it was repressed. Because of his low self-concept, feelings of inadequacy, and inability to be loved by his parents whom he loved, he felt totally helpless, small, and desperate in his dilemma. When he married, this rage was displaced onto the new love object—his wife," Dr. Lex patiently explained. "The only hope of ever escaping his overwhelming helplessness was to ventilate his rage onto the love object in monstrous fashion, gaining a temporary feeling of omnipotence.

"Yet, there was much guilt after the drunken ordeal, wrecked house, and beaten wife because he loved his family and knew they didn't deserve such treatment. So he felt even more inept, totally lacking in understanding, unable and unwilling to ask for assistance."

Shari continued her anonymous report, stating that this cycle masqueraded as normalcy for this particular family for many years. Then the day came when the family separated themselves and relocated at the wife's doctor's advice. She finally could endure no more beatings. Although she loved her husband she could no longer tolerate the effects of his alcoholism on their lives. Faced with an intolerable situation, the husband prayed (what is now known as a vending-machine prayer), "God, take away my desire to drink, and I will not tempt myself. I can't stop on my own. But if you'll remove the desire, I swear to You, I'll never drink again."

Shari related that the news that he had ceased drinking was carried to the family by his foreman. The family returned home hopeful, yet with reservations and an element of fear. His wife feared that if he should ever drink again, she would be killed because of his deep resentment over her leaving. Dr. Lex and the entire staff pensively followed her "case presentation" as usual, while she continued to glance at the file, carefully recounting the details. She knew this was her miracle moment.

"The drinking was never again resumed. However, a new practice began. He developed a passion for detective magazines and would buy several at a time, then avidly read them late into the night."

Another member of the staffing session asked Dr. Lex, "What about his prayer, and why the murder mystery magazines?"

"The prayer," he explained, "was not a submission of himself, of his will to God, or even of his confusion and his pain to God. It was really a fix-it prayer, a negotiation, a business deal. The drinking ceased, but a psychotic process had begun long ago. Now the rage continued to mount with no outlet for ventilation as would occur when he previously drank alcohol. The magazines became his fantasy world that promised hope by destroying the love object who had (seemingly) hurt him so badly. The victims in the magazines were the villains who deserved to be punished by death. The murderers were justified in retaliation and consequently overcame their helplessness through attainment of omnipotence. Over a period of time, the fantasy became his reality. In other words, he was conceptualizing the magazines gradually as they became his reality or point of reference."

Shari later recalled her dad's statement, "When you're dead, you're just dead, and that's all there is to it." In that he had once prayed to God and received an answer, it was most difficult to understand why he would come to say that.

Dr. Lex explained that in this man's quest for omnipotence he also had to destroy God, which he had done and revealed by his statement. The last obstacle to his freedom from rage and despair was to destroy the love object: his wife. "She'd better get away from him. He'll kill her one of these days."

The others nodded, seriously.

At that point Shari blurted out, "The wife was killed!"

"You're confirming everything we've just said," the psychiatrist said. The other psychologists and therapists nodded again, this time in amazement. Some squirmed in their seats or got up to take a breath. At some level, Shari was hoping for flaws in the doctors' reasoning. But it was clear that what Dr. Lex was saying must be the truth—now discovered after thirteen years of waiting!

So now she had confirmation of what she had suspected for so long. Yet what can a person do when she knows deep in her heart that her father killed her mother? Who can she tell? To make matters worse, Shari was also convinced that there were people who had known from the very beginning. Why did they cover for him? They didn't even really like him. Was it for the Lewis name, as some had speculated?

She knew she had to tell someone about this, but would she be disrespecting her father by announcing such a thing? Shari wasn't sure, but she knew she had to approach this out of love for her mother. Mama already had been judged and condemned for her "suicide," despite heaps of contradicting evidence!

Shari did have one consolation, though. Even without understanding exactly what had transpired to lead to her death, at the very least, she was in perfect peace regarding her mom's spiritual condition. Her mother had been, throughout her life, warm, loving, and responsive. She loved God, people, life, her children and her two little grandbabies. She'd been so pleased to learn of Shari's own conversion in the Tennessee revival, loved the record album she gave her (Mama loved Elvis Presley's gospel records), and they'd discussed spiritual things on their last visit together. NO, for her there was no doubt.

For a long time, Shari had harbored all sorts of guilt about herself because, subconsciously, she was trying to spare her father the guilt that he rightly deserved. For a long time, she remembered only the bad things she had ever done—including how she had left home and married at an early age, to the disappointment of her parents. Knowing that her own parents had spent the first year of their marriage in Washington State in the apple orchards, she often wondered whether she would have left home and married had her husband been stationed in any other state? Shari seemed almost predisposed to repeat her mother's life. Still, not once did she complain to either parent about her marriage.

Despite the mounting evidence, she couldn't accept the guilt of judging her father "without proof." Having found that magazine in his desk, describing in detail the manner that he had apparently chosen for her mother's execution, she knew the truth, but still she could not accept it fully without a great deal of arduous investigation. But she couldn't reject what she knew, either, so the two versions became a power play of forces, always battling in her mind.

Then it hit her. *Of course!* she thought. That's exactly why families are entitled to investigations and explanations, so that all of this inner wrangling isn't left to the grieving relatives of a victim. They don't need unnecessary guilt. They need to grieve and be comforted in their grief.

Buy why? Why did even Mama's relatives protect Daddy when they all hated him? And why were they even angry at Shari for wanting to know what really happened? The miraculous relief of that staffing session had been worth the thirteen-year wait. Shari would appreciate it forever.

By the same token, new questions were already forming. "'Dear God, will they never stop?" Shari asked her Creator. "Or will they never stop until the truth—the whole truth—is discovered? It just doesn't matter, however, because I'm committed to a profession that I love and appreciate so greatly, in which I can continue to work and enjoy and learn and investigate and do all those things the rest of my life. So what, and why not?"

Shari related the staffing session to Aubrey and Cecelia at dinner, and they were as excited about it as she was. Aubrey himself put words to his mother's earlier thoughts when he said, "Well, you may have just scratched the surface. You've proven beyond a shadow of a doubt what it wasn't, but they're a tight bunch, your crooked relatives. You probably need to just plan on it being a lifetime task to get it all straightened out."

"A lifetime task? I'll buy that, partly because there aren't other options available. But it sure has been an uphill battle. The irony is that I have to live away from them to do it, and yet the distance is what makes it so slow and costly."

"Yeah, and probably safer, too."

"Well, do either one of you think I ought not to stay with it?" Shari valued her children's opinions more than anyone else's and always had. She found that they were usually on target. She waited for their words of wisdom. "To be honest, we'd rather you let it go and went on with your life, like a good little Southerner's supposed to do. You're really causing us a lot of embarrassment." Cecelia was always one who could think quickly and lighten situations with soft humor. The trio laughed.

"You know, I wonder what I could have done with my life that would have pleased all those home folks, relatives and all?"

"You would have stayed out of sight and out of mind. Then once in awhile someone could ask about you, and they'd answer, 'Oh, she's just fine out there in California. Very happy. We're so proud for her too, poor thing, for her mother to have killed herself, but she's bearing up just fine. We really can go on with life; we just have to.'" Both kids chimed in building on the dialogue as though they were the ones who were raised in that area, rather than Shari. But she never doubted that her kids were in full support. They and all their teenage friends talked about it from time to time and agreed that Shari's reaction to the events surrounding her mother's death was clearly normal. Indeed, it was the resistance to her normal reaction that was abnormal! There was only one problem, her children said: "There was just one of you, and many of them," referring to her relatives who'd tried to stop her inquiries.

Certainly, in retrospect, Shari realized that a lot of brainwashing was implemented early on; the guilt trips were unrelenting, combined with the shock reaction and her fear of Daddy after emotionally regressing to a younger age. It seemed carefully planned that only Lewises were at Daddy's house, and none of the Deevenses, while Mama lay in the funeral parlor, far away. Later Stan had said the kids could have come to his house where the Deevenses were. But Shari didn't know that at the time. She'd never been invited there. It seemed that they belonged at home with Daddy.

Shari's cousin, Debra Faye, did come to their house, though, as the representative of Stan's group. Shari was glad to see her. When she wanted to see the pistol that killed her mother, Debra took her to the state trooper's house across the street to see it. Shari never asked her why they boycotted the kids. Perhaps, had she asked, her cousin would have told her. So many complications result from the failure to simply ask. In her newly found courage, after Dr. Lex's exposé, Shari telephoned Uncle Darren and blurted out, "Darren, I know Daddy killed Mama. I know he did!"

To her total shock came Uncle Darren's steady response, almost as though he were both relieved that his niece knew at last, while also somewhat defensive of Daddy. "Well Shari, I can tell you he wasn't by himself. He wasn't alone down there. He didn't do it alone."

How Shari has wished she could have asked one poignant question of him at that moment. But instead, she instinctively did as she had done when Grover Lewis answered Mama's phone and tried to tell her she was dead. Would it take another thirteen years to unearth the second layer here? It was as though a long period of time was needed to adjust emotionally with each minute step of progress made. A grain of truth was grasped and gleaned for all it held. But that was followed by days and weeks of thinking about it, crying over it, and discussing it with confidants. When it was finally incorporated into her psyche, then the truth could lead toward the next step.

Later, Shari asked her (theistic existential) therapist friend for his diagnosis of her father's condition. "Exaggerated blindness," he said. So often did Jesus relate to people who "had eyes but cannot see" that the diagnosis seemed appropriate in the existential sense. Shari knew that Daddy had always been colorblind and depended on Mama to match his socks and clothes. Now she realized his entire life had been colorless and his blindness extended beyond colors to all of life. He had depended on Mama to compensate for his blindness; he had depended on her entirely, as a child relies on a mother. As another psychiatrist said to Shari later, "It really was suicide after all; your father killed the better part of himself."

Of all the words of tongue and pen
The saddest are these, "It might have been."
And yet, there may be one equivalent sadness,
That of Unexpressed.
To have an idea and not express it is withholding,
To have an emotion and not express it is deception, To
have a kind word and not express it is deprivation, But
to be a human being and not express humanness is
Excruciation.
To see people and not see people is blindness
To miss their words and thoughts, needs and hope is
Deafness.
In not seeing, not hearing, ye shall become
Invisible.

CHAPTER TWENTY

SHARI'S LIFE COASTED ALONG somewhere between childhood and maturity, when quite unexpectedly another psychiatrist walked onto the stage. He was a physically large man, yet sorely lacking in self-esteem, virtually withdrawing from the world to escape a multitude of family problems. She later learned that he was an alcoholic. She found herself filling so many different roles with him—a child helping her poor, discouraged "father," a social worker fixing others' circumstances, a woman wanting to relate to a man, and a mother doing her best to nurture. In the midst of it all, she occasionally wished she had someone to lean on rather than always being the one providing support.

Still, she would have settled for just his appreciation. But there was little of that. In her effort to relate with this man, at one point she forfeited her own eagerly anticipated summer plans because she thought sacrifice was appropriate. One evening her psychiatrist-friend made reference to actual servitude, to which Shari laughingly responded, "I'm not a servant."

Yet, servitude was exactly what he was expecting of her! She continued to ponder that area for further insight. A week later, alone in the night, she awakened, sat up in bed, and clearly reflected upon it. "I watched my mother serve and be viewed as a servant. I tried to serve in marriage and failed. A woman can't be a servant to a man, or they both lose," she said aloud.

Later in their staffing session at the counseling clinic, Dr. Lex assigned her a case who needed 'mothering.' He was a fifty-year-old man who was still living in what was referred to psychologically as the Oedipal phase. But what about Shari's own Oedipal conflict? Why, in the midst of agonizing grief over her mother's death, did she struggle to protect her father from guilt? Why the need to protect him? Did she pity him even after strongly suspecting that he had killed her mother, and so brutally? She could not put him in prison; she could only put herself in prison—both emotionally and in the employment setting.

Other questions sprang into her mind. Why had she initially chosen a husband who was so much like her father? To "rescue" him? Why had it seemed so important to rescue the tall, dark, handsome youth counselor/ gambler? Why did she choose social work? The men she became involved with were usually older and appeared to need mothering. She served them—and then paid the consequences. She mothered older, weak men— weak father figures. She remembered her mother telling her that she had wanted to become a nurse but figured the training would be too costly. So Mama got married instead, to a patient-equivalent!

Now so many years later, it seemed astonishingly clear that a pattern was being repeated. But this time something was different: the psychiatrist. As surely as truth liberates, understanding transforms! And a change had indeed occurred. Shari's sick, distorted servitude came to a sudden halt. He accused her of being vindictive.

Her whole being smiled. "Yes, I am being vindictive." For the first time in her life, she finally transcended her roles of social worker, woman, mother, and servant. Here stood a new creature, able to speak freely to an equal. And speak she did. Vindictive? Perhaps. That would be refined with time. But the Oedipal phase lessened with that smile.

Dr. Lex laughed when she began waving aside with disinterest the cases who needed "mothering," particularly when she told him she'd retired from that role. He understood fully. As psychological growth continued, her family's material situation also improved. They sold their home at a significant profit and paid all of their debts. They replaced it with the purchase of an even nicer home.

Shari remembered Dr. Schuller's prayer with her and her children, on that special Thanksgiving Day, that they find a house near his church. And the home they ultimately bought was immediately adjacent to the Garden Grove Community Church. The family enjoyed the richness of the ministry, and participating there was a benefit to each of them individually and as a family.

Though some might have seen the trio as an incomplete family, they never for one moment lacked the warmth and presence of their Father-Husband (Isa. 54:5). He guided all their decisions, comforted them in their trials, and encouraged them as they matured to adulthood. They knew that theirs had been a journey of growing up together. There had been almost insurmountable obstacles, such that without their Father-Husband they might have succumbed. He gave the strength, and they shared the work, and the love between them overcame each hurdle.

In their new area, the children completed high school. They each did a fine job, made meaningful contacts and contributions. On their graduations, Shari almost burst with joy that they had come through it all so successfully. Their smiles were radiant, their friends shared in their joy, and their teachers expressed a great love for them. She knew they were indeed, "home free."

Before long she progressed to the position of supervisor in both of the large church counseling centers in the area, where she designed a program, coordinating students and fieldwork experience. With her large salary increase, she and the kids decided to take their dream vacation: a trip to Europe. They obtained passports, purchased tickets, and then Shari was abruptly fired from one of her jobs.

All the college instructors at one of her employment sites had decided to call some issues to the attention of the director of the school. As her moment to speak began, she discovered how wonderful it felt to express dissatisfaction to a white man in charge. She was unconsciously transferring years of suppressed anger toward other white men in charge onto this man, her employer! She heard her voice increase in volume and her words become sharper and sharper. She even noticed the shocked expressions on the faces of the other instructors. But her words continued with ever increasing volume and venom.

The director winced a few times and grew very red, but he braced himself until she finally finished. Then he spoke very briefly, saying only that she was fired and would gather her things and leave immediately. The dismissal hurt in many ways, yet Shari realized it was individual progress that needed to be achieved. It had felt so good to speak freely and release pent-up anger! But the three as a family soon began to feel the decrease in income. They canceled their travels, of course, and before long the crunch manifested itself in other areas as well.

To make matters worse, she'd entered another school program and now felt foolish to be pursuing an expensive and intensive degree again. It had seemed important to study advanced psychology. She also knew that many others in her family, including her sister and brother, were still struggling alone. She felt she needed to understand their struggles if she were to be helpful to them and their families.

Meanwhile, both Aubrey and Cecelia were doing a fine job of assuming adult responsibilities. They, too, were employed and studying in college, but the strain of their situation had an effect on them all. Shari was inclined to forfeit her school program since she had been going to college for many years, and it was their turn now. But she could not leave without losing all credit for the program, and she had thousands of dollars invested in it—not to mention the work, books, and credit toward the doctorate degree. Most significantly, she felt certain that in this program, she would discover the parasitic, psychological leech that would not go away until she fully comprehended it. She was torn by inner conflict, wanting badly to assist her two deserving young people, always her life's priority, while containing the grueling need to "know the entire truth."

The school granted her a temporary leave just to rest up a bit. She sought other employment and, unsuccessful, settled for obtaining a home-equity loan. This bought them some time, and she hoped to regain her strength and senses. She wanted to be strong for her children, yet the harder she tried, the more consistently she crumpled. Naturally, the more concerned she became, the worse it grew. The children were responsible and even protective, but it seemed unfair at the time in their lives when they needed guidance and support.

There were additional requirements from her instructors, and one admonished her to work on her discernible lisp. She hated that particular instructor, although she did not actually know him.

Apparently, she hated what he represented through transference; he was the persecutor or authority figure that seemingly sought to annihilate her. She felt her extinction rapidly approaching. Though she had grown skillful at running away, evading and avoiding such people, this time she grew weary and chose not to run. She asked him, "Will you conduct the therapy yourself?" This time, she would face her fear.

He agreed. She resented approaching him with acquiescence and questioned the source of her resentment. She felt his demands were ill-founded, unjust, laden with ulterior motives—and he seemed in many respects much like her father. When he offered coffee, the similarity to her father was even more pronounced and all the more so as she feared his power. He was the president of the school with the authority to promptly dismiss her from the doctorate program. It seemed she would die if she lost her school.

She had hoped the haunting mystery would be solved once and for all. The bachelor's degree helped as did the master's degree, but the work invested in them had not completed the quest for deeper understanding. Shari needed to know the psychological factors that contributed to her mother's death. This must be fully understood for some larger purpose, but what the purpose was, she didn't know yet. She simply had to understand how her father became the way he was, why her mother endured so long, and why the whole town refused her an investigation and seemingly blamed and rejected them.

So there she was, teetering, while engulfed in a doctorate-level psychology program. Yet much as she disliked this man, this therapist, this president of her college who found great fault with her, somehow she felt a measure of progress in facing him. She remembered how her father could never face directly those he hated or became angry with. Rather, he would curse them to Mama. She also knew she didn't want to continue launching obsolete anger onto a convenient target, as she had recently done (having also suffered the consequences). She told this therapist she did not like him, and she told him who he reminded her of and why. That helped; he accepted it. It felt good to talk back to a man of such authority and not to be stricken down.

On one occasion, he held a medicated cloth over his eye because he had injured it. He explained that was necessary for his eye but it need not hinder their progress. However, it did. She could not speak negatively toward a man, even of authority, who was obviously ill. This wasn't clear, however, until on another occasion when his foot was hurt and he sat with it elevated on a pillowed chair. Again he instructed her to disregard his condition and continue her therapy. Instead, she blurted out, "I weaken around weakened men of authority. I want to help them and feel helpless and sad when I can't. Certainly I could never add to the pain of a weak man."

He sharply corrected her analogy. "I'll have you know I am not a weak man." But he never again doctored his eye or foot during their sessions. She was not rejected from the program, but she later encountered difficulty seeking out a supervisor, an essential requirement of the school. When she attempted to approach a female instructor, the woman bombarded her with her nonstop verbiage and blasted away with numerous criticisms of her speech (again), her manners, and so on. Shari knew that she could not work with her.

She began supervision with a male instructor who sized her up early in their working relationship: she dressed and looked dowdy and needed to socialize more. He insisted that she converse with another student on the phone from his office because it was the sensible, social thing to do. True enough, but her experience of that ordeal was reaction to invasion. She felt attacked, overpowered, and disrespected. She ran from there, desiring never to return. As on similar occasions, she could not explain her experience. She had no argument, no defense. Her only option was to give it up, to flee, and to stay away.

Another male instructor seemed safe enough as a classroom lecturer, and she still needed that mandated supervision. When she inquired, he replied, "I will be happy to be your supervisor." She rejoiced and eagerly anticipated working with him.

On one of their initial sessions, he asked what she experienced, and she answered honestly (unfortunately): "I feel as though the Hulk monster lives inside me, always raging, and I often have to run so as not to become conspicuous."

This man was a noted psychologist. He abruptly dismissed her from that particular session and from the supervision. She returned again to her inner domain.

Until I am permitted to be
And to speak all that needs to be spoken
Then your words cannot help me
As does my refuge from noise,
Your pointless noise, your senseless words.
In my silence, I'm safe and I can patiently wait
In my refuge, In my silence, Silence.

CHAPTER TWENTY-ONE

THEIR FAMILY PLIGHT BECAME increasingly depressing as their options narrowed. Both Aubrey and Cecelia chose to attend college, but with finances seriously faltering, they later withdrew from school, looking elsewhere. Jobs were easily enough found, for they had worked since young teenagers for their spending money. Now they desired to assume more responsibility for themselves, embarking on young adulthood, but were in a quandary as to just how to emancipate without some direction.

Then Cecelia's father offered a solution which she excitedly accepted: an invitation to live with him and attend Shari's own alma mater, University of Arkansas. But upon her arrival, he immediately rescinded his offer, as he had done through the years when Cecelia and Aubrey had trusted him for assistance. Being practical minded, she knew she must make some important decisions soon. She went to the recruiting offices of all the military branches, making comparisons.

"I would like to travel, live in Europe, have some rough and rugged experiences," (the movie Private Benjamin was recently out), "and study nursing. So, I have discovered that the army is the one that guarantees all these things in writing. SO, I think that Uncle Sam needs me, and I hear him calling my name. I want to go." She signed her contract before leaving Arkansas, then returned to recruit her brother. She grinned and beamed with the same angelic aura Shari had observed when she first viewed her in the delivery room only eighteen years earlier.

Aubrey grinned back at his sister, then commenced to query about the myriad details she'd already obtained before making her lavish announcement. He had long ago come to trust her, knowing that she was extremely thorough, missing no essentials. She welcomed his questions with, "I just happened to have all this information, just waiting for you to ask." They both laughed and talked well into the night. Within a few days, they were equally excited about the joint decision they'd made. "We're going into the army! The navy gets the gravy, but the army gets the beans, beans, beans, beans."

Shari knew that they were more mature than her, in some ways, and while she was unable to assist them in making decisions about their futures, they were helping themselves and their mom. They knew she was floundering financially and they wanted to remove some of the burden. Yet they really did enjoy the dirt-and-mud fun, and all three of them enjoyed traveling and staying in a strange land long enough to know the people, experience the culture, and speak the language. Maybe Uncle Sam would be the helpful family member that they sorely needed.

At least the three would have some time to prepare for their departure, and they would enjoy each other and strengthen each other concomitantly. As happy as they had been to discover and obtain their home, to be a part of the church they loved, and near their adored pastor, Dr. Schuller, they had also learned to let go. Their time had been wonderful and now, soon, "Somebody else can get a good deal." They knew they each were about to embark on new adventures. Only time would show them exactly what and where.

This was Shari's opportunity to delve more intrinsically into therapy, because so many factors were interrelated and she was determined to complete the puzzle. Soon she began to understand there was a distinct correlation between the jobs where she worked with men, and the male relationships she had known in her upbringing. She was carrying with her former feelings of "castles" run by men, powerful men, guided by their own weaknesses, thus exploiting others for their own selfish benefit.

The psychological dynamics were so clear and amazing that she became totally absorbed, totally committed to her supervision-therapy hours with psychologist Dr. Robert Anthony. She was at last able to admit to the Hulk-type of rage she harbored and the anger toward men in authority, without being rejected. He was, in his own words, "Strong enough to let you be strong too."

The ugly memories of her repressed rage spilled forth, and here was a man who could allow it. She began to catch glimpses of what true strength and power were, what real manliness was. He never once took issue with her manner of communication (restricted vocabulary, having emotionally regressed back to primary process thinking, accent, lisp). Rather, he listened to her at a deep, deep level. Her pain and scars had never been permitted lancing before, and their presence was rotting her psyche. She explained to him all those symptoms she experienced: anguish in the night, repeating dreams, guilt—tremendous guilt for her family's plight.

Soon she discovered a specific and relevant name for these symptoms. She had begun to manifest a syndrome with a distinct diagnosis of which few are aware. As she read her symptoms in the book Massive Psychic Trauma by H. Krystal, it did not matter that she was reading about European Jews. They recognized the symptoms to be exactly the same, and her spirit rejoiced in newfound recognition and identity. She was discovering who she was. She was experiencing Survivor Syndrome. At last she made sense.

Their home had been a concentration-camp early environment. She obediently awaited her eighteenth birthday to emancipate (liberate) from her home. However, that effort was unsuccessful, because she married a husband much like her own father, thus perpetuating concentration-camp home environment. Then, when her mother was murdered (that word "murdered" has a beautiful ring to it, because truth is melodious), it seemed that the household, the town, the entire community, and in fact, her whole world, was now a concentration camp. She responded to everything as she had in earlier years, to her father, and later, to her husband: in stunned silence, inner rage, total helplessness.

In a concentration camp, one doesn't mourn or do a lot of other similar and normal things. A person only survives, whatever that may require. Sequentially, the cost is exorbitantly great, for the original person gets lost among the mastery of camouflage. For Shari, her children had became her focus via regression. Emotionally, she returned again to age six, for that was the point in time in which her dad had shown her his power by destroying her cherished, red table-and-chair set, which she tried so hard to protect from destruction. With each piece, she failed and he convinced her of his message: he was the strong one, and the powerfully strong man reigns rampant... always.

Shari's mother was silent that day and helpless to intervene. She had her own problems, especially the damage to her body. So the little girl turned to her dolls for comfort and interaction (a safe fantasy world) in the midst of chaos. She read stories of good fairies, angels with wings and magic wands (like in the Cinderella story), who make good things happen despite the bad. She adored her heroes, Roy Rogers, Gene Autry, and other good men, doing good things and righting wrongs. They kept hope alive, however minute. She pretended Roy and Dale adopted her as she corresponded with their fan club and pasted the pictures of their ever increasing family into her cherished scrapbook. She loved Jesus and His Father, God, for They, too, were strong and did good things for people. It hurt dreadfully to learn that Santa Claus was fake, but because she hated fakes and deceptive appearances, he wasn't missed for long. She had to believe that the good was real and lasting.

Then once again, in December 1964, her mother lay silent and helpless to intervene or come to her aid. Her father again was powerful and she clearly understood his message when he stood in the doorway, silently informing her that he was in charge as always, the king in his castle. She would not speak against him or indicate any opposition to him, because they both knew who was strong and in charge and who was weak and insignificant. She turned to her doll-like children, ages two and three, who were so precious. The three of them had fun and good serendipity times, as they continued to pray to God, seek angels' protection, and recognize miracles. They grew close to this realm and remain so today. They have learned from whence miracles come, even against great odds. They know a closeness that not all families are privileged to know. Their separation could hardly be easy, perhaps even if circumstances had been altogether different.

But they were embarking upon their separation-individuation processes, a prerequisite for a happy, stable, positive, successful, purposeful, rewarding adult life. They were "on time," and she was twenty years late. But as Dr. Anthony assured them, "You're all the same age emotionally, eighteen and nineteen."

As Aubrey's army entry date crept closer, Cecelia and Shari prepared a fantastic surprise going-away party for him. It was indeed one spectacular night. The American flag covered one wall, Cecelia made him a camouflaged cake with little jeeps on it, and his friends brought love, gifts, prayers, and best wishes. Amidst the inner layers of separation pain she felt, Shari also perceived a man in this soldier-to-be, a good man with a source of strength that would never fail him. For that, she's eternally thankful.

Cecelia and Shari were privileged to share a little time together before the young woman left for basic training. Mom was pleased that her daughter would be trained in the nursing field, having no doubt that she would be a most beneficial presence to those patients who fortunately came her way. Although Shari felt in many ways that she had probably failed her children, they both argued to the contrary and seemed honestly satisfied to get what they warmly called, "care packages"—boxes of cookies and candy mailed to them wherever they happened to be stationed—as they proudly wore the uniform of the United States Army.

Shari's own task of disintegrating the Hulk monster within continued, revealing gradually the Personlichkitzwandel who would become permanent. She had learned the term from her studies of the Jewish Holocaust and she'd come to love its meaning, a word for which there is no English translation. It is the person left after the trauma has been worked through and incorporated into the original personality. But parts of the original personality are lost forever, having been replaced with the experience of the trauma. There is no doubt that as her quest to solve the mysteries of 1964 is finally completed, then doing whatever needs to be done toward rectification will be next.

For now, however, the most challenging thing for her would be going into the world as an adult, after years of fearful postponement. She was grateful that God had allowed them to migrate from her family homeland of Arkansas to the warmly received homeland of California. For in her newly adopted homeland, she could seek good men who would help to right the wrongs, eventually leading to healing. A girlfriend asked her years later, "Did you move there to be near Roy and Dale?"

Smiling even now in reflection, it was tremendously heart warming, to greet Roy and Dale as they approached their regular pew in their church, for morning services.

Shari usually managed to sit directly behind them and then hold the door for them as they exited. One morning while they stood, singing a hymn, Dale's large purse fell over, onto Roy's seat and both of them were unaware of it. Roy seemed fragile, and seated on the end of the pew, Shari feared the purse might cause him to fall and be injured, when he tried to be seated again after the song ended. Just at the moment he started to sit, she snatched Dale's purse! Dale was indeed grateful and expressed it. Roy never realized that an early admirer of his had just protected her hero!

Shari enjoyed giving them poems on their birthdays and they always had time to be attentive and show personal gratitude. These are just among the many reasons that so many people have loved them over the years, as she has.

No, she didn't consciously move to California because of these delightful people, but their sweet spirit contributed tremendously to her healing process and to her enjoyment of California.

> *To our American Heroes, a tribute once more*
> *A new note of "Thanks," from friends who adore.*
> *You've given to us so many fine years,*
> *Many years of smiles... diminishing fears. As distance*
> *has narrowed between us and you,*
> *The healings have hastened, the scars left are few.*
> *You represent mothers and daddies we knew,*
> *You've lessened their absence - their errors seem few.*
> *You've transformed our pasts into memories dear,*
> *Forgiveness has surfaced, as you've simply been near.*
> *Much like the dear lady who longed to be healed*
> *Reached out, His garment to touch, lowly kneeled.*
> *For God Himself promises, Desires of our Hearts,*
> *He alone understands, He alone, Love imparts.*
> *And only He knew how much it would mean,*
> *To be near my Hero and my Hero's Queen.*

CHAPTER TWENTY-TWO

THE WAY OF THE Beatitudes, as described in Matt 5:3-12, is the route of the most unpleasant, unpopular, unwanted, unappreciated. Yet this route is referred to by Jesus as "blessed." We are told that herein we can rejoice, for in this way, we become the "salt of the earth" and the "light of the world."

Are these idle metaphors? Can it be that only through the beatitudes, we can truly discover our own self-insufficiency, thereby becoming receptive to Him who is all-sufficient? Could this be the quintessential position in life? If a man does not keep pace with his companions, perhaps it is because he hears a different drummer. *Let him step to the music he hears, However measured or far away,* wrote Henry David Thoreau.

As symptoms of Survival Syndrome continued to dissipate, greater relaxation prevailed and Shari found herself making decisions respectfully, without the life-or-death urgency of recent times. Looking back, it seemed a particular route was chosen at an early age, and although interrupted by various detours, the way was returned to and the detours only confirmed the way chosen. When she was deeply troubled by a friend's crisis, someone made this statement, "He has suffered a setback in the game of life." The statement intended no disrespect, nor was it received as such. But she found herself pondering it for quite some time. It seemed simplistically amusing to view life as a magnanimous game board, with multiple routes for our choosing as access to our individual journey across the board. What criteria will we use to produce and support our choices onto and throughout the board?

Years ago her mother had given her a little white Bible, which grew in value as the years passed and the questions and turbulence mounted. She committed Psalm 100 to memory, because it seemed to describe not only the nature of God Himself but also our relationship, or our "pasture-ship" with Him. The words conveyed purpose and truth. Although the evidence was not at all seen, it was sorely hoped for. Psalm 1 revealed the way not to choose, and the courage not to choose it. The story of Ruth conveyed what a true authority figure was in Boaz—one who ruled in the power of wisdom, understanding, compassion, and love. It's been said that we can know something and yet have to discover it. From her earliest years, the way of God and of life was known, but the darkness and the struggle made the discovery of that which was known all the more vivid.

Einstein was once considered a simple man who asked simple questions, and Plato contended that an un-reflected life was not worth living. The simple have always had an advantage over the intellectual, for they are willing to admit that they do not know and can thus learn. Those who believe they know already refrain from asking, seeking, or knocking. Socrates himself discovered that wisdom rested in the bosoms of the simple.

Shari often wondered how much similarity there may be between the simple and that which we often view as the backward and misfits? What could tenderness and true authority share in common, and how is strength made perfect in weakness? Where is the narrow way if not in the answers to these questions? Is one major clue seen in Jesus' own words: "The first shall be the last and the last shall be first" (Matt. 20:16)? It also states, "There is a way that seems to be right, but..." (Prov. 14:12). Did not Jesus' own life illustrate the unconventional and was not He too met with extreme opposition? What could He have meant when He instructed us, "Take up the cross and follow me" (Mark 8:34)? Or to *be in the world, but not of the world* (John 15:19)? Do we need to cultivate the art of doing things backward to social norms?

Her experience in being "backward" oftentimes was that of burdensome hindrances to living and definitely out-of-step with the preferred "normal." She had never grown comfortable as a misfit. The best she could do regarding this dilemma was be as inconspicuous as possible in maintaining her individuality, however ridiculous or unpopular.

When she first saw the poem Different Drummer, Shari felt grateful because her own world had seemingly been redefined with a measure of respect. But when her Uncle Stan remarked, "You did all the right things," it came as quite a blow. Then why was everything she had ever done met with extreme opposition at the time and with subsequent excruciating turmoil and pain, which she thought resulted from having done the wrong things?

But now as her attention became drawn more to the sublime, more of the sublime was discovered. As surely as a day to us is as a thousand years to God, and vice versa, as 2 Peter 3:8 says, so who is to say that backward to society is not, in fact, His way? We know that Jesus was describing in the Beatitudes all the undesirable, uncomfortable, unpopular, and backward places in which we find ourselves inevitably reaching, which seem at the time out of step. If we had eyes that see, would that be truly the case?

As a high-school girl, her mother poetically penned the words that would become prophetic to Shari years later after a long, laborious journey—a journey that would find home to be that of returning to live in Psalm 100, valuing the truth that endures to all generations, the truth that sets us free. Wrote Olive Deevens:

> *More than I thought you meant to me.*
> *Gold of the sunlight, blue of the sea.*
> *Sunlight has failed, the sea grown gray,*
> *Gulls are silent since you went away*
> *Many the miles are, pathless to track,*
> *Still I am hoping, you will come back.*

CHAPTER TWENTY-THREE

AT THE FIRST AMERICAN reunion of Holocaust survivors, many profound truths were stated and a devout commitment was made to honor those who'd paid such a tremendous price for the world's apathy. Some of these statements deserve a place here:

"The world should never again ignore evil as it ignored Hitler's Germany, and we will never shut our eyes, never refuse to acknowledge the truth, no matter how unpleasant," stated President Ronald Reagan. "Good and decent people must not close their eyes to evil, must not ignore the suffering of the innocent, and must never remain silent and inactive in times of moral crises."

Dr. Sam Geotz, a Los Angeles optometrist, was not quite seventeen on the day his camp was liberated. He began to examine the events that took away his family and his childhood.

"I was too young to ask questions during the war; I only thought of survival," he said. "I felt the pain of losing my parents and my family, but I couldn't rationalize why they were doing this. I just didn't have the mental capacity of asking those adult questions." He later returned to the camps, drawn by his need to see them again and to better understand what had happened there. And he noted the strong bond and kinship among other people who survived.

Elie Wiesel, chairman of the U.S. Holocaust Memorial Council, recalled the moment, decades ago, when the American army liberated the inmates of the Buchenwald concentration camp. He, too, was seventeen at the time. The message he would spend the rest of his life trying to communicate is simply: "The opposite of love is not hate but indifference. And indifference to evil, is evil."

Said Rose Toren, another survivor, "I believe in miracles because my whole life is a miracle." Although her pain came from a different source, Shari could relate to the words of these courageous Holocaust survivors. They brought her comfort, even in her most trying times, and especially in her search to find herself.

Decisions had been extremely difficult to make after Shari's children had joined the army and moved away. One tough decision concerned suitable employment, because she didn't really want to remain in the area. When someone approached her with an offer to purchase her home, she agreed, although she had no other direction in mind for herself. So she sought direction. Shortly before their escrow was to close, she concluded in absolute despair that it did not matter where she went or what she did, for she would only be miserable. She had no place. She remembered Jesus' words, "The Son of man hath nowhere to lay His head" (Matt. 8:20). It helped to know that He had, many many years before, tested her experience.

But then, soon after she resigned to a lack of direction, a direction was given, much as a good fairy or a fairy godmother grants a miracle. It was far greater than her wildest imagination could have conceived. It was an opportunity to purchase a condo in France, in a very desirable location. Naturally, she needed to learn the language. She also knew that she would visit her soldier-son in Europe, for she missed him even though she was proud of his newfound independence and travel.

As she prepared to sell their family home, she knew that she must move, uncertain as to where or for how long. She remembered the one and only compliment her husband had ever given her: "She can stretch a dollar farther than anyone." Although she would have only a few dollars, they would be sufficient to take her wherever it was that she desperately longed to experience. Consequently, from the first discussions of the condominium in Europe, a smile accompanied her, often even in the night when she awoke. It was a simple reminder that, "Something good is going to happen to me," to borrow Rev. Oral Roberts' theme.

It didn't even matter whether the purchase offer actually materialized; what mattered was that she had a direction at last. She had a journey to joyfully anticipate. She had a place!

Faith in an Angel

Faith is a common word and something that, undoubtedly, everyone has in something. This is evidenced in the fact that we cross the street, trusting the unknown drivers not to overrun us, and multitudes of other such everyday examples. But, angel is another common word and perhaps one that is less utilized in our daily lives. We normally affirm that such beings exist, and we even delight in reading about or listening to someone else's supernatural experience depicting such. If we could have our "druthers," likely we would wish an angel to come very plainly into our lives (as a genie from a lamp), and grant us the desires of our hearts. Sounds delightful for sure.

Yet what would we do, just how would we react if such a thing actually transpired? We have eyes that sometimes fail to see clearly what is obvious. That, of course, is ignorance— innocent—yet still ignorance, for it ignores the real. But suppose an angel comes into our midst and introduces himself to us as such? Would we reject him? No, if we have truly desired the visitation of an angel and we have conditioned our eyes to see the unseen, the real, then we will welcome him. We'll be honored to serve him coffee or soda and enjoy every word he utters. Most importantly, we will notice the quality of his presence, of his conversation, and of his very thoughts. And these we will hold to, even after the angel has departed. The miracle that he ushers into our life will be recognized as just that and will be both accepted and appreciated.

Yet when others cast doubt upon the essence of our angel, or upon the validity of his gift—the miracle—what will be our response? It is one thing to have faith and to see clearly what is. But when the majority's voice grows firm, discounting our own vision, it can be distressing and discouraging. Yet having once met the angel, one cannot return to where she formerly was. One cannot eradicate a miracle. Again, what is faith? What is hope? What is the desire of the heart?

As she penned these words, the telephone rang.

"Hello, this is Mr. Angell. What can I do for you?" And the gift of the miracle was resumed. For the angel had become a friend.

The gentleman in charge of arranging her overseas purchase was actually named Lloyd Angell. That added a measure of unique amusement to the discussions between her attorney, her friends, herself, and Mr. Angell. Thus, for the following weeks, it became possible to sort through twenty years of family possessions, packing the most treasured mementos and discarding the remainder.

One weekend, Cecelia visited from her assigned base, and they held a yard sale. It became so taxing that they walked away and left it long enough to attend a movie and have dinner with friends. They hoped that someone would be kind enough to steal all of it so that their task would be less arduous. Upon their return they were surprised to observe that an artificial flower arrangement had been taken from the vase, but the vase remained. From a set of dishes, someone had removed three place settings. From a free yard sale, patrons had taken only what they needed. Shari learned the relief of letting go of unnecessary trappings, of "things and stuff," as her daughter aptly described them.

Her postgraduate school program was in its final stage after four years of course work. She reluctantly packed the finished chapters of her dissertation as she packed to move out of their house. She hoped that the chapters that still needed to be written would not become lost through the inevitable delay of transferring them from her head to her typewriter. For a while she stayed with friends and lived out of her boxes, but she needed to complete her final chapters. So she stayed at a motel, where she was able to give her dissertation the attention it deserved. Soon the chapters began to emerge. It was truly an exciting event. They lay in stacks across the floor, daring anyone to enter, step on them, or touch them. Even the motel's maid respected her paper stacks and handed linens to her at the door.

Tension mounted as the degree drew to a conclusion. *Me, a doctor!* Shari thought. Whoever would have imagined? It had taken only twenty-three years! Of course, there were a few years during which she had not attended academic classes, but at last she was completing her Ph.D. in clinical psychology. Whereas previously, it had seemed undeserved, she now felt a strong identification with the word doctor (meaning teacher) and with philosophy. Had not her life become a vivid portrayal of her philosophy? Was she not truly living her most heartfelt, existential beliefs? Could she not teach what she had experienced, understood, and painfully discovered? Most certainly!

One last thing remained to be done before she went out into the world on her own. She needed a name, her own name. With both children now grown and emancipated, she no longer needed to share their father's name with them, and she had no intention of retrieving her maiden name. So something clearly needed to be done. She wished to become just herself, with no man's name. Perhaps society needs to recognize women as solely themselves, not someone else's property. As more women recognize their own value, it will become easier for others to recognize it as well.

It is a fairly simple procedure to enact a legal name change, and thus she set about the task with her attorney. Upon entering the courtroom, she found herself somewhat mesmerized in observation of the judge in his black robe. She momentarily confused that scene with a male executioner in black, sensing the magnanimous power that a person of such authority held over the "just me" types of society. She became extremely uncomfortable.

Her attorney attempted to dissuade her anxiety. He reiterated the simplicity of their exchange when they would face the judge with her name-change request. Though she believed his words, her apprehension mounted. She envisioned the judge sentencing her to life in prison, perhaps capital punishment, although she was innocent. After all, what does innocence have to do with conviction?

Her fears subsided, however, when she placed her arm on the armrest next to the attorney's. She felt the strength of contact with a person stronger than herself. He never even realized that she was borrowing strength from him, much as the woman who had crawled to touch the hem of Jesus' garment. As strength flows from one, others are strengthened. The last time she had borrowed strength was during the few seconds she leaned on the governor's arm, walking away from her mother's grave. Those few seconds had carried her a long, long way.

My heart is weeping, mine eyes are dry.
My soul is bleeding, but must not die.
It hurts, it aches, how well You know,
While I'm alone it must not show
And on and on and on I'll go...
Alone.

CHAPTER TWENTY-FOUR

AT LAST, WITH HER completed dissertation and degree, plus a modest down payment from the sale of their home, Shari left California behind and journeyed to her place in Europe. Traveling alone was difficult, and occasionally she wished for someone to help carry luggage. At least her suitcases had wheels and leashes, and she found the Eurorail system to be extremely efficient. She visited her tentatively purchased condominium in Evian, France. Its breathtaking beauty took her by surprise. She spent several hours there each day, overlooking lovely, sparkling-blue Lake Geneva. When she learned that a certain businessman wanted to purchase her condominium to add to his collection, she figured he could have it—in time.

Why was the idea of living in Europe so appealing to Shari that it had consumed her those last weeks and months in California? The answer never came totally, but the idea did lead her to Europe, and that sense of direction had certainly terminated her distress about lacking a plan and a place. Perhaps the condo had seemingly justified her trip? Perhaps it had introduced the idea of separating herself even further from all that comprised the past? She had left hometown, home state, and now homeland. She was leaving fellow Americans to seek out French, Swiss, Germans, and European Jews. Was she searching for home and family and common kin? The answers never came, only more questions, as usually occurs when a seeker seeks. A seeker always finds more to seek, but the search itself is most illuminating.

She was utterly fascinated with Switzerland to the extent that she almost forgot there were other places to visit, see, explore, and experience.

She preferred to absorb Geneva. Certainly Geneva was esthetically beautiful, but it was more than that. The character of Geneva was beautiful. Everywhere she found kindness, politeness, courtesy, assistance, and respect. Yet efficiency in work and quality production were never forfeited in the process. She recalled years ago, when she had felt that Hawaii must be much like heaven. It, too, is a happy, beautiful, restful place with only lovely and pleasant music. (Hawaii has no sad or negative music.) Something apart from that diversion existed in Geneva. All of the loveliness was incorporated, but she felt something she had often longed for, yet never hoped for. There was total absence of fear or the need for fear, an absence of deception, calculated manipulation of the vulnerable. A woman could go alone to a movie at night and walk back to her hotel at two o'clock in the morning with no fear. She could meet other people to whom she might speak, or not speak. They respectfully responded to her preference to be left alone or to engage in conversation and friendship.

Shari questioned the citizens of Geneva about crime, particularly violent crime. They hardly grasped her concept. There was an innocence, a purity, an authenticity that she had believed in through the years but had stopped looking for beyond the world of children and the uniquely wise elderly.

The police were highly visible—and highly esteemed. They maintained a vigil over this country of order, safety, and efficiency. They were helpful and reliable when help was needed. They were the authority who firmly handled any minor disturbance before it had opportunity to escalate. She was reminded of her own elementary school years, which included reading the Bible, pledging allegiance to the flag, and showing respect for authority.

Many customs in Switzerland were based on trust, such as the purchase of bus tickets (which were not collected by the driver or anyone else), newspapers purchased at unlocked public stands, and items displayed openly on sidewalks, unsupervised. It seemed that thefts not only failed to occur but also failed to develop as thoughts or temptations. The people manifested a quality of naivete, the healthy naivete greatly needed by all humans.

She noticed that most Europeans knew several languages, enjoyed long intellectual discussions, were extremely adept at whatever job they held, and maintained high, healthy values in general. Here, young and middle-aged adults also conveyed authenticity. A foreigner or tourist need never be lonely in Europe, particularly in Switzerland, specifically in Geneva.

The locals communicated an interest by their friendliness, rather than a probing or passing curiosity. Often in her own country (outside her home state), she was asked that stale question, "You have an accent; where in the South are you from?"

But most Europeans were not merely curious; they were genuinely interested in the whole person. They knew themselves and their own preferences, and they eagerly and openly discussed both. If they did not like a person, they did not pretend otherwise. They seemed to be conscious of a desire to learn, rather than a desire to impose their ideas or standards on others. One visiting in Europe would not encounter the "ego trips" that are so commonly found in the States. There was, instead, a genuineness that was enthralling to the visitor who truly valued authenticity.

It was hard for Shari to believe this experience even as it transpired. She awakened early in the morning in her inexpensive hotel, eager to eat the hearty breakfast of rolls, butter, jelly, and hot chocolate. Then she hurried out the door to walk. It never mattered which direction she walked, and she seldom had a plan for the day. All directions held good things. She looked forward to the people she met wherever she went. Almost everyone spoke English and fielded numerous questions about the United States. Many enjoyed showing her how much they knew, and they were indeed quite knowledgeable.

They were entertaining, too. Everyone had an excitement, an alertness, a note of expectancy in his or her eyes, tone, and manner—an expectancy of good things.

Shari wondered, why was she born in the United States, when conversing and relating with the Europeans seemed more natural to her? She made friends easily and no time was wasted on the games Americans played. It seemed as though she'd found her *home* in Europe. Then a dear Swiss friend of hers asked Shari, "Why are you angry at the United States?"

That question startled her. She'd never realized she was angry at the United States. She thought the United States was angry at her. She felt rejected by it. After all, from her earliest years, she had loved her country, its flag, its Statue of Liberty, its Pledge of Allegiance. She remembered the end of World War II, although she was only three at the time. She remembered how joyful everyone was and all the soldiers who passed in caravans of army trucks, throwing out boxes of Hershey's candy bars to the children alongside the road. She knew the U.S. soldiers had done well, and Americans were proud of them, and they were proud of themselves, and everyone rejoiced together as a people.

Had she not worked hard all her life to abide respectfully by American laws, even teaching their history and government in schools, taking the students to the police station and courtrooms to instill the same admiration and respect in them? Then she had even submitted her own two highest achievements in life to the defense of this same country, because her children loved it as she did and wished to serve it as soldiers.

Why should she be angry at the United States? Just because the Bill of Rights, all the laws of justice and decency, had made an exception with regard to her mother and had treated her as less than an American citizen, less than a foreign citizen or tourist, less than an expensive or even cared-for animal, she thought. Just because she continued to reside in her birth country, finding no refuge, but feeling herself falling in between the cracks while other upright citizens watched passively, extending no hand, lending no ear. She felt they were no longer a people, E Pluribus Unum, as had been the case when she was three years old and the soldiers had passed, tossing Hershey bars because the war was at last over and everybody was happy.

Thus it became clearer. She had generalized the pain from her hometown to her home country. At any rate, she was elated when another dear friend in Geneva, Aaron Zweig, suggested she might work with him. He was a psychiatrist who had lived in a concentration camp as a young man. As they shared their stories about their mothers' "insignificant" murders, they instantly shared a unique friendship. Aaron suggested that she was running away from her country.

"You, too, have run away to Geneva, and I only wish to do the same," she retorted. He was originally from Hungary, and he told her much about his home, which he had not spoken of in decades. It was easier for both of them to talk and to listen deeply as they savored the delectable French foods in the finest restaurants throughout the city. He had enough brotherly communion and compassion to maintain a colleague-to-colleague friendship while also psychologically removing the last cords of her burdensome trauma. He particularly loved her poems, for they expressed his own feelings, which he had never been able to express. She felt it was an honor to give him copies of them.

"You are as my sister," he warmly concluded.

Of course, Aaron was partially accurate. She was running away, but she was also running to freedom. She was bathing and basking in the neutral air and the quality, character, nonviolence, and genuineness of Geneva. She wept when she visited the United Nations buildings, where great decisions are made for all the world. She went to the Alps and found only more of the same liberation and inspiration. She talked to the snow and to the green grass and to the cows and the cheese fondue. Most people would not believe that they all spoke back to her, but they really did listen to her respectfully, and that made her feel important.

With her son only a short distance away, she pulled herself from the haven of Geneva to visit him. Seven months had passed—the longest separation they had ever experienced—when they visited again in Germany. The meeting was truly delightful for the seven months had seemed like seven years, and Aubrey had grown from her young son to a wonderful young man. The two talked late into the night as they had often done through the years. The level of his conversation was stimulating and refreshing, for his was a blend of humor, philosophy, scientific facts, inquiry, and creativity. Shari knew as they talked and laughed that her existence had been purposeful, for truly the world was a much better place for his presence in it.

She could not resist venturing on to Austria, for that was where Dr. Viktor Frankl, the author whom she greatly admired, actually lived. More importantly, he was a Jew who had been imprisoned in a Nazi concentration camp, where the Nazis had killed his young wife, other family members, and friends. His life was committed to service for others, allowing not even a vacation in the past twenty years. His writings noted there was purpose in such magnitudes of suffering. Purpose she had glimpsed, but she wanted and needed to more fully comprehend.

It was a unique honor for her to be invited to his home to meet him and his wife. They were most gracious and discussed some of the items in her dissertation at length. She felt a strong sense of family kinship, sitting in the presence of this concentration-camp survivor—a man who'd experienced the murder of his loved ones and the awful feeling of disinterest from the outside world. Consequently, he had borne the trauma alone, but for the help of God and support of others who had shared the ordeal and similar losses. She felt validated.

As they discussed the area of common symptoms of such survivors, he shared his strong conviction with her: Survivors feel that the remainder of their lives is for service to others and that no time can be wasted in this endeavor, for time is of utmost significance. Even behind his relaxed smile and humor, an extreme seriousness prevailed and left no room for the trivial or superfluous. Thus, at seventy-seven, he maintained a hectic schedule of writing, editing, and meetings. Yet he asked her to accompany him as he went to the bank and then shopping for a comb for his thick, unruly hair. As she stepped toward the elevator, he bounded down the stairs. Laughingly, she hurried to catch up with him, remarking that she never imagined she would ever be chasing Dr. Viktor Frankl down the stairs in Vienna! He laughed warmly.

As she strolled along the streets in the vast city of Vienna, she felt that the beautiful, large, old buildings maintained a demeanor of sadness, seriousness, and endurance. She heard their message. She met a lady in her hotel who did not try to stifle her interest in the war years. They talked late into the night regarding these topics. The next day Shari's phone rang. The lady she had spoken with the previous night was the owner of the hotel and was calling to invite Shari to her family's residence floor. There, they resumed their discussion, viewed movies and documentaries of the war and interviews of survivors. The lady translated German into English for her and seemed appreciative that someone greatly desired to understand and listen to her feelings, memories, and lingering fears. Shari met her entire family, and they made her feel like an honored guest.

Her knowledge was extensive and as she spoke, in drifted the congruent mixture of sadness, seriousness, and endurance. For the first time, Shari realized the Jews had initially heard the stories of the destruction occurring in the camps, but they did not really believe the stories, because they considered themselves Germans. They actually knew, at some level, yet they unconsciously chose to deny what they knew because, "Hitler was our leader; we trusted him."

The gracious woman made it all so clear to Shari. "Feeling themselves family with the Germans, their leader was as their father, provider, and protector. Their trust was more valuable to them than the knowledge they received, which would require them to relinquish their trust." The hotel lady went into detail, wanting this to be clearly understood by her guest because it was important to her.

"Because of their childlike trust, they were vulnerable?" Shari asked, tears in her eyes.

"Yes, dear, now you do understand. They trusted and they died, they and their children. They could not comprehend the truth, because of their unwavering trust. Hitler was their leader and their enemy. They thought he was their leader and their friend. They loved Hitler, and they trusted him, so he easily deceived them." With those words tears softly scuttled over her cheeks as well. The two hugged each other for what seemed like ages. At least the hug helped to compensate for the evils of their trusted leaders, over the ages and across the continents.

They continued to dab at their tears as they respectfully sorted a few more details. The lady's husband and sons had the same somber essence as did she and were equally gracious. When they opened their finest wine to share the honor of their expedition with Shari, she felt most honored indeed. Wine in this home did not represent to her what "drinking" in general had come to represent back in the United States. They hugged goodbye, richly extending invitations to each other to visit again when time would make it possible.

Now she was ready to travel back to Geneva, as she had so much to think about. She had come to discover that the train is a remarkable place to meditate. Her head was full of many thoughts and analogies; her heart was bursting from newfound truths, quickly penetrating her very soul. She needed the refuge of the train where she could think, write, cry, sleep, and then begin the cycle again until her destination appeared. She thought of the abused child who is unable and unwilling to perceive the abusive parent as bad, even as the child draws his final breath beneath the blows. She always wondered why these children do not attempt escape but remain as sheep for the slaughter? Now she knew.

She remembered her experience of returning to her parents' home after Mama's death. She recalled her earlier words, "If you ever come in and find he's killed me, get out, for you will be next." Shari inwardly feared her father, but in those first three weeks following their trauma, she remained within his reach. On the nights in which she awakened and observed him standing in the doorway (just as when the minister and his wife had tried to talk) she already knew that her father controlled all the escape routes, both symbolically and literally. She never considered resisting, because they were his doorways to block as he chose, his house to rule, and his family to do with at will, just as is the abusive parent's and as was Hitler's domain. She understood clearly now her proximity to the Jews, even though they had been oceans apart. They were as one.

She also came to a new realization of the biblical term chosen people. Jesus was first described as "a lamb for the slaughter." He resisted not his assailants, because His suffering was necessary in order to redeem all assailants and all other sufferers. All assailants would be examples of exaggerated blindness and the assailants' innocent victims, who could not understand their plight, would also serve as examples. Jesus, on various occasions and in numerous manners, reminded the people that they needed a vision, that their problem was a misguided, limited, or immature focus. Their eyes were not seeing.

Thus, it would appear that all such horrible suffering was for a distinct purpose. Alas! One of the most significant symptoms common to Holocaust Jews was the need for their suffering to not have been in vain. They shared an inner need for purpose. Were not all Dr. Viktor Frankl's books actually addressing the very meaning of suffering? He reiterated to her during their time together that the purpose was twofold: that the suffering not be in vain and that through it others might be reached. The light was dawning ever more clearly now, the Jews were a special people, for they were chosen to suffer for an honorable purpose—that blind eyes everywhere could be opened. Jesus Himself, so greatly loved by God, was chosen for the same purpose.

Shari remembered how Jesus, in His innocence, was nevertheless pronounced guilty by the authorities for having committed a crime. In His place, Barabbas (the murderer) was preferred and released. Pontius Pilate even felt badly about the way it went down, but he washed his hands of the matter because of politics. He had a status quo to maintain. With a sigh of relief, she realized that victim-blaming had been occurring for a long time. Their family had suffered greatly, and yet the worst torment was that it might all be pointless, senseless, that no one would ever benefit from it, that no lesson would be found in it, that nothing would be seen or revealed through it. Lord God, she prayed, that is what would be more than she could bear.

People programmed her, into and throughout her automaton state, not to talk about her loss, her own mother, but to suppress what happened and not ask questions. This had been the most frustrating of all. It had emphasized society's preference not to investigate. To not investigate is to not ask, seek, or knock. To refuse to ask, seek, and knock is to forfeit receptivity, learning, growth, healing. To forfeit these valuable experiences is to remain stagnant, blind, and separate from God—a wasted life, a purposeless life.

She thought of Helen Keller. What was so remarkable about this woman? Although plenty of excuses availed themselves for her to remain stagnant, blind and separated from all others, her spirit longed for purpose. Her spirit was receptive. She asked, sought, and knocked, not because it was easy. Indeed, it was extremely difficult having to surmount many serious obstacles. Yet it was necessary in order for her to transcend the alternative: stagnation. Thank God for Helen Keller, for all persons handicapped, and for their heroes—for all who dare to reach beyond where they are, for a purpose. Thank God for the Jews, for her mom, for the abused children, and for all who suffer that their suffering not be in vain, but that through their suffering, we will be prompted to seek to understand it all.

CHAPTER TWENTY-FIVE

THE RETURN TO GENEVA was a blessed time of renewal as she ferried to various ports, visited with old friends, and made new ones. She even grew more adept at the local language as folks were eager to be of assistance. In short order, however, a reminder of the Austrian family's enticement began to gnaw at her. They had firmly stated that her visit would not be complete unless she added the experience of a Communist country to her travels. They further explained that a visit to Hungary would be less complicated than some Communist countries and not as far away. Because that was Aaron's homeland, she felt intrigued to visit, knowing fully well she could not prepare for whatever she would encounter.

So she joined a weekend tour group traveling into Budapest, Hungary. She wanted to walk on Communist soil and personally observe people living under Soviet rule, not because these would be pleasant events but because it seemed a necessary piece of her own puzzle that was quickly promising completion. Shari befriended people from countries all over the world as she ventured into Communist territory. Their commonality was the English language. She will always hold close to her heart the wondrous experience of walking down the banks of the Danube River in Budapest, holding hands with a handsome Spaniard from Madrid. Little could he know that, at forty years of age, she was consciously becoming an adult there in Budapest. She appreciated the fact that he had neither known her before nor would he know her after that weekend.

Thus, for one weekend, she was free to be spontaneously herself in an oppressed environment. It felt as though a reiteration of December, 1964 was occurring and she was able to react to that bizarre event as a confident adult rather than as a terror-stricken, twenty-two-year-old, regressed child. Furthermore, in Budapest, as she looked into the cold, staring eyes of the Soviet soldiers, someone was holding her hand, and this time, she was neither alone nor afraid. It did not change the situation, of course, but the human contact of this fine, adult man kept her from slipping away from meaningful human contact as a way of life because of the vultures in control.

Marchello marveled at her youthful personality, for spontaneity was that part of her former personality, which was now returning. She welcomed it. She knew she was retrieving a healthy emotional place that had been lost for almost eighteen years. Marchello was an intelligent computer expert, and she called him Mr. Spock (as in Star Trek) because his every thought was predicated on logic. He loved her humor, and it permeated the duration of their time there. She felt her spirit celebrating. She talked with him freely about her albatross of eighteen years, and because he was non-emotional, he never encouraged her to avoid the issue. Rather, he supplied many logical and valuable observations.

They made plans for their return to Vienna, and she anxiously anticipated them. Vienna was lovely, yet when her visit to Soviet soil was completed, Vienna was not quite far enough away to fully relax and enjoy her newfound liberation. She longed to return to Geneva once again—to her home away from home, and family away from family. She did not take the time to explain to Marchello why she must leave quickly but knew he would understand sufficiently, and if he did not, that too would be all right.

In Geneva, she met another of the famous authors she had long admired and wished to know and consult: Dr. Paul Tournier. He was eighty-four, actively retired from the medical profession, and probably the wisest human being she'd ever known personally. He was also adorably delightful in his childlike joy, love, and soft wit. This was, undoubtedly, the man with whom she could clear the last remnant of her emotional debris. She had read his many books and had never encountered more spiritual, insightful, human brilliance than this man held.

He was gracious, warm, and receptive from the moment he opened the door to her. She sensed that, at last, her time had come! Soon she was actually sitting in Dr. Paul Tournier's home, having tea and cakes with him, and permitted—even welcomed—to ask her questions to her heart's content! She noticed that his books were printed in many, many languages, and he reminded her, "The human dilemma exists throughout the world."

She thanked him again: "Your book, *The Violence Within*, has intrigued me especially, although I love all your books. But violence is a topic I particularly wish to understand."

"If you particularly wish to understand violence then you must have a particular reason for wishing to understand it. You do not seem to me to be a violent person by nature. So what is behind your wish to explore the vast configuration of violence?"

"Violence invaded my own family many years ago when I was young. I could not understand it at the time, and it had so many ramifications that I was overwhelmed by it all. I just knew that someday I absolutely must understand it. I went to college for years and learned some valuable things but not thoroughly enough. When I read your book, *The Violence Within*, I thought, 'This is it. Paul Tournier has the understanding I am seeking.'"

Dr. Tournier asked, "What is your present understanding of the roots of physical violence?"

"In school we studied the work of psychologist Lawrence Kohlberg, pertaining to levels of maturity and how those various levels contribute to one's resorting to violence."

"Tell me about Dr. Kohlberg's *levels of maturity*."

Shari suddenly felt like a first grader in a show-and-tell class. Could she possibly present her information well enough to this highly acclaimed mentor? As he sat patiently, smiling with full confidence in her, she proceeded to try.

"Well, Dr. Kohlberg says that people are functioning at different levels of moral development—not to be confused with moral behavior. He thus examines the reasons for peoples' specific decisions and actions in certain situations. These 'reasons' are related to the level of maturity from which the people are functioning."

"Yes, yes. Please continue."

"The levels of functioning range from 'pre conventional' to 'conventional' to 'post conventional' or even 'principled level of maturity.' The pre conventional level of moral development is seen typically in adolescence, ten to thirteen years old. Here, the individual feels small, weak, and dependent on others for receiving pleasure or pain. In an authority relationship, he feels himself inferior. He relates on a reactionary level to his environment and to people. He is basically unable, or too immature, to empathize with others. Immediate gratification and selfish interests direct him. He has disregard for others' rights and for the social order in general. If an adult is functioning on this level, he is said to be 'fixated,' failing to mature emotionally and mentally at even a reasonably simultaneous pace with his physical maturity."

"And if he does mature beyond the adolescent level?"

"Then he moves into the conventional level of functioning and of moral development, in which he demonstrates a preference for involvement with others, a growing sense of self- respect, and a general concern for the social order. This is the level at which most adults do function."

"Yes, I would tend to concur. What do you feel—or what have you learned from your studies—is the determining factor as to whether or not an individual will mature?"

"This I feel is determined by what an individual, having reached adolescence, has chosen—consciously or unconsciously—as his basic "life position." This is not something I learned in school, by the way, but is something I learned from classes given at Dr. Schuller's Crystal Cathedral in Garden Grove, California. Are you familiar with Dr. Robert Schuller and the Crystal Cathedral?"

"Yes, somewhat. You see, Dr. Schuller is much like my own books; he is of many translations, because the human dilemma is worldwide." He smiled pleasantly, then asked, "And these two basic positions in life? Tell me about them."

"One position is that of being open, responsive, and receptive, and the second position is that of being closed, rigid, controlled. The open position is interested in investing himself in his own development and will be willing to take the risks involved, to accept delays of gratification, to allow fairness to others, and will accept responsibility for his good accomplishments as well as for his failures. He is likened to a student in a classroom, because he values new, expanded thoughts, others' contributions, and the learning arena in general. He feels himself to be a small, yet valuable part of the very large scheme of things and is respectfully grateful.

"The controlled position lacks receptivity, patience, and regard for others. Those whom he does value are valued primarily for however they tend to benefit him, rather than for themselves. He functions competitively, needing to be seen as superior in some way, yet is lacking in basic self-respect."

Dr. Tournier continued my discourse: "And when adults from different levels of maturity are interacting, there will, inevitably, be problems because of the difference in maturity. But when these two basic life positions are also at odds, additional problems are created, because they are each marching to different drummers. We see this in the workplace, in relationships, and in every place that humans interact. Do we not?"

"Absolutely," Shari replied. "Here is where Dr. Kohlberg breaks it down to specifics. He says that if a pre conventional adult (extremely immature) were conversing with a conventional person, the former would soon feel himself to be at a disadvantage."

"And he must make a decision about the disadvantage, which he feels himself to possess?"

"Exactly. Dr. Kohlberg says one of three things will likely occur: (1) the disadvantage will serve as an incentive to develop the pre conventional person toward the next higher level; (2) it can discourage the person to give up and fixate, give up trying to improve himself; (3) it can frustrate the person to the point of seeking an impulsive or calculated means of gaining the 'superior position.'"

"He will become a student of the universe, or he will become the dictatorial teacher, yes?"

"You understand these positions very well, I see."

"Have I told you that the human dilemma is universal?" Dr. Tournier smiled, obviously pleased with his own gentle humor. "Once we can understand that, then it is easier to deal with specifics. It is extremely difficult to deal with specifics without understanding that, because we become too engrossed in the small picture. Is this what you call... tunnel vision?"

"Actually, I was so consumed with tunnel vision for a long time that I finally realized I had to separate from my locality to see it all more clearly. I moved to a faraway state, and now I'm in a farther away country! But it has helped. It's been absolutely essential.

"If the pre conventional person had already cultivated a receptive nature, he will, as the student, attain to the next higher level—though difficulty is entailed in doing so. He will invest himself and evolve into the conventional, finally the post conventional, and possibly the principled level of functioning, although few are said to attain the latter. Abraham Lincoln and Martin Luther King, Jr. are two individuals who did so in the United States. But most adults remain at the conventional level, and the prisons are found to contain a larger majority of the pre conventional adults. However, if the pre conventional person had thus far cultivated a controlling nature, he will retreat from the person he feels himself inferior to, or lacking in some way by comparison, and will fixate. He may simply seek out non threatening peers to hang out with—"

"Or," Dr. Tournier continued her thought, "he will resort to a form of violence to gain the advantage he lacks by overpowering his competitor."

Shari recognized this statement from his recent book, *The Violence Within*.

Dr. Tournier had done much research and writing in this field, but more importantly, as both a medical doctor and as a psychotherapist, he had counseled untold numbers of individuals.

He continued, "I like Dr. Frederick Hacker's statement that, 'Violence comes from a lazy mind giving up the patient search for a true solution through thought and negotiation; yet, negotiation is hardly ever possible except when the two parties are obviously equal in strength.' Here of course, the strength referred to is the strength of basic maturity. Otherwise, one seems to overpower and the other feels himself to be overwhelmed."

"Here is a line from your book, Dr. Tournier, that I've reflected on since first reading it: 'Aggressiveness and violence scarcely lend themselves to reflective thought. For when a person is gripped by violent passion, it stifles in him all capacity for rational thought.'"

Dr. Tournier only nodded in affirmation and waved her to continue.

"So what we are actually looking at is a deficiency disease of inner strength and self-esteem. On this note, Harold Lyon says that, 'Toughness is merely a compensation for a lack which is feared to exist,' in his book, *Tenderness Is Strength*."

"This is because, despite appearances, violence is more a sign of weakness than of strength. Violence is actually the opposite of strength, for the energy it brings to bear is only the energy of despair. Despair of winning the argument, by argument, despair of being strong enough to sustain the dialogue. The stronger one is, the less one needs to show one's strength."

As he spoke, she remembered her dear mentor, Dr. Anthony, in her doctorate research, who said he was, "Strong enough to let you be strong, too. Therefore, we will move at your pace, not mine."

Dr. Tournier slowly turned a few pages of his own book, which she had carried with her for this opportunity. Looking up at her from time to time, he both read the words and pensively reflected on their truths, "Man's need for beauty, for poetry, for mystery and dreams, his need to find a meaning in his life, his need for love, for personal contact with others, with Nature and with God, all these go for nothing, so far as personal power is concerned.

"The glorification of the powerful has gone along with the devaluation of the weak, the old, the sensitive, the shy, the odd, the abandoned and the dreamer...."

Listening to his words, she thought of the minorities, the handicapped, the increasing homeless who remained weak in the political game.

"Society proclaims it is dangerous to be weak. Perhaps it is dangerous to be powerful, for power obstructs true dialogue between men. As true dialogue becomes more and more rare, then the following ensues: the exchange of threats and reciprocal aggressiveness, a dialogue of the deaf, confrontation by adversaries—each of whom is sure his views are right and is anxious only to impose them, not to engage in conversation between partners desirous of mutual understanding.

"A colleague of mine, Mme. Elaine Amado Leiz Valense (a French psychoanalyst) says, 'Aggressiveness is the result of a decay of dialogue.' We live the drama of the lost dialogue."

"Does that mean we have forgotten how to simply discuss things?" Shari asked. "Or do many people never learn how in the first place?"

"Most people do know how. But they have become afraid to engage themselves because of the competitiveness. They feel they must win, or be on top, or be number one, or else they are nothing, a failure, of no worth. That is not true, but it is believed by many people, and that is why they are afraid to trust in their own ability to use dialogue—sufficiently. Then they feel a need to place their trust in something else, in something more assuring than their own communication skills."

"One of the authors I studied was William Ryan. He did much research in this area and he explains that, 'The common substitute for a personal power based on loving intelligence, self, and other respect, social status and income earning ability, is a weapon. For a weapon can destroy a party who possesses these things. A beating, a rape, a murder, etc., of such an endowed person, by a fixated, pre conventional person is an extreme form of robbery, for he is attempting to rob the self-esteem of the other via the other's annihilation.' Is this what you mean, by placing their trust in something else?"

"Certainly. Why do you suppose that in your country, wives are beaten up by these husbands? The husbands lack sufficient self-esteem and personal confidence, so they resort to the advantage of a weapon, in order to gain the power position. The weapons are their fists and their overall superior physical strength. If they possessed self-esteem and confidence in themselves, they could stay with the dialogue, or they could walk away from the wife if dialogue proved futile. Please excuse me, I say, 'in *your* country,' only because your country is known to be more competitive and, therefore, more violence-prone than the European countries."

"Has this always been the case, or has our society deteriorated to this level?"

"If you consider the Garden of Eden and the two brothers, it would seem to have always been the case. Otherwise, it has been evolving through all cultures to varying extents. Much, of course, depends on the levels of maturity you have been studying. Cultures, even nations, differ in maturity levels of functioning—which may also help to explain why some cultures thrive while others do well for a time, then fall. Fear and the need for control can collapse an individual or a nation.

"The tenderness that we as children all possessed unknowingly has become lost in toughening ourselves as adults to avoid the pain of our competitive society. This tenderness can be regained by simply acknowledging our fears. The opposite is to deny our fears and then feel compelled to eradicate those who seem to be a threat to us. This is demonstrated in the use of violence for 'personal power' and serves instead to augment our own depletion."

Shari felt compelled to ask, "So how do the passive ones fit in here? I mean, those individuals who do not use violence directly but do nothing to interfere with others' use of it?"

Dr. Tournier hardly needed her question, as he continued: "Indirectly, they condone the use of violence as long as it does not affect them directly. Then they would probably react differently. From a base of personal fear or uncertainty as to what to do, frequently people choose to do nothing, to say nothing, to look away, pretend they do not know what is happening, or to say, "It is not my business."

"As in, *not my problem,* huh?"

This conversation was touching her very heartstrings. She didn't want to be greedy with his time, but she knew that this discussion was a profoundly unique opportunity, and she had to grasp it for all it was worth. Dr. Tournier was an octogenarian, retired, and living alone with no obligations demanding his time. He did not rush her. He seemed to be enjoying their discourse very much himself, as well as being conscious of how much it meant to her. She continued.

"Are you familiar with the concept of 'blaming the victim'? This is one route to the denial you were describing." She was glad she had also brought William Ryan's book with her. Dr. Tournier began to read from some of her marked pages, which clearly pertained to their present focus. One example in William Ryan's book illustrates how "victim blaming" can in fact be applied in any situation. It states:

They must analyze the victims carefully, dispassionately, objectively, scientifically, empathetically, mathematically and hardheadedly, to see what made them so vulnerable in the first place. What was Pearl Harbor doing in the Pacific!

There is something about the oppressed, whatever kind the oppression— that when it is known, it makes those who are not oppressed uncomfortable having "it" (the oppressed) in their midst. They tolerate it, for the non oppressed are good people themselves, just not oppressed. They don't fully understand how the oppressed came to be that way and figure someone must be to blame for the oppression. Yet "good people" prefer not to blame, so it is easier to assume that the oppressed are simply an inferior people and, thus, live inferior, oppressed lives.

Simple! When good people don't wish to take responsibility, just blame the victim. Then the good people can go on with their lives. And they feel they have, 'dealt with It' sufficiently, so they are satisfied. They can sleep at night. They suffer little pain or guilt.

In times past, it was generally assumed that victims were born inferior, a minority race, poor, physically deformed, etc. But now, prejudice has "progressed." Now the inferiority is primarily due to his "oppressed environment." But the inferiority is still located 'within the victim, inside his skin.' This is a vitally important distinction that must be made in order to consistently dispel any and all traces of community guilt.

Thus, the humanitarian can concentrate his charitable interest on the defects of the victim, justifying a perverse form of social action designed to change, not society, but rather, society's victim—to perpetrator!

Blaming the victim is an ideal, almost painless evasion.

The second step in applying this explanation is to look sympathetically at those who have the problem in question, to separate them out and define them in some way as a special group, a group that is different from the population in general. This is a crucial and essential step in the process, for the difference is in itself hampering and maladaptive. The "different ones" are seen as less competent, less skilled, less knowing—in short, less human.

The ancient Greeks deduced from a single characteristic a difference in language—that the barbarians, the babblers who spoke a strange tongue, were wild, uncivilized, dangerous, rapacious, uneducated, lawless, and indeed, scarcely more than animals. Automatically labeling strangers as savages, weird and inhuman creatures, not infrequently justified mistreatment, enslavement, or even extermination of the different ones.

In essence, "blaming the victim" is actually an ideological process, for it is a set of ideas and concepts deriving from systematically motivated, but unintended distortions of reality.

Karl Mannheim explains that such an ideology develops from the "collective unconscious" of a group or class and is rooted in a class-based interest in maintaining the status quo. However, to maintain the status quo for the "satisfied group" means to maintain the status quo for the oppressed, simultaneously. One cannot be affected (positively or negatively) without affecting the other; if one improves, both improve. If one stagnates, both stagnate; if one deteriorates, both deteriorate.

An ideology has several components:

1. The belief system itself, the way of looking at the world, the set of ideas and concepts.
2. The systematic distortion of reality reflected in those ideas.
3. The condition that the distortion must not be a conscious, intentional process.

Finally, though they are not intentional, the ideas must serve a specific function: maintaining the status quo in the interest of a specific group.

This practice has a rich ancestry in American thought about social problems and how to deal with them.

Blaming the victim is necessary for those whose personal security lies in the status quo of the social system. Yet the fruits of this ideology appear to be so fraught with altruism and humanitarianism that it is hard to believe that it has principally functioned to block social change!

"Yes, this man is very scholarly, very wise, this William Ryan," Dr. Tournier observed.

"I believe this explains what has occurred throughout history, at least in our countries. I think of the slaughter of the American Indians in order to take their lands, the early slavery system in order to exploit Blacks and the Jewish Holocaust—"

"To create a superior race?" Dr. Tournier continued her thought. "The consistent theme in these examples and many more that could be listed, is man's need to control—to establish himself as superior by overpowering those he deems inferior, yet still finding a way to justify himself, absolving himself of true responsibility or subsequent guilt and remaining among the 'good.'"

"Would you agree that adherence to 'victim blaming' fixates an entire community at a pre conventional level of moral development?"

"Oh, of course. Of that there is no doubt. But it becomes far more complicated toward correcting. That is why most minority groups remain helpless. Their status quo cannot change, because the status quo of the majority (those with the power) does not wish to change."

"Then what is the solution? Is there no solution to be found and one need not exhaust oneself in attempting to find it?"

"My dear, you ask many questions in one breath. But that is good because that is the solution."

"I don't understand. What do you mean?" Shari implored.

"The solution, or the healing of the closed, non receptive individual is the same as the solution and healing of a status-quo protective society. Both need to ask the questions: What has happened? What is wrong?"

"In blaming, there is no question, and that is the problem. In refusal to ask a question and reach further from where we currently are, is to choose to fixate, stagnate, and deteriorate. This can be done on an individual and/ or on a societal level."

Wow! Having come full circle, the two went on to discuss Christian concepts such as <u>asking, seeking and knocking</u>, which leads to <u>receiving, discovering and arrival</u>. They also discussed, "You have not, because you ask not," (James 4:2) and, "Ye shall know the truth and the truth shall set you free," (John 8:32). She even remembered her therapist at the Crystal Cathedral, encouraging her that she would probably pass her state boards because, "No good thing doth He withhold from them that walk uprightly."

Thus, an open, receptive, and forthright attitude results in a low interest in violence and a high interest in tenderness, and a low interest in victim blaming and a high interest in moral development.

The people who have authority and fail to use it rightly lower the standard of their society. They open the door for more discrimination to occur and for further injustices to abound. In failing to do that which needs to be done, they are, in essence, the 'blind leading the blind.' Even when the blindness is that of simple denial.

"Far better to cultivate seeing with awareness. For human awareness is a precious and awesome instrument," read the last page of Harold Lyon's book, she noticed as she picked it up.

A psychiatrist friend of Shari's, Dr. Thomas Hora, puts it this way, 'As thou see-est, so thou be-est.'

It was a rare occasion when she was too exhausted even to think, yet that was how she felt as she began to digest these valuable truths. Dr. Tournier, fully aware, led her outdoors to view his lovely gardens. They talked about the places in Switzerland she had thus far seen and what her future plans held. He was pleased that she was so partial to Geneva and that she enjoyed the people she met so very much.

As their conversations eventually ended, Dr. Tournier drove her in his own car the few miles through the lovely countryside back to her hotel in town. If anyone would assume this eighty-four-year-old gentleman would be a slow, cautious driver, then they do not know Paul Tournier. He drove his compact, economy car like an eager, newly licensed teenager. Of course, laughing on these drives, she told him as much and he smiled all the way. She was later honored to be his guest at a lecture he conducted, and watching the multitudes of scholars vying for a moment of his attention, she knew she was indeed blessed. It was difficult to say goodbye to this absolutely delightful, most enchanting gentleman who stole her heart away in restoration of trust and respect for the Caucasian male. They agreed that they would write letters upon her return to the United States, and that made it a little easier.

No doubt Geneva had become the playground for this adult of twenty-two emotionally, and forty chronologically. The disparity was always obvious to Shari. An example was in the selection of her clothes. She had much difficulty, without help, in dressing appropriately, according to the social norms of her own country. However the problem was nonexistent in Geneva. All their clothes were comfortable, practical, colorful, youthful. She devoured the freedom. After all, she had waited eighteen years to be twenty-two again!

Perhaps her vacation of vacations would have lasted indefinitely, but when her daughter wrote her that she was seriously considering marriage and wished her to help with decisions, Shari decided that it was time to return. The earlier visit with her son in Germany had been most enriching and they'd shared a glorious reunion. But now her attention returned to the States, to the daughter she also adored. Cecelia had always had wisdom and friendship for her mother through the years whenever she'd needed either. Now it was Shari's opportunity to reciprocate.

It was also time to go "home" to Arkansas. After a time with Cecelia, she knew she'd be going back.

Easter morning outing.

Olive with Sherry, age 6.

Pals–mother and daughter outdoors.

Sherry and Mother–indoors.

CHAPTER TWENTY-SIX

SHARI WAS BACK AT "home" in Arkansas, at Christmas time, no less. It had been so many years, and yet it seemed that only yesterday, at Christmas time, did her existence turn inside out. She found the town looked much the same, with very few changes. The people looked about the same too—a few wrinkles here and there, grayed heads.

She found herself still silently asking the question with everyone she met on the street who had been her friend: Why didn't somebody care? Were there explanations that would make sense today as to why such an exception was made with her mother? Why did she have to go to Europe and find strangers and other cultures to talk about her mother when so many of her friends, even now, would not speak about *It?* Yet as she milled around the town among friends and enemies alike, she realized that her own previous inhibition was now absent. Did she leave it in Geneva? In Budapest? At last, at age forty, she was an adult in her hometown. It had taken so long, yet she had hurried so.

She just had to visit her Uncle Stan when she noticed his car at a public gathering place. No one was seated around him except for his family, and she was invited to join them. They first exchanged the usual social nonessentials, then as though they were waiting, she complied and brought "it" up.

"Stan, I still am interested in knowing why you chose to let Mama's death go unresolved as you did."

Immediately, his wife, Begonia, responded, "Now, Shari, you could have had it investigated if you'd wanted it investigated. You didn't choose to then, and it's too late now."

"No," replied Shari, lowering her gaze to Begonia. As she did, so did Uncle Stan.

"Oh, no, she couldn't. She couldn't get it investigated."

"You knew all the time I was trying, didn't you, Stan? Why did you block it? You're Mama's brother and a lawyer. Oh why, Stan, did you put us through so much?"

"Well, what do you want to do about it now?" he retorted with obvious impatience.

"The same thing I wanted years ago. I want an investigation. There never was one and I can't rest until there is one. Mama deserved it, and it still needs to be done." When she heard those words come from her own mouth, she knew what it was that she wanted to do about it now. At last, she knew.

He refused to help, although he was politically the most powerful figure there. Powerful enough, she thought, to block her efforts then; powerful enough to block her efforts now. Through the years, numerous individuals had asked, "Why didn't Stan have it investigated? There had to be some reason."

Her memory wandered back to the times she had discussed with the governor her deep desire for an investigation. He had been at this uncle's home. The governor had even attended Mama's funeral with him. Stan knew what was going on all the time; he *knew*.

What else did he know? Why was he keeping it a secret? As warden of the state prison system, didn't he want Shari's father—his brother-in-law—placed there for the murder of his sister? Or would that have been too much for him to deal with day in and day out? Would it cost him his job, or invite unwelcome publicity to him and his prison? Was it coincidence that a short time later, the Arkansas prison system underwent its scandal of bodies buried nearby, resulting in the movie Brubaker? She deliberately avoided seeing that movie in defense of Uncle Stan, who left the prison under unfavorable publicity as a result of that investigation. Did she avoid seeing more than a movie? Was she like the Jews, too trusting of the wrong person? With renewed hope, she borrowed money and hired an investigation firm.

Then a strange thing occurred: a major flood came to that little town in December just before Christmas. They called it a 500-year-flood, an event that statistically happens no more than twice in a millenium. Fifteen feet of water stood in the business zone, and boats were used to rescue people from the roofs of their businesses. It was a literal and symbolic washout. Declared a disaster area, Shari's hometown made the national news.

Throughout the entire town people were gravely upset and depressed. Everyone talked about how much worse it was to have it occurring right at Christmas time, which was supposed to be a happy time... deja vu. As she walked those streets and observed the ravaged town, still plagued with debris and mud, Shari inwardly prayed: *God, I can't feel good about people's pain. But somehow after what this town and these people did to my mother's name and to her rights as an American citizen and to her kids—and right at Christmas time—somehow this ghastly event seems appropriate. No one ever even said, "I'm sorry," to me.*

Many of the merchants wept and said, "We're wiped out, ruined financially, everything's gone." Shari answered them, "You still have your family."

Her private investigation began. Needless to say, it was less than exhaustive, only helpful. After just four interviews by her investigators (a far cry from "Colombo") it was obvious what the missing link was. All those interviewed merely supported each other, circumventing factual information.

For eighteen years, she'd been unaware that the name of the game was politics. The game was taken so seriously that basic American concepts of law and justice were cast aside. She remembered the coroner emphatically telling Shari and her sister, merely days after their mother's death, that he knew it was not suicide for several reasons: "Her severe arthritic condition wouldn't have permitted her to hold such a large, awkward pistol in the position that had occurred."

Further, he was certain that, "From the area that the bullet entered she did not die quickly. She flopped around for quite a long time, like a chicken with its head wrung off." Shari remembered watching chickens with their heads wrung off, flopping around, walking and falling, getting up, and walking and falling more before they finally died.

He continued, this family doctor, friend to her mother: "But don't worry, girls, because your mother did not feel any pain during that time, and she did not know anything; she was unconscious, her brain was dead. It just took quite some time for her body to die also."

It had been meticulously explained to Shari that Mama was found lying on her back, arms in a surrendering position, palms up and body straight, so straight that her dress was pulled down neatly over her knees.

"How could her dress be straight?" she had asked her Uncle Darren, who explained all this to her as her father stood, silent and staring, beside him the night she first returned upon hearing of her mother's death. "Women are vain. She sat flat on the floor and straightened her dress, so she would be nice and neat when found."

She listened to his words, looked at her father's eyes, and accepted those explanations, not wanting any more answers from "them," at least not then. But she had never doubted that what this trusted doctor reported officially was what he'd reported to her and her sister. After all, his father had been her mother's doctor during all those years of beatings. He had been the one who advised Mama to leave Daddy when her body could endure no more. He was also the one who had told her mother, "Cecil should have stopped drinking slowly and with assistance, because his body had been saturated with alcohol for so long that everything about him broke down when he suddenly ceased the heavy alcohol intake."

Old Dr. Ball had plenty of professional integrity and patient-friend compassion. It never occurred to her all these years that his son, Dr. Ron J. Ball, who was the coroner at the time, was the person responsible for the actual investigation and that what he told Shari and her sister "was the actual investigation"—that which **did not get reported officially.**

But the law books don't lie. They say that the coroner is the official in charge of the investigation in an unnatural death. Shari telephoned the coroner-doctor and told him, "I would like to come and visit with you for a short while, Dr. Ball."

"Alright," he said, and hung up.

When she arrived, he appeared nervous, immediately asking her, "Are you here to talk about your mother?" A somewhat strange question to ask eighteen years after her mother's death.

"Yes. Your professional opinion of how my mother died, which you gave to my sister and me, did not seem to go down on record, Doctor."

"I changed my mind. I changed my mind."

"You changed your medical opinion based on my mother's arthritic hands and the area where the bullet entered her head? Those two facts did not change. How come you changed your mind?"

He immediately replied, "Go see Harold C. I changed my mind based on evidence he had. Go talk to him."

She thanked the doctor and left. She did not go see this Harold C., however. All these years, she barely recalled his name mentioned in regard to her mother's death. She knew that he was a state police officer now, but she was not sure what he had been eighteen years ago. She figured there'd be time for him later. Instead, she went to her attorney-uncle's house.

He seemed glad to see her; his wife, as usual, did not. When Shari brought up the topic of her visit, both women exchanged adverse opinions as to whether she had a right to bring it up or whether she should just leave it alone. Begonia felt that since it had happened so long ago, it did not need to be brought up now.

"Nobody ever wanted to talk about it even when it happened. The reason there's no statute of limitations on murder is because it is always important to reopen a case if new evidence is found," Shari said.

"Leave my house!" Begonia shouted at her niece. Then she picked up the telephone and started dialing. "I'm going to call the sheriff!"

"You stay here," Uncle Stan said, and instructed his wife to hang up the phone. "This is still my house too, at least partly. I think."

Shari had loved him for a long time. He was the one she'd come to visit, so she stayed, telling him that she wanted to discuss legal matters. Because he was an attorney, a practicing judge, her uncle, and her mother's brother, he seemed the appropriate person with whom to talk. He nodded in uncomfortable agreement. He also noted that he was sixty-three and would not be living long. His niece sensed diversionary tactics—again.

"Nobody knows how long he or she has to live, Stan. Mama didn't know she'd die at fifty, and Faye didn't know she'd be dying in her forties." Then she told him that she had looked up the correct procedure an investigation was supposed to follow when a death occurred; she had spent a good deal of time in the law library in Little Rock. She'd discovered that there are certain things a coroner is supposed to do, which Dr. Ball did not do.

"Now, Shari, Ron J. (the coroner) has come to me all through the years, admitting that he felt bad because he did not properly investigate Olive's death. He came up to me again, right after your dad died, still feeling bad about the way things went down," he confided.

"Stan, he took an oath for honesty and assistance to life. This has been torture to Roberta and me, and he knows it. Besides, he is responsible as coroner, and he didn't do the job. He knows that too! He ought to feel bad. But that's not enough. He ought to straighten it out now." Shari went on to tell him what Dr. Ball had told her and her sister from the first.

"Honey, Ron J. faced a class situation," he said.

"What do you mean by that?"

"He was on the spot. He faced the Lewises and didn't have the courage to call it as he saw it, because the Lewis name is an important name in this town—particularly Grover Lewis, and he was there at the house. So the doctor just said nothing, but he has always felt bad about it."

"What about what he told Roberta and me?"

"He committed a serious offense in not reporting that. A serious offense."

Then she asked him, for the record, "To your knowledge, was there ever any investigation of any kind by the sheriff or anyone else? Did they ever learn where the gun came from or anything? Do you know where the gun is now?"

"I know of nothing except that they found her there and concluded that's what happened. I, myself, called for the ballistics tests, but it was too late. They couldn't run the tests since her hands had been washed. Your dad had instructed the morticians to hurry up and embalm her, and they had. I found Olive's grocery list that she had made out that day on the piano and I wondered why a person would plan to buy groceries and Christmas things before committing suicide."

"But, Stan, where did the word suicide come from, with no investigation?" Shari asked.

"It looked like suicide. She was lying there dead, and there was a pistol at her feet."

"That's not evidence! That's a dead person and a pistol. The dead person can't speak in her own defense, and that's why an investigation is necessary. You, an attorney and judge, know that!"

He shook his head, like an all-knowing judge. "If a person is lying there dead and a pistol is there, suicide is just assumed."

"Stan, how can you look at her and say that? You, an attorney, you, a judge! I spoke with Sid McMath and he told me—"

"You went to see Sid McMath?" he asked gravely.

"Yes, I did. I knew he wouldn't lie to me. Remember you introduced me to him when I was just a little girl? And I helped campaign for him for governor and all my friends helped, remember?"

Stan put his head in his hands a moment and Bea walked over to Shari, bringing her hand up as if she was going to slap her. Shari looked at her and said, "You just go right ahead if that's what you want to do. What you do just doesn't bother me in the least, Bea. I'm here to see Stan."

Uncle Stan told his wife to leave, and she left in a huff. His niece continued from her meeting with former governor Sid McMath. "He told me that Arkansas law presumes against suicide, based on the assumption that the strongest drive common to people is the drive to survive. Thus, suicide can be concluded only when there is a **preponderance** of evidence to prove that it was definitely suicide. Unless that is the case, the death has to be reported as unresolved. I want the cause of death on the death certificate changed from Suicide to Unresolved or Homicide."

"You'll have a hard time getting Dr. Ball to change it, and he's the one who'll have to do it," he said.

"Will you help me?" she asked, mostly for the record.

"I don't want to be involved in any way."

"Actually, you are. We all are." After informing him that she had started an investigation and that he would be approached for an interview, he consented to speak with the investigator who arrived just as she was leaving.

From there, Shari went to visit her mother's other brother. They socialized for a little while, and then she engaged him in the area of her interest, that of clearing her mother's name from premeditated suicide.

"How old were you at the time of your mom's death?" he asked.

"I had just turned twenty-two."

"You were an adult and could have done whatever you wished," he said. "You did nothing. The rest of the family members were being considerate to you by staying away, staying quiet, and letting you do whatever you wished about the situation. It was your father. Here you've waited eighteen years, and now you want to stir up something?"

Shari sat still for several moments, trying to see it all. As he spoke, it sounded reasonable enough. She was past twenty-one, a legal adult, free to do what needed to be done when her mother died. But Mama had been dead for two days before she'd been informed. By the time she had learned about her death and arrived, much had already been done. Could Shari have undone what had already been done just because she was twenty-two years old?

Thinking about how she'd worked nonstop for the past eighteen years to sort it all out and make sense of it, she knew that she could not condense those years of efforts into a few statements that would make him understand. Besides, he didn't seem very receptive to hearing anything different. Shari remembered her mother confiding her concerns about her husband and her situation to her brothers, and they had explained to her how it was and that she had no room to complain. She soon caught on and stopped complaining to them. Perhaps they assumed she was happier when she no longer complained to them; perhaps they felt better. They also felt better to not view her in her coffin, just as they chose not to view their own parents or others after death. That is everyone's choice, of course, but perhaps it also conveyed a preference to deny uncomfortable realities. Had they viewed their sister's bruised arms and felt the.38 hole in her head, they might have found it more difficult to stay away and remain silent, 'for the children's sake,' as so many people had put it.

That excuse, or smokescreen—for the children's sake—seemed a little too close to 'victim blaming.' It sounded reasonable enough when explained, yet it was so misleading with the misplaced hint of kindness it carried. Such reasoning involved a gross distortion, and a significant reality was blatantly rejected, even denied.

Shari shared with her aunt and uncle her new discoveries and hopes, and although they expected that the hope was futile, they wished her well in her efforts.

Ironically, on the street in town, she later met a man whom she had not seen in almost two decades. She was not absolutely certain that she recognized him at first. As she came closer to him, she asked, "Are you Harold C. Blevens?" He nodded. She then asked when and where would be a good time to talk with him.

"Right here and right now is OK," he said.

"I understand that you're the person who has some specific evidence regarding my mother's death, evidence that verified suicide, and I'm wondering what that evidence was?"

"We just figured that's what happened," he said.

"Wait. Did you find a suicide note?"

"No."

"Did she have powder burns on her hands?"

"No tests were done."

"Had she bought the gun or the shells?"

"Not to my knowledge."

"What about fingerprints? Were her prints on the gun?"

"No."

"Harold, how was suicide determined without some of this evidence?"

"We just looked at her and figured that's what happened."

"Did you question anyone?"

"No. Nobody was there except your dad, so we didn't question anyone."

"You didn't question him?"

"That's right."

"Harold, if that had been your mother or your wife, would you have just looked at her and figured?"

"No, I would have investigated it."

"So, was my mother just not important enough? She didn't matter?"

"Don't get horsy with me, Shari," he said as he straightened up his six-foot frame and towered over her.

She hadn't heard that term in years, but she knew it was a type of "kin" hint to remember her "place" as a woman. She remembered and left.

Later she was privileged to talk with two of her father's brothers, both of whom firmly noted that if either her mother or her father carried out that fatal deed, their brother was certainly the one more likely for several reasons. He was socially isolated with no friends, totally dependent, and had problems. Her mother, by comparison, was socially healthy, friendly, responsible, and a good, stable person. Uncle Darren who claimed he was first to the scene, beckoned by her dad, said Cecil was saying, "They'll blame me; they'll blame me."

He continued his story. "Then, Harold (Blevens) picked up the gun like this." He simulated the use of one finger so as to protect fingerprints on the gun.

"What was Harold, anyway?" she asked.

"I'm not sure but I think he was with the state police," Darren answered.

Shari later found out that Harold C., at that time, worked in the licensing department. Currently he was a lieutenant in the state police department.

Her father's other brother added that as soon as he heard what had happened to her mother, he went to his father's house (Shari's grandfather). He knew that his dad owned a.38 pistol and knew where it was always kept. He looked for it, and the gun was gone. He asked his dad where the gun was.

"Poppy said he didn't know where it was," Shari's uncle said. "I always figured that's where the gun came from. I also thought that it was your father's deed, not your mother's."

Undoubtedly, it was plain old politics as usual. The name of Grover Lewis, according to her judge uncle, meant a great deal. Since Grover Lewis was her father's cousin, also a Lewis, the name had to be protected. Sadly enough, none of the cover-up was even for the purpose of protecting her father. Had that been the case, he might have enjoyed the protective warmth extended him. But no one actually cared about her father, only the Lewis *name*. She could not recall Grover Lewis visiting their home ever in all her years growing up. Her dad had not liked him, the cause stemming back decades ago to a family feud involving their fathers, who were brothers.

However, Grover Lewis had been the one to man her mother's telephone when Shari had called home to speak to her Mama and had discovered that she couldn't come to the phone. She also recalled hearing that it was Grover Lewis who personally and forcefully escorted her sister across the street and up the hill to her aunt's house, rather than let her remain with the crowd at her house. Why? Why not be at her own house with her own mother and the spectators and the questions and her father? After taking Roberta there, Grover Lewis had stayed at her aunt's place long enough to literally barricade the door while instructing others to keep her there. They followed his instructions without question, for he was Grover Lewis.

Yes, she guessed Grover Lewis was an important person in that town. She always liked him, despite the fact that he was a Lewis. She forgave him for that—it's nobody's fault what family they're born into. She remembered how he'd given her fifty dollars one year to buy an evening gown so she could represent his insurance company in a beauty contest. That was an honor, but instead of getting one knockout dress for fifty dollars, she bought two pretty dresses for twenty-five dollars each so that she could take them with her to college the next year. She never told him, but figured he wouldn't mind. She didn't win the contest for him, but he seemed pleased when she came in second place. Perhaps if she had bought one fifty-dollar dress as he had instructed, she might have won.

He attended the Methodist church she went to, and she liked both him and his wife. She particularly liked their only son, Earl. He died at a young age from cancer and spent his last months making his beautiful home comfortable for the wife and two little girls he was leaving behind. Shari always admired that kind of thinking, even though others saw it as simply doing what needed to be done.

She remembered the last time she saw Grover Lewis. It was in a nursing home, where he looked unhappy. He also seemed so small in his wheelchair; no one would have realized that he was more important than anyone else. When she visited him, she asked, "Grover, do you know who I am?"

"Yes. You're Shari."

She and Robbie were standing there together, looking at him. Shari wondered what he was thinking as he looked at them. She held his hand and tried to make meaningful small talk, but he was clearly uncomfortable. She felt sad for him. A few months later, she learned that he had died. But why was Grover Lewis more powerful than her politically powerful uncle who worked closely with the governor of the state? How could Grover Lewis be more powerful than both these men? How could Grover Lewis protect his family name by shielding his cousin from a murder investigation, when to do so required that a powerful attorney ignore it himself and manipulate his family's trust by collectively boycotting his sister's residence and isolating her children? What could cause a lawyer and governor to conspire to stop legal procedures and to withhold the truth? And why would he leave the victim's children in the care of the victim's in-laws, where they would themselves be subtly redefined as the perpetrators of the grisly crime?

Grover Lewis was not more influential than her lawyer-uncle or the governor. He just was not intimidated by them because like them, he too used any tactics at hand to achieve his own means. He knew what was occurring there. He knew her uncle and the governor had much to keep concealed from the public and the news media. He knew how to persuade both these political figures to use their legal influence for his cause. He understood their cause. What none of them knew was that the prison mess would be disclosed very soon, anyway, and the public would learn from the newspapers and the famed movie Brubaker what the warden and governor had allowed to happen.

The bottom line was that a prominent lawyer had betrayed his own sister, her children, and the legal system. But for what? The truth he conspired to hide became known and he felt the scandal of the prison situation as it exploded. By this time, the larger picture was finally becoming more focused. Politics and the status quo of the town's elite were at stake when her mother met her death, and that had become the issue—not her death.

In the thirty years that her parents had lived in that town, it seemed that they always managed to be missed. Her mother used to mention that she had wondered why she never got a baby shower when she had babies, even though it was customary to give them in those days. She received invitations to all the others. And when her daddy's business burned and his mental and physical health broke, people noticed, but no one offered to assist. The church and townspeople left them alone. Finally, when Mama died, she was actually ignored.

And Shari's father? He was tolerated around town all those years, and most folks had nothing negative to say about him, but they didn't have anything positive to say about him, either. Most people recognized him, but no one really knew him or particularly cared to get to know him. When he had problems, they were his alone. When he was suspected by many for the murder of his wife, he was again ignored. He was not the one protected, for he was not an important person in that town. He happened to have an important name, though, and that name was protected. He wasn't even questioned, and he might have been delighted to have been questioned, who knows? Nobody bothered to find out. He became somewhat of a spectacle as he continued to run his business selling lumber. Most folks would go there to buy lumber just to observe him and wonder, *Did he do it?*

Shari's lawyer uncle once asked whether her father took some type of drugs. He said that he and others observed her father's strange expressions and questionable behavior following the December episode. Did they permit a psychotic person to wander on aimlessly until he shrank to half his own weight and died? Many things they did, but one thing the people of that town consistently avoided doing was whatever-needed-to-be-done.

Shari could think of one person in particular, though, who dared to be different from the small-town profile. Her cousin Debra Faye invited her away from a large group of relatives to discuss some of Shari's questions regarding the 1964 events and her current investigation. To Debra, her cousin's questions mattered, and she strongly encouraged her to continue the investigation. She confirmed some of Shari's new distrusts of Uncle Stan, whom they'd both loved in their early years, when she indicated that he was consistently, "The fly in the soup, all along; you just didn't know it."

But Shari's primary concern, which kept resurfacing, was, "What will the investigation do to Uncle Stan?" She kept asking that at frequent intervals. Then finally, she wondered, "Why do I keep worrying about Uncle Stan when it is Uncle Tim who had bypass surgery? Our whole family has been conditioned to believe that Stan is the important person. I wonder why that is?"

She didn't know for sure, but she certainly found it strange. Maybe it was because Stan was the older brother, the "golden boy," so to speak. Or maybe because he was more responsible for the murder cover-up. Uncle Tim only followed Stan's lead; he always followed his older brother. Perhaps he didn't even know the truth about everything himself.

The last time they'd discussed the matter, he'd told her that he really didn't figure Daddy had the nerve to kill Mama himself. Tim had said, "Cecil probably paid somebody to do it for him. But it's the same thing."

> *Many songs are written and many more shall be*
> *To help our hearts imagine that great Eternity.*
> *We're told, there will be streets of gold*
> *And beauty everywhere - that we shall meet*
> *With friends of old and loved ones in the air.*
> *All this and more so glorious - I know that day will be,*
> *For in that lovely city, my mother waits for me.*

I know she waits there patiently, for patient here was she,
Yet still, I know she's longing, her daughters yet to see
And oh how we do miss her and look beyond this life
Toward that heavenly meeting place, where never enters strife.
But still I feel that there will be most wonderful of all,
My Lord Who died on Calvary, Who hastened to my call.
'Twas He Who built that home so fair,
'Twas He Who told me so,
'Twas He Who loves beyond compare,
Protects me from each worldly snare,
'Tis He Who takes my every care...
'Tis why I want to go.

CHAPTER TWENTY-SEVEN

AS THE INVESTIGATION CONTINUED on, so did the cleanup of the flood-ravaged town. The family took time out, though, to hold one beautiful wedding event on the evening of Christmas. The red poinsettias and nativity scene were still in place as Christmas decorations. Cecelia was breathtakingly lovely in her Southern-bride attire; she had made her own wide-brimmed hat with flowing red ribbons, matching those on her bridal bouquet. Her dress had a full skirt made of billows and billows of white taffeta. She was, in Shari's unbiased opinion, the most gorgeous bride ever, and she was pleased that her daughter could be wed in the church they'd attended for so many years before leaving for California. There in Little Rock in their home church, with Jesus, Mary and Joseph on the stage with her, her spouse-to-be and the preacher known for many years, they put together the vows as they went along.

Only one word impeccably described Cecelia's spouse-to-be: nervous. As the preacher ran late and later, Mark eyed the back door more and more seriously. He admitted to everyone later that he was timing the preacher, trying to give him a fair chance, but that, "When my last cigarette was gone, then I was going to be gone too if that guy still hadn't shown up."

Mark was a handsome groom. But more importantly, a fine young man whom Cecelia aptly described: "He's a Northerner; the main criteria I used in selecting a husband was that he could not be a Southern man and he had to be good father material."

Shari marveled at the wisdom her daughter used, and both factors have served their family well as they are devoted parents of two very special young adults. As she viewed their family, she somehow felt her mother smiling at her from a distance, as though to say, "You did well, Shari. You broke the cycle of dysfunction, and I'm proud of you both." Shari had found the courage to end her abusive marriage, and her daughter chose a healthier partner to begin with.

After the wedding, Cecelia and Mark eventually returned to their army base where they prepared to deploy to Germany. Shari permitted herself a few weeks in the area, visiting people she had not seen for years. One such friend was a woman about her age who had been a neighbor from birth, and their friendship had continued right into their college years when they were roommates. She was the one who, unknown to Shari, had gotten word back to her mother that she was both pregnant and starving in their unfurnished room in Washington, DC. In the meantime, she occasionally brought her food to eat while they visited, since she had, "so little time otherwise to visit."

Shari became curious as to why the two had never discussed her mother's death at all. Her friend's first child was born within a day of when Mama had died, and she remembered buying a baby gift and taking it to her, but she thought, *She never came up to the house to see me, and she was just next door.* Shari had stayed there for three weeks. After recovering from giving birth, why had her friend never come?

Always before, Shari had assumed people were angry at her—at the family—for being so bad (having "killed their mother"). But now with her vision so much clearer, she wanted to see her friend again. She went to her workplace in another city, and there they visited and made plans to go out for dinner after she closed up; her spouse would watch the kids. Shortly after the old friends settled in at the restaurant, Shari gathered her courage and broached the subject, apologetically asking if she could bring up the "taboo topic," as it would mean a great deal to her.

"Of course," she said, hardly fazed at all.

Inwardly Shari collapsed. *Oh God!* she thought, *Why had it taken me so long to get the nerve to ask that question?* Shari began talking, and her friend did not stop her. She kept talking. Both talked nonstop, drinking coffee all the while. At midnight, the restaurant closed. That six hours of permitted, nonstop talking about the taboo topic was the best meal Shari had ever consumed. Nevertheless, nineteen years had gone by since that bleak December. She had discovered much and experienced even more through her inner battle of fear and deception. She had been seeking the truth on a moment-by-moment basis, for everything depended on its discovery. For without those preliminary small steps, it would be more than she could bear.

Fear reigned fervently, for fear was paramount on that day when Mama met her death, and fear continued to order the decisions made by everyone. Deception was shared by all the authority figures who lacked truth and integrity of character. Silence was the response shared by all who were not themselves victims to a murder disguised-as-suicide. Perhaps some of the silent ones meant well, but the others? Perhaps it took the passive silent to make the evil deed possible. Are the silent often those who allow a leader to lead and silently condone his leadership by their silence?

Who in his or her right mind could really consider it a kindness to allow a mother's children to believe that their mother chose to give them her suicide for their Christmas present? The children were simply left to sink or swim in their abyss of excruciating pain.

Uncle Stan informed Shari of an event in which he seemingly took a good deal of pride, yet it conjured up additional anguish in her. He noted that, "Roberta had been drinking heavily; she was crying, hysterical, guilt-ridden, and wallowing in the mud. I lay down in the mud myself and talked to her awhile and finally talked her into coming to the house for coffee. Yeah, I brought her around, I did."

Shari looked at that smug, self-proud grin and answered, "Yeah, you're good at handling things, aren't you? And little Robbie needed handling by a big 'ol judge who knows how to handle things, didn't she? But did you ever wonder why she had a need to drink heavily in the first place, and why she resorted to guilt-ridden hysteria in the mud? Did you remember to thank her for making you look good, once again, Mr. Politician?"

He shifted his feet, then eyed his niece directly. "Now you hold your tongue, young lady. You're gettin' a bit feisty these days. I've been meaning to tell you, you ought to watch it."

"Yeah, I'll crawl back under my rock, Uncle Judge, don't you worry about me. I knows my place, I does." She left frightened, thinking, *I really do know my place,* and that was to act as insignificant around him as he considered her to be. She mustn't say too much, reveal too much, or show her anger because *they* had the upper hand and she had to remember that. Shari knew she could conveniently 'die' as had Aunt Faye back when they couldn't stop them from talking, and that would not serve any worthwhile purpose, so she'd play their game for the time being.

But away from her uncle, she felt an ache for Robbie and for all the mental and emotional torment her sister had experienced. She wanted so desperately to ease it for her, and she'd tried so hard, but this task was too big and it sometimes seemed that she was regressing two steps for each one she progressed. *But please, Robbie, trust me and someday you will know the truth.* They all would. Shari, her sister, and her brother had survived, more or less, and left to sink or swim, they learned to swim. It was a hell of a lesson in learning. They'd lost each other along the way, and that's a price that can never be reimbursed. They may forever be isolated from each other. It seemed they'd shared a nightmare too hideous to be reminded of by each other's presence. The last time her brother, Ellis, had spoken to Shari was in 1977 at a class reunion, and he didn't seem to want to talk then; she had initiated a conversation.

Then Stan appeared and monopolized the rest of the visit. Over the years, she had so often wished that she and Ellis could have further discussed that phone call she had made to Uncle Darren, when he had said, "But he wasn't by himself; he didn't do it alone." Had he hired someone to kill Mama? Did both of them chase her, torture her? Did they kill her upstairs, (as indicated by the wet spot Robbie saw there) and drag her downstairs, or was she chased through the circular house, and that's how the bathroom stove broke?

But when Shari immediately phoned Ellis and related Uncle Darren's message, Ellis just wanted, "to think about it," not to discuss it at all, ever.

Some people had told her that Ellis just couldn't think of his dad in that way, it was too painful. She'd studied psychology and knew that identity issues are pretty serious ones, no doubt. Others had theorized that Ellis didn't want to see her because she reminded him of Mama, and that was unpleasant for him. She had no problem with respecting others' rights to be as they are and do as they choose. Yet sometimes she found it hard to believe that the three siblings never had one single conversation about their past, their parents, their dead mother, nothing. Robbie and Shari had suffered together and separately, but never once the three of them together.

Yet she respected Ellis' right to handle his pain in his own way, assuming that since he is male, his needs must be altogether different from the sisters'. She stopped missing him long ago and acknowledged that she would just never be acquainted with his children, because he wanted it that way, just as he had no interest in knowing her two children.

But Shari does know her nephew Ken, Robbie's son. He's a fine young man who's suffered in ways that the people of their town could never imagine because, for the most part, he suffered quietly and out of the public view. Shari was thankful that she knew Ken.

Still, what had happened to their mother—first the murder, then the cover-up—took from the three siblings their good memories with their parents and the freedom to discuss their merits and mistakes with love and understanding. When eighteen years are spent in aloneness, upheaval, fear, deception, and guilt, good memories are lost, and love between siblings is replaced with loathing. Being a part of that horrendous event and its aftermath, they remained apart from each other as adults.

Only one question remained: What should be done from this point on? Shari hoped the truth would be revealed one way or another, and she preferred that it be done by those who needed to rectify their deeds. If not, perhaps another way to the truth would be provided. At any rate, she didn't believe that all this has been for no purpose. Her mother did not die in vain, and their many years of struggle had not been in vain. If even one other person who struggled similarly could find some measure of meaning as a result of their pain, their lives would be purposeful.

Some might object to the way Shari's told her story, but it is made up of her experiences and her perceptions. As Viktor Frankl said, "No one can take away our attitude... the way we perceive a situation and react to it is our choice." That is a universal freedom. Certainly no one can argue with an experience, and this has been Shari's. In becoming a psychologist, she'd grown to appreciate the painful experiences that people have because, in them, there is significance, and that significance must be discovered for healing to occur.

Her father's problems had meaning to him also, but it was never found in time for him and others to benefit. Shari hopes that the reader of these pages might develop a new respect for the person with such problems and invite him or her to ask, seek, and knock for assistance. She hopes that others, particularly those in authority, would refrain from playing politics when the price of the game must be paid by those deemed less important.

Some might wonder why Shari went to such lengths to write this account. It was Robert Kennedy who said, "Some men look at things as they are and ask, Why? I dream of things that never have been and ask, Why not?"

Whether her own answer is, "Because it needed to be done," or simply, "Why not?" or perhaps to confirm that the strongest drive in mankind is indeed the drive to survive, as a theistic, existential psychotherapist by nature and by profession, she could do no less. She recalled Uncle Stan's statement a few years back, "You did all the right things." Now she realized that she had his approval and respect, even though they were serious contenders.

And although she admitted to having realized feelings of intense resentment and anger toward some people for a time, such human emotions are no more or less than common in the course of interacting with people in life. The negative emotions subside (through lots of prayer and lots of emotional work), love continues on. But there must be communication before each can occur, and this presentation is Shari's gift toward that communication. For sure, many of her own efforts, decisions, and actions acknowledged herein would be viewed critically by some. In that they already have been properly dealt with, no further apology or defense is necessary. They seemed at the time to be essential in the quest for total liberation.

She's grateful that when Jesus was hanging on the cross and the criminal next to Him asked for mercy, the man was given mercy rather than scorn and condemnation. He was quickly accepted by Jesus, who was hurting alongside him. For those who wish to judge, perhaps their own time of hurting has not yet arrived by which their own empathetic understanding will be opened for mercy to follow. Perhaps Jesus knew that the criminal—as we all are, at least for a time—had paid his dues in full.

Upon mentioning to a friend recently that she was about to complete her autobiography, he laughed, replying, "You've not lived long enough to write an autobiography." His statement brought to mind a song that had been popular in Nashville in the early 1960s, "By the Time You've Learned How to Really Live, You're Old Enough to Die." It always left her with the question, Why? It seemed to her imperative that people learn to live early so that everyone can live long and fully or, as Jesus put it in John 10:10, "*abundantly.*"

In her elementary and high school years, she remembered often studying about some really admirable person, reading his or her biography. In so doing, she came to know that person, how he thought, what he valued, how he made decisions, and so on. Consistently, these individuals were engaged in wondering, questioning, searching for those things they deemed important to know. In doing that, they fulfilled their "impossible dream." Sure enough, the *world was better by far, because they reached their unreachable star.* Shari knew of no more important message to understand in a lifetime.

Sometimes in despair, in loneliness and pain,
His sweet tender voice I hear,
"My child you have chosen the greatest of gifts
And the path will not always be clear.
You have chosen to go when I say to go,
To come when I speak the word,
You have chosen to stand alone,
If alone, is where for a time I afford
You have no request of your own origin,
You have no complaints of My ways
You have only love and tenderness
And have committed to Me all your days.
You've chosen to climb the mountain,
The highest of the high.
You've chosen to swim the deepest and wide
Or the valley to live or die.
My kingdom lives within your heart
My love will see you through
My grace still stands sufficient for all that you may do".

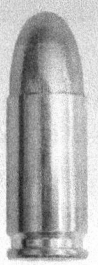

CHAPTER TWENTY-EIGHT

WHAT KIND OF PERSON merits such a petition of inquiry twenty years after her demise? How can such a body—exhumed— convey the story of her death to the pathologist? These questions and many more raced through Shari's mind as she filed the appropriate papers.

In the Circuit Court of Van Buren County, Arkansas, No. DH3954. In the Matter of: Olive Deevens Lewis, Deceased. Petition for Exhumation. The petitioner, Shari Anne Lewis, petitions the court pursuant to Ark. Stat. Ann. 24-661 (Supp.1984:) for an order of the court for the exhumation of the body of Olive Lewis, and further ordering the State Medical Examiner to perform an autopsy on the body and in support thereon, states:

1. The deceased, Olive Deevens Lewis, was a resident of Van Buren County, Arkansas, who died of a gunshot wound to the head on December 18, 1964. She is buried in City Cemetery in Van Buren County, Arkansas.
2. The petitioner, Shari Anne Lewis, is the daughter of the deceased and is a resident of the State of California.
3. At the time of the death of Mrs. Lewis, no autopsy was performed, although one was authorized by applicable law at that time.
4. No investigation of the death was performed and no evidence of suicide was discovered.
5. Nonetheless, the death certificate lists the death as a suicide.
6. Because of the allegation of suicide by her mother, the petitioner and her family have suffered severe emotional trauma.

7. An autopsy would show unequivocally that the wound could not have been self-inflicted.

8. The petitioner and her family have a right and the State has an obligation to correct the death certificate.

9. The deceased had a right to an investigation before being declared to have taken her own life and the State had an obligation to overcome the presumption against suicide. The petitioner alleges that the circumstances surrounding the death of her mother were purposefully covered up in order to prevent a murder charge being filed.

10. The petitioner will produce evidence at the hearing on this petition, supporting the allegations herein and notice will be served on all the interested parties. Attorney for Petitioner

Verification—I hereby verify that the above allegations are true and correct to the best of my knowledge. Shari Anne Lewis, Petitioner.

She was well aware that many people would scoff at her actions and that others had already turned away in disgust or anger. Some valued the "rest" of the dead above the "rest" of the living. But others simply inquired, "How can the exhumation reveal anything pertinent? It's been so long. Isn't it too long?"

Nonetheless, she'd enjoyed a new and liberating peace ever since she learned that a date had been scheduled for the court to hear her petition. She planned to attend the hearing. If the petition was denied, she'd appeal it. After all, that was the procedure of the legal system. However, deep in her heart, she knew that the final moments were at hand, irrespective of the court's findings or whether the exhumation ever occurred. Once, she even considered the fact that the best professional people sometimes make mistakes, and what if the state pathologist erred in her mother's autopsy and confirmed suicide? Would that usher in any regret on her part? The answer flowed from her soul as warmly and respectfully as did the few quiet tears that slid from her eyes. There would be no regret for doing what needed to be done. All that had been done thus far was sorely needed.

As for the final declarations? Well, perhaps they were in themselves somewhat irrelevant, after all. The belated investigation was done. The legal system at last turned a respectful ear to her mother's life and death and to its own previous errors. Rectification was sought and now set in motion; official publication was made. Even if the truth of December 18, 1964, became no more than a case of not knowing, that was the truth that was needed to replace the false accusation, which had caused so much damage for so long.

What kind of person merits this much of her own mental, emotional, physical, and financial energy for half her lifetime? Shari wondered as she recollected her mother's jet black hair and quiet, soft smile. Olive could be seen only as a good person by anyone's standards in that she brought no ill to others and attempted, over a lifetime, to provide warmth and pleasant, peaceful simplicity to others. Although her greatest efforts were manifested at home, she also extended lesser but similar efforts to the outside community, for she felt a oneness with people in general, and in particular with those in crisis, hardship or sorrow. Her overall disposition was kind, confident, and consistent with her highest priorities, and in that sense she could only be considered a success, for she never relented. Her priorities were changing in her last days, and she was accommodating the change by switching her own goals, expectations, and commitments as she planned her divorce and relocation. Yes, she truly exemplified an authentic person in today's society, although she likely would have smiled to have heard such a complimentary description. Her mode-of-being was receptive, responsive, and gracious. Thus she lived harmoniously with herself.

Olive greatly valued the traditional family system and took seriously her marriage vows. She lacked a vision of her children without their father or their home and of herself without her husband. So for many years, she maintained the traditional family. She was nurturing to her husband, who needed and demanded much care. Her three children had various mixtures of their parents' opposite personalities, thus they accepted her nurturing from different positions, forming different conclusions. Olive nurtured because she needed to and because that was all she knew to do and to be. She did not expect anything in return for what she gave, but she wasn't simpleminded and didn't fail to recognize that something was amiss when she received stones for her fishes, as described in Matthew 7:9. She allowed plenty of space for the individuals in her life to be themselves, because that represented fairness in her own value system and because she wanted to be herself.

Shari remembered the time her mother had said that she would always keep a prayer going for one specific young man in their town. Olive and Cecil had been the first to arrive at an automobile accident near their home. This young man was driving and there were fatalities. "That will be a terrible burden for him to live with for a long, long time, and he's such a fine boy. He'll need our prayers to get over it, and he sure has mine." She had a special place in her heart for people who were struggling. Shari wondered if the young man ever knew Olive was praying for him all through the years?

In this respect, her mother was guilty of practicing the Golden Rule. In her earlier years she traded in a martyr's burden for a separated lifestyle at her doctor's advice. That indicated that it was not her desire to be a martyr, per se. She had been willing to pay a high toll in order to maintain the traditional family system. When her doctor brought up the issue of her own health and noted that she might not survive long enough to rear her children, that superseded the priority of the traditional family. She shifted gears and claimed a new priority—that she must live to rear her children, with or without the traditional family system.

Later when Olive was offered a business-type proposition—returning to the same husband and the same home but without the alcohol—she accepted the proposition. Although she was never formally a businesswoman, she had worked behind the scenes in her husband's business, and she had a knack for recognizing a good opportunity when she saw one. Having earlier concluded that her husband and home were basically good, contaminated only by his consumption of alcohol, she consequently decided that, minus the contamination, both the husband and home would become "good."

However, being of a sound business mind, she also realized the possibility of false advertising and pondered whether or not she might be buying into false promises. On the other hand, she also had some simple faith. In weighing the pros and cons, the pros won out. She was hoping that her husband would remain free of alcohol and that she could maintain the traditional family system, remaining true to "for better or worse." This would enable her and her family to grow to be fully themselves, individuals within the family unit. She accepted the business proposition as would any good business person, totally oblivious to the long-term effects of both Cecil's weakness and the strength of the disease of alcoholism.

Olive recognized family members' rights to be themselves and seldom used words like "should." She properly disciplined the children in a manner that literally left its mark—for the hickory switch continued to sting long hours after its use. Yet despite the red stripes it left on legs, it could hardly cause severe damage. Even in its use, though, she was fair, resorting to it rarely. Shari often outran her mother, managing to avoid the switch for the entire day. On those occasions, she let it go, assuming that her daughter had suffered enough through the fear of being found, doing without food, or missing whatever was planned for the day. She was seldom one to hold grudges, partly because they had been held against her by Cecil so often, and she knew their negating effect.

On many occasions she conveyed intelligence, common sense, and intuition, which would be recognized today as wisdom-psychology. Once when Shari returned home sooner than expected from a friend's house with a mouthful of bubble gum that she'd gotten from her friend, Olive questioned her about it. Shari was unaware that her friend's mother had telephoned Mama and laughingly reported that she, in anger, had stolen her friend's piece of bubble gum (lying alongside the one actually offered to her).

"Isn't it nice to have friends who would give you so much gum? We'll stop by Macie's house and see if she wants to go to town with us," Mama said.

Shari insisted that Macie didn't want to go to town. Then she insisted that she did not want to go to town either. However, Mama put her into the car and stopped by to thank Macie for her generosity and offered her a trip to the store. Sure enough, as Shari had feared, Macie came out the front door, crying loudly, angry that she had stolen her bubble gum. That event was so distasteful in itself that Shari relinquished all interest in criminal behavior at the age of six. Her mother's wise handling of that event left its mark even better than the hickory switch.

Mama also discouraged her from any attempts to lie by letting her know that she couldn't lie well, because her eyes told the truth even when she tried to be dishonest. Thus, Shari often chose silence as a defense but seldom considered trying to lie.

There were times in her teenage years when she was not totally sure that she liked having Olive for a mother. One such time was when Mama absolutely refused to allow her to date a shady character—even though she knew how important it was for Shari to have her friends see them going out together. The teen even promised her parents that if she could date him, they would go straight to church on Sunday morning and straight home afterward.

"No," Mama said.

She resented the rigidity that her folks displayed on that issue and later suspected that had she been allowed that one date, she might not have married the jerk later. Her mom certainly was a sport when she did actually marry him, however, and shipped all her clothes, plus dishes and extra gifts, to the newlyweds. Yes, for the most part, Shari considered her to be quite a trooper.

Whenever she knew Mama to be angry with her, she felt badly about it, but she was usually at a loss to defend her position. She was never quite certain what her position actually was. Besides, she knew that Mama was probably right, so she usually preferred not to verbalize her own wrongful stand. She just maintained her anger, conceded silently, and knew the time would come that she'd be elsewhere.

For example, when their family raised laying hens, Shari was the family's egg-crater. She developed an artistic system of crating eggs and took great pride in it. As she became engrossed in the process, she also became lost in her own thoughts. One day Mama walked into the storm cellar when "the pro" was at work. Startled at the suddenness of hearing her name spoken, Shari slung fresh eggs left and right simultaneously, accidentally sending them crashing against the cement walls instead of finding their slots in the cardboard crates. When she turned around, Mama slapped her once across the face. The slap itself was not painful, but the insult it carried was.

Mama announced that she had opened Shari's private box using the private key and had examined the box's private contents. She was angry because she had discovered a letter from a youth minister that Shari had received after summer church camp. That confirmed Mama's suspicions that her daughter had become too interested in the youth minister. The incident let Shari know that she had to work even harder to maintain her privacy.

Again, she was saddened to have hurt, upset, or disappointed her mother. That was the last thing she wished to do. However, as she resumed the egg-crating, her thoughts returned to that minister. Yes, he was several years older than her. That was why they hired him as a youth minister for the kids at camp. He had allowed her to confide her private thoughts and feelings to him as no one else had ever permitted. That helped a lot, so much so that she wrote to him after camp to thank him again. He had answered her letter, and that letter symbolized respect for her private existence. That privacy had just been invaded, and it hurt. Even worse, her privacy had been discounted. Her mother had then concluded from the letter that she was infatuated with an adult man. *But what if I were,* young Shari wondered. He was twenty-one and single, a nice person and had been helpful when help was sorely needed. What was so terribly wrong about a kid being infatuated with such a person? She even wondered why she was speechless under accusation. Why hadn't she offered her mom the simple explanation of the confidential discussion she'd held with the minister? In the absence of defense, Mama assumed her guilty of something, and it hurt to be thought guilty when she knew she was not.

Nonetheless, she felt the guilt, the guilt of breaking an important rule. Shari had talked to an outsider about their family and had spared no details about its ghastliness. She had not been able to admit this to her mother because she preferred to be thought guilty of a silly crush on a preacher rather than to admit revealing the family's secrets. The latter would surely be more upsetting to her mother than the former.

Then her thoughts wandered back to the youth minister. He listened, he understood, and he seemed to care about the whole family—although he didn't know them all. And he prayed and encouraged her to pray often. Plus he promised to remember their family and to pray for all of them, long after camp was over. That helped a lot. He soon discovered that Shari was seriously wondering how their family would all turn out and how she could get out and away from it. The "it" had been released in the privacy of the counselor's office, where she talked freely of her home situation, the morbidity there, and the conflicting facade that all of them conveyed to those outside of her family's walls. She was tired of it and it was difficult thinking clearly, for it seemed necessary to properly decode everything as she passed between the inside and the outside worlds.

There was also the constant fear of what might happen if she failed to properly decipher, or failed to do so in sufficient time. The two worlds were exhausting and exasperating, and she felt resentment toward the entire situation. She could not rightfully feel resentment toward the persons involved, because having scrutinized them, she felt fully convinced that they were all innocent. How could she be angry at innocent people, the ones she loved the most? Yet she did feel resentment and thus assumed guilt for such unfair feelings. It would be simple, she admitted to herself, to just exit via the second-story window. But she knew she would not take that option because it would only help her while increasing the pain for the rest of her family. God knew, they had enough of that—all of them.

The counselor understood and promised to keep their conversation secret. Shari appreciated both, so much that she wrote him a letter conveying that. He answered her letter. She felt honored, validated, and respected because of that private letter. As her face stung lightly from the slap, her thoughts wandered to the egg-crating ritual. And now she felt invaded and judged and damned and doomed and angry. She felt so angry at Mama. Although she wasn't certain why, she felt angry that her mother let it all happen.

And now it can't stop, and I can't even tell you how I feel. I want to help you, and instead, I hurt you. I have to pretend and be quiet, and I'm so tired of both and angry at you, Mama. And I'm so very, very sorry.

Tears began to softly flow as the eggs found their places in the crates more slowly. Amidst the tears and privacy of her storm-cellar workshop, Shari peered through the tiny window and viewed her dad working hard at the planer mill, oblivious to the pain of her world. Perhaps, she thought, his pain is much greater. She locked her private thoughts into a private compartment of her mind with a make-believe key and counted the eggs aloud as she crated them side by side in their comfortable little slots, where they would rest as they made their journey to various stores. For now, they were her means of escape.

Decades after her mother's death, a lawyer made a statement to both Shari and an acquaintance. "It is difficult and nearly impossible to rectify a situation after time has passed," he said, "for with the passing of time, folks come to believe that the wrong deeds they committed were actually right." The comment came as a surprise to both of them and also as a disappointment.

No, Shari never wished to idealize her mother. Olive Lewis was no more perfect than other good mothers, but she received a bum rap and had been denied representation.

"Therefore, just go on with your life and leave it alone, huh?" she replied to the attorney.

Very seriously, he nodded, as if to say 'exactly.' "Best thing to do, under the circumstances," he added.

Perhaps he disclosed only one man's philosophy, but Shari believed he conveyed the mentality of their entire town as well. Nevertheless, that mentality is in stark contrast to the American democratic system, and that difference is what has made this nation so great. She'd doubted that greatness for a time and had placed trust in the wrong sources. Dare she place trust in the American system and its alleged greatness yet again? Is that in itself a worthwhile pursuit? *Yes, because Mama is still entitled to her American right of representation*, she thought. It took more than a year to get the formal petition hearing. When it was but a few days away, Shari surveyed the past year, which she'd spent working at an agency assisting others with family, interpersonal, and intrapersonal problems. She grew up a lot during that year, encumbered with responsibilities. Her life in a one-room efficiency apartment provided rest, and the meager salary was sufficient for her modest lifestyle. She realized the emotional and professional validation as they concomitantly occurred. Both were liberating achievements.

She smiled in amusement upon recalling those who assisted her in the process. Upon her return to California from Europe, she sought out another therapist to help her complete her self-restoration task (having reluctantly left her Jewish colleagues in Europe). The psychiatrist she found proved to be uniquely quintessential. After several weeks of work, she delightfully and ecstatically discovered that the physician was Jewish. That further validated the significance of their work and seemed a special addition to her own mission, which the Jewish physician well understood. She had earlier concluded that life's survivors were special people. As a race, the Jews were known to be survivors, and she considered them special. "Maybe even chosen?" Henry, the physician, remarked to her.

Yes, she strongly recognized the Jews as God's chosen people and felt special with her close identification with the Jews and other survivors. She also felt special in her relationship with God. Yes, she loved special things and special people and special meanings. And she was grateful for the many special blessings that she and her children had received through the years. As far back as she could reflect, she always sensed a special purpose. During her early years the purpose was to fortify, endure, and assist. In her teen years, it was that of escape. Following her mother's death, it had returned to a survival level—via regression—combined with the purpose of freeing her children and herself from their family's bondage. Always there had been the prevailing purpose of seeking the meaning of it all.

She recalled her visits with Viktor Frankl in Vienna and his vivid explanation as to the purpose of survivors—to convey to the world a multidimensional meaning. As others were being helped by the message, the medium of the message (the survivor) also benefited, for in proving his own experience not to have been in vain, he was validated and restored. Thus, his unique purpose—his survivor's mission.

It seemed certain that there was a level of understanding, of relating, that was not quite possible or available to non-survivors (unless conveyed to them by survivors). She valued this unique and special level and privately enjoyed its occasional presence in her work with others. She also valued her professional integrity and kept those special moments private for the welfare of her clientele.

She made an exception only once. In her fantasy, she had desired the experience of a conversation that would be of such transpersonal momentum that all else would be forgotten in the ecstasy of the encounter. She suspected, though, that such intimacy might be available only later in the luxury of heaven itself. Recently, however, while sitting in a therapy session with a client she'd had for several months, she became so totally enthralled in the width, depth, and magnitude of the client's wisdom that she felt as though she were sitting at the feet of Jesus. At the conclusion of the therapy hour, the client waited for her to write out his next appointment. She was reluctant to do it, asking, "Why would you want to make an appointment?"

"You mean I'm cured?" the very special client asked, smiling.

At last, she had encountered a true public servant in the purest definition. It should not have come as a surprise, although it did, when she later discovered that this public servant, the pharmacist, was also a Jew. As she eagerly shared that monumental event with her supervisor, she transcended their conference momentarily and smiled globally, remembering that this supervisor himself was one of them, a Jew.

She secretly whispered her question to God, "Whatever is the meaning of all this?" A year before she'd sold her home and belongings to travel to Europe to seek out and query Jews. Now, left and right, those special folk appeared. Twenty years ago, she had lost her own nuclear family. Today a new family was hers. As in the experience of Job, it was even better than before—twice restored.

Captivity Turned

Look to the days of Job - the love he had was great.
It stood the fiery trials - and withstood others' hate.
He never questioned God - about why this must be
But in the midst of problems, his eyes ne'er failed to see
That God was ever, over all, and true to Him he'd stay
No matter what the purpose, nor what the price he'd pay.
The losses seemed forever - without a hope in sight
His pain increased as others scoffed, condemning him, his plight.
But at last the nightmare ended - his losses twice restored
The trial had proved him worthy - and God was still his Lord.

CHAPTER TWENTY-NINE

TO COURT AT LONG last. It took twenty years to get to that courthouse in the hometown where Shari grew up, the town where her mother had lived for thirty years. During those thirty years, she was usually seen on Saturday mornings buying groceries for her family at the little grocery store across the narrow street from the courthouse. For the last decade of her life, she also had purchased her insulin at the drugstore adjacent to the grocer's. Olive was known by everyone who worked in the courthouse, and she often stopped to visit with the workers as she passed through its main corridor on her way to the post office. She also visited the courthouse offices frequently to take care of the family's taxes and other legal business.

Because the courthouse sat in the middle of town, people would walk through it rather than walk all the way around it to reach stores located on the other side of the street. The benches outside of the courthouse were usually occupied by old men, a hangout where these retired guys socialized and stayed abreast of the busy and still-active lives of others. There they could recognize folks they knew and loved, and could reminisce with others who shared many of their own memories. The kids often referred to them as the Spit-and-Whittle Club but enjoyed the warm greetings of the old men, as did their parents. Local farmers parked their truckloads of produce to sell alongside the court square, and the elderly men sat on the curb, on the trucks, and on benches, talking, laughing, and passing time with the shoppers.

Inside the courthouse, people were usually seen lingering with little purpose other than to greet the local passersby. After all, most of the lingerers, as well as most of the employees of the courthouse, were related to the other townsfolk, so conversation usually centered on families. Olive Lewis was always in a hurry, but she nevertheless took time to stop for brief, warm visits. She asked about folks' relatives because she cared about them. She knew she had to hurry, for Cecil kept her that way. But she knew that no matter how much she hurried, she gained little for her conscientious efforts. She smiled, visited, inquired about folks' health, their families, their children. She talked about herself, Cecil, their children, and grandchildren.

Shari's first job after high school was in the courthouse as a stenographer. She enjoyed that job, and Mama was proud of her. During that summer employment, she had even more reason to pass through the courthouse corridor often. Mama's brother, her Uncle Stan, managed to get Shari the job through his political contacts in Little Rock. Mama was close to Stan and spoke highly of him. Stan had worked his way through college, which was commendable, considering that their parents had no means of assisting the kids beyond high school. Stan first became a schoolteacher and then an attorney; Olive admired that, and he knew she did.

All through the years, Stan would stop by their house without notice and usually announce that he'd stopped by for, "some of those good ol' cold biscuits and bacon of yours, Olive." They were leftovers from breakfast, and he always found them on top of the kitchen stove. Their visit would begin and continue in the kitchen as had so many of their good times down on their parents' farm. Sometimes Daddy joined in. Occasionally he would be in a hurry and just say hello as he passed through. Other times, he would have a cup of coffee and join them, but only passively. When Daddy was present, Stan usually had less time to visit and the visit was less jovial and relaxed. However, the difference was understood by all, because it was Daddy's house, and he certainly could occupy it. It just changed the tone whenever he did, for Daddy seldom saw humor in anything or cared much about friendly dialogue.

Mama was especially proud of her brother when, as prosecuting attorney, he tried a case in their county courthouse. For particularly significant trials, she knew she could count on Stan to assure her a seat. Most often she encouraged her daughter to attend the events and to ask Stan to find her a place to sit. When it was extremely crowded, as in a highly publicized trial, people even sat in the windows.

Once Shari wanted to get inside the courtroom to watch Uncle Stan prosecute a man accused of killing his own parents. The courtroom was packed to capacity, so she nervously motioned her concern to her uncle as the trial was in progress. He called her inside and directed her to occupy his own chair— right near the judge and the infamous, brutal defendant. Shari was so proud of her uncle that day when she heard him press hard for justice and defend those two victims who had, as he said, "Given birth to the accused and raised him to be grown and strong, strong enough to kill the ones that fed him." Even though those parents were dead by their son's hand, Uncle Stan respectfully represented them that day in the public courtroom, and to her that merited the highest praise.

Little did anyone know then that this same prosecuting attorney, this same Uncle Stan, would be the judge in this same courtroom. Neither could any of them know how difficult it would be nor that it would take two decades against the resistance of all authorities in the town, including this same uncle-attorney-judge, for her to succeed in being granted a court hearing to address her own mother's brutal, hushed-up death. No prosecuting attorney had defended her mother's death; no attorney had prepared any case. No authority had asked any questions and no laws had been enforced on her mother's behalf. After thirty years of living in that town and passing through that small courthouse, her mother's life and death had passed silently as though she were a non-person, unworthy of a courtroom hearing.

In sadness Shari thought, *It's much easier and more practical and appropriate when folks simply do what needs to be done.* When the appointed folks resist their appointed tasks, other folks have to assume those additional jobs. What needs to be done continues to need to be done. Many times when a responsibility is ignored, the ramifications expand like ripples in a lake, making rectification more complex and complicated than had the problem been given the attention it required at the beginning. She recalled J. Edgar Hoover's famous statement: "Justice is incidental to law and order." And she sensed an interesting correlation. He, being head of the Federal Bureau of Investigation at the time, well knew the difference between indoor crimes that only break the law, and crimes that disturb the social order. With this in mind, she considered the many factors involved in successfully concealing a murder when it happened to her mother.

A fairly simple event occurred in Clinton on December 18, 1964. A woman was found dead in her home, shot in the head. What needed to be done?

1. An investigation needed to occur. It did not. No report whatsoever was written by any official concerning Olive's unnatural death. No fingerprints were taken off the gun that was used; no check was made to locate the owner of the gun; no tests were administered of the victim's hands; there was no questioning of any witnesses, or gathering of any evidence, although much was obvious.
2. The coroner needed to confirm "unnatural death" and order an autopsy. He did neither, although both were required by law.
3. The victim's brothers and sisters should have warmly and openly talked with the children as the first priority. Instead the victim's brothers and sisters boycotted the victim's residence where her children remained. They were boycotting only Cecil for having "murdered their sister." They were persuaded by Stan that they must refrain from any further actions or words toward Cecil "for the children's sake." Thus the victim's in-laws (Cecil's relatives) were given full reign over Olive's home and controlled all the spoken messages, which became in essence, "Olive killed herself because of her children."

Normally in absence of the appropriate legal procedures, the *family* would initiate action, but because of the passive and active co-conspirators who withheld legal procedures, and because many of these were family members, there was no united *family* to take action. 'Divide and Conquer.'

Shari and her sister not only lost their mother that day, but in time they'd be separated from each other as well. They were alienated from both sides of the entire family of uncles, aunts, cousins, and so forth. Ironically, the maternal kin ostracized them "out of kindness" to them, having no doubt that Daddy had killed Mama. They didn't interpret it as kindness, however. They felt they and the townspeople were isolating them because they were so terrible. The paternal kin kindly assured and reassured them that their mother had elaborately premeditated and carried out suicide in her home amidst preparations for the family Christmas holiday a few days away. The sisters lost their own rootedness, family centeredness, home and town enmeshment, friends, and all that had ever been familiar, warm, trusting, and binding to them. With such massive disconnectedness, the same also occurred within themselves. Their existential foundation was gone. Thus a traumatic and mesmerizing toll wreaked havoc on their young adult emotions. The effects were devastatingly irreparable, but deemed insignificant to the unconcerned or unaware bystanders and relatives, except for the fact that it successfully provided the silence of their mother's deepest mourners.

It must not be overlooked that even in the best of families and circumstances, when the word suicide is attached to the loved one's death, there is an inevitable assumption of guilt by the family members. This is a global occurrence. This automatic stigma of guilt hinders the normal grief process. In Olive Lewis' case, this stigma was multiplied tremendously and was deliberately handed to the victim's children on a silver platter, so to speak, by the passive and active co-conspirators who were interested in concealing a murder.

Calling a death a "suicide" when it clearly isn't is a unique form of "victim blaming." Victim blaming is usually subtle, cloaked in kindness and concern. Humans prefer not to endanger themselves physically or with extra responsibilities, or with the guilt of evading those responsibilities. The solution is to blame the victim. Now it is *her fault* that she suffered. In observing the process of blaming the victim, one tends to be confused and disoriented because those who practice this art display a deep concern for the victim. As the humanitarian concentrates his charitable interests on the victim's defects, a perverse form of social action occurs: The victim is changed to "perpetrator" through the *systematic distortion of reality,* overtly and covertly agreed upon and applied by the collective group with a common interest—maintaining their status quo. Thus the quote of J. Edgar Hoover, *"Justice is incidental to law and order."*

Blaming the victim is an ideal, almost painless evasion. In the death of Olive Lewis, it worked. Perhaps her children would recover, perhaps only in part, perhaps there would be no recovery at all. Perhaps the children would find for themselves again, a new connectedness with reality and a reunion with each other, someday. Maybe they would reconnect only partially and perhaps they never would.

What did happen, was that the children became strangers to each other. Never once did the three siblings sit down together to discuss their parents, their losses, or the events of that traumatic time. Sitting down and discussing anything was something that their family never did, unless it was initiated by the healthiest family member, and she could guide them no more.

Thus, each sibling formulated a separate value system by which he or she would live a separate life. As her mother's oldest daughter, Shari could not rest until she had exhausted all efforts to correct that asinine, obscene, hideous, heinous injustice of 1964. First, she had to make an arduous and meticulous endeavor to understand all that had occurred. Yet this could not be her top priority, because the living—her own children—would remain her first commitment. While she reared Aubrey and Cecelia (being much to them as her own mother was with Shari), she also studied sociology and psychology, for she was desperately trying to retrieve her own connectedness and find much needed answers. The belief tenaciously clung to her mind and soul that if she just searched hard enough, the answers could be found!

Her church family replaced the former family losses, and her love of God gave ever-renewing strength for the journey: the steps of which she realized, had no number. The journey was, as her mother had written decades earlier, "pathless to track." But it needed to be continued on toward completion in order to fully "come back." Sometimes she felt like the Israelites whom she studied. She wondered if perhaps she, too, were wandering in a circular motion without progress. Bit by bit she realized the progress though, and it motivated her to continue the task, for the task became her own Survivor's Mission.

Rousing from her memories, she picked up the official court document bearing her mother's name. She read her own name listed as the petitioner. She did not even have to wonder what her relatives' reactions would be to the petition. One relative had angrily questioned, "Are you wanting to prove your dad innocent?"

She responded, "He was proclaimed innocent by virtue of the suicide assumption. I'm wanting to exonerate Mama. Can't you see that?"

As the grieving and struggling process drew to an end, a new awareness dawned. This action on her part was undoubtedly perceived by many as the greatest crime ever committed by her family. For anyone to break the unspoken law of silence surrounding a town's secret of someone's death, for anyone to disrupt the status quo, was far worse in their eyes even after two decades, than wife beating, alcoholism, child abuse, or even murder. She wanted to prove her entire family innocent of December 18, 1964. They were guilty of some degree of ignorance, as was the rest of the town. They all paid for that crime, and at last, through the legal system and the printed page, they would be pardoned. The family was disintegrated, but the surviving children and grandchildren had the right to be free of guilt of Mama's death.

Survival Guilt is a terrible sentence, for it is a form of torment. Ignorance is often a prerequisite for such torment, and in the case of her family and hometown, those dual factors produced a hellish nightmare. It was time for the nightmare to end.

There's so many, many choices
And so easy to go wrong
Let my presence be supportive
To the weak who would be strong
Nothing else in this life matters...
For all else, soon fades away
Help our blinded eyes to see now,
That our hearts were led astray
Only Truth remains our real friend,
While deception's been our foe
Let our hearts today repent Lord...
So Your vast love we can know.

CHAPTER THIRTY

Uncle Stan's Poem

Shari Anne is a sweet little girl,
She's pretty as can be, with her hair all curled.
She goes to school and studies hard,
She knows darn well that I'm her Pard'
I'm struck on her to beat the band...
I ought to be, I'm her Uncle Stan.

SHARI REMEMBERED THE POEM her uncle used to recite to her from her earliest years, and his rendition always made her feel very special. She'd trusted him perhaps more than ever because he, too, was special. So how can it be that she was about to face her own beloved Uncle Stan to combat him in his own courtroom? Was there some element of disloyalty there? If so, perhaps not her disloyalty, as she was conditioned for years to believe. Otherwise, just what did Debra Faye mean when she jokingly suggested, "You might not want to use the word 'precious' when you refer to Uncle Stan in your book, Shari."

During her entire lifetime Shari had adored Uncle Stan, as did Mama. Both assumed they knew him. Olive knew him as the brother she grew up with, and Shari knew him as she experienced him up until December 18,

1964. Now, however, the pieces were forming an identifiable portrait of a man whom, perhaps, she didn't know at all.

She always considered him remarkably different from Daddy and therefore some compensation for Daddy's ineptness. She still remembered the meal that she and Uncle Stan enjoyed at the Chinese restaurant in Little Rock the day he took her to get her first job at sixteen. Actually, she was flattered to have an uncle who knew people in high places and could pull strings to get her a job. She was even impressed that he knew the Chinese owner and employees at the restaurant and joked with them as they ate chicken gizzards and rice.

During her high-school years, it was known that all the liquor confiscated by the local police was taken to Stan's house. It was fun to take her friends to view the loot in his garage— all sorts of containers and quantities of liquor. Her friends could also accompany her right into the governor's office, and when he was in, they could have the privilege of shaking his hand. As a teenager, Shari had eight by ten inch pictures of herself with the governor, and she always knew she was special because her uncle was special and knew exciting people in high places.

She was stunned one day when Stan revealed to her something he considered a special advantage. He was often present when someone was electrocuted for crimes. She understood that to be a chore that someone had to do—or to be present as witnesses. She even realized that someone had the gruesome job of pulling the switch. However, she was shocked when Stan revealed that he himself occasionally pulled the switch, bringing death to condemned persons. It was not his job. Rather, it was his voluntary choice to personally terminate life. Shari never dwelled on it, yet she never forgot it. Neither did she brag to her friends about this "special privilege" of her powerful uncle.

One day Stan asked her for her favorite picture of Mama—a recent picture of her smiling so sweetly. She reluctantly loaned it to him, only because he promised to return it soon with a lovely surprise. The surprise turned out to be a large picture of her, a charcoal portrait made from the photo by one of the inmates at the famed Arkansas prison. Again, her uncle as prison warden was able to pull strings to accomplish something he wanted. Shari never questioned that Stan might have told rather than asked the artistic prisoner to do it. But at that time, her view of Uncle Stan was untarnished.

Whenever she looks at her mother's portrait now she cannot regard it separate from the provider of the portrait. Stan "had it done" at the prison. Stan "gave her the picture" that he wanted her to have, to see her mother the way he wanted her to see her. But he gave the public a picture of her as a suicidal maniac, and then he gave Shari a beautiful, fancy gold-framed private portrait of the mother and grandmother She already knew her to be lovely, smiling, gentle, happy.

Stan also gave Robbie a similar portrait, drawn by the same prisoner. Could it be that his guilt persuaded him to attempt some compensation to his sister's daughters for his skillful deception in parlaying their feelings and their lives? Even his words in reference to no investigation—"for the children"—continued to burn savagely at her heart.

The pieces were less jumbled now. Stan was always there and in authority, although she never thought in such terms in her youth. Stan held the gun on Daddy as Mama packed for them to leave him when they moved to their apartment in Little Rock. He even checked her out of school as Shari packed the things from her desk and told her fourth-grade friends goodbye. He later arranged her summer job in the courthouse. When she was tempted to date someone against her parents' consent, Stan had the boy drafted into the army. When her mother needed money, she borrowed from Stan. He even since referred, smiling, to her manner of returning it: "All neatly tied up in a little handkerchief, as only Olive would do."

And there was more. Once, when Shari was terrified and alone with her babies and called Stan long distance, he told her what to do, and she did it. "Take your babies and go next door to your friends' place and tell them that you want to spend the night at their house." Later when she was about to be divorced and kept meeting obstructions, he fixed them also. After many hearings and hassles, the judge walked into the courtroom one day. "Write it up as she says," he instructed the attorneys. Over at last, her ex-husband said, "Stan Deevens can fix anything."

Later still, with Shari's sister and her stormy episodes, it was Stan who calmed her down. "We both lay in the mud on our bellies while she cried hysterically," he beamingly explained, his own heroism the emphasis. Again he fixed it. He had handed Robbie a gift also—a distorted picture of her mother which at her tender age of seventeen was simply more than she was able to bear. Having always experienced her dear and trusted uncle as highly competent, it was a grueling torment to her that even he was obviously unable to persuade an investigation of her mother's death, even though he was an attorney. Why was she so different and their family so insignificant that such a powerful man could not get an investigation achieved, even with the governor in his home and accompanying him to the funeral? Why was the governor himself so helpless when it came to their family's case? He could do so only if and when Shari would accuse someone—her father, of whom she was terrified—and accept full responsibility for the investigation and the consequences!

She recalled the conversation well in which the governor spoke to her: "If your dad were tried and convicted, he would get seven years and get out in four." She was too cowardly to take action and accepted the guilt instead. She also accepted the responsibility that the governor forfeited to her—not understanding then that it was his and the state's responsibility to have an investigation done. He too presented her a gift disguised as a kindness. So true are those famed words: Power corrupts, absolute power corrupts absolutely.

Why was she so blind for so long, so trustingly naive that she projected her own helplessness onto those two powerful figures? What purpose did it serve? The familiar biblical tenet comes to mind again, here: There will never be more put upon you than you are able to bear. As a young adult, she gave up her mother to death, her dad to psychosis, her brother and sister to oblivion, her own personality to emotional regression, and her hometown to total apathy. But she had to maintain belief in someone and something, trust in someone and something, and love, confidence, and connectedness in someone and something. That was her uncle, and that something was the American legal system—justice itself, what their nation proclaimed. Had she given up her trust in Uncle Stan and American justice, she would have ceased to exist. That would have been more than she could bear.

Only after readjusting her life and accepting multiple traumatic losses and incorporating the fear, guilt, and never-ending bereavement, could she become emotionally reestablished sufficiently to accept the ultimate betrayal. That took two decades.

Now another Mother's Day has just come and gone since her mother died. The day itself was incidental. She took herself out to dinner and then returned to her seclusion. She viewed herself in the mirror. *Where am I, twenty years later? I look OK, so why am I not married or even dating?* She liked men, yet she felt a distance and distrust that obstructed potential closeness. She appreciated her men friends, mostly men who were happily married to her women friends. She looked again into the mirror and saw someone who was not at all lonely in her preferred solitude but someone in waiting. *What am I waiting for?* She had accomplished the greatest desires of her heart: her children were now reared into healthy, wise, God-loving adults. The prayer she began twenty years ago—God protect them spiritually, mentally, emotionally, and physically—had been answered. She was appreciative. Now what? Her eyes smiled warmly in response to her question. Now she knew that there was a new desire of her heart. It was to fight back, face to face, with her ultimate betrayer, to remove him from his proverbial bench as a man in high places, controlling the legal system.

Why? Does she want to proclaim a cause, to lead a revolution, to make noise, to get revenge? No to all these questions. A survivor has a mission, and her mission was to complete her project to reveal the truth and become free—to fight back, to retrieve and establish herself. Her existential existence required that she complete what was begun and her heart longed to do it. She recalled Dr. Martin Luther King's references to such. He had said he would rather live thirty-nine years of a meaningful life with a purpose than live eighty years without a purpose. Thus far, she had lived fully with purpose and agreed with the friend in the mirror that it was the quality not the quantity that really mattered. The survivor's mission compelled her to go on. Godspeed.

The hill is ooh, so steep
I'd like to rest awhile
Can hardly drag my feet
To go another mile,
But still I hear God say
"If you'll stay on the way,
Each mile and step you take
I promise I will make,
Worthwhile."

CHAPTER THIRTY-ONE

THE CASE WAS WELL prepared. She had the conflicting and incriminating testimonies of the following:

1. Her paternal uncle, who was among the most active in the cover up. He was the first to the scene and alone with her father for a period of time prior to putting the word out.

2. The lieutenant of the state police, (whom the above uncle observed picking up the murder weapon apparently to preserve prints for testing, yet he himself stated that he played no official part at the murder scene - obtaining no prints, writing no report, etc.). He was referred to her by the coroner as the primary person verifying suicide, yet the lieutenant stated to her, "No evidence... we just figured."

3. The coroner, who stated to Shari and her sister his adamant professional diagnosis of murder and the reasons supporting it, yet did not order an autopsy, as required by law. One year later, he instead signed the death certificate stating Suicide.

4. Non statements and non efforts of the then-sheriff and now-mayor of the town who conducted no investigation whatsoever.

5. The pathetically conflicting statements and actions of the victim's brother recently retired (coincidence?) judge, who at the time of his sister's death was a powerfully influential, political person and attorney. It was his explanation to her that "a class situation

occurred, preventing the coroner and himself from acting with the integrity that their professions represented and required."

6. The statement of the state medical pathologist, verifying that if the victim's wound occurred on the left side of the head, suicide would be definitely ruled out.

7. Shari has the picture of herself feeling the wound in her mother's head, which was on the left side. A former classmate and his wife had learned that she was alone at the morgue with no ride back home in the early morning hours, and they came to offer her a ride. Before entering the room they took a photo of her examining her mother's head and she's always appreciated their thoughtful initiative. It certainly was their last photograph together.

8. Next, she has the unfinished garments that the victim was sewing in preparation for Christmas gifts for her grandchildren to be given to them one week later had she lived.

9. She has letters from her mother, showing her state of mind days prior to her death and written statements referring to the rapid deterioration of her parents' marriage and referring to her father's increased belligerence and demands upon her.

10. She also has a letter from the governor responding to her pleas for an investigation, indicating his full knowledge of the situation and that a foul-play finding would point to a family member. His letter was obviously designed to discourage her pursuit of an investigation.

11. She has testimonies from two paternal uncles, each verifying his own belief of her father having committed murder rather than of a suicide having occurred, based on their comparison of their own brother to the victim, that their brother had never made friends and had serious problems, that he was a dependent and basically unhealthy person, whereas the victim was healthy and stable, thus equally unlikely to have taken her own life. One uncle volunteered his firm belief that the murder weapon used belonged to their father and that the uncle had inquired into its whereabouts after learning that her mother had been killed by a .38 pistol.

It was a joyous privilege to have a specific date and hour officially assigned for the hearing of Olive Lewis. Only animals are thrown into the ground with no official investigation or hearing. Mrs. Olive Lewis, her mother, was designated by this court petition to be a person, a human being, meriting the dignity of an official hearing. It was a joyous day, indeed! On that day, it was insignificant that it took twenty years to earn that court date. All that mattered was that it had at last been acquired and that witnesses had been subpoenaed. That day, the courtroom was Shari's and her mother's, as the courtroom belongs to all, not just to the politicians or elite. That day, the laws of Arkansas, the laws of the United States, the U.S. Constitution and the Bill of Rights were theirs at last. That day, her mother, Olive Deevens Lewis, and Shari restored their citizenship.

She felt tears swelling her eyelids from overwhelming joy. She was cautioned not to cry, however, in that her tears would be misinterpreted as emotional weakness. So her joy, gratitude, and tears presented themselves silently to God. She looked around the empty courtroom and recalled occasions when she was there as a youth and some occasions when she was there with her mother. Today surpassed any occasion that they ever attended together, for none had represented the restoration of their dignity as did this prized occasion.

The approaching footsteps outside the door caught her full attention. In walked the lieutenant of the state police. She spoke to him by calling his name. Today, he did not observe her in quite the same manner as he did on the sidewalk when she last conversed with him. Then it was with obvious disdain. Today his expression showed a mixture of respect (at least for the courtroom), of personal concern (even a policeman feels fear and guilt prior to being exposed), and of awe, as though the occasion itself and its purpose were unique to him. Certainly that was true. The purpose of the hearing was unique, particularly to this town. He sat on the front seat of the courtroom to wait for the other subpoenaed witnesses to join him.

A couple entered whom she did not recognize; then a man entered and sat alone. They cared enough to attend the hearing, and she did not know who they were. She wished she did, but she didn't ask. She was glad, though, that they came. Soon her two paternal aunts appeared, and she visited briefly with them. One was her mother's best friend from high school days; they lived across the road from each other for three decades. Her sister was with her, her face taut with sadness and stunned bewilderment due to the recent suicide of her oldest daughter. Shari's heart ached for her grief, yet she had not seen her in the many years after she vehemently insisted that her mom, "Killed herself because of you kids." On this day, she was able to communicate compassion for her only nonverbally. However, she seemed to receive that and to reciprocate.

The coroner walked in and immediately looked the opposite direction from her. He sat with his back turned, as he talked with those he joined. Next appeared her brother-in-law, Chuck. How greatly she appreciated his presence, for she well knew that he understood the significance of the day better than anyone else. He and her sister needlessly suffered excruciating pain together, during and after December, 1964. Then their pain continued as a black cloud over their marriage for eighteen years. During those years, they buried two babies, became entangled with alcoholism, and the marriage ended. For Chuck, this day was a restoration of his dignity as well. Somehow she wanted to apologize to him for the unending chaos he experienced after joining their family at the age of nineteen. Perhaps this day was an apology to him and he had come in acceptance of it.

Entering next was her attorney-judge-uncle, on crutches, but this time he was not exclusively using diversionary tactics, for he really had fallen and broken his foot. Shari called his name and said hello to the uncle she had loved and trusted so greatly—until late in life when she realized she no longer knew him. She still loved him as she had thought him to be, but she had no love whatsoever for empty politicians or for ruthless politics. His expression was painstakingly grave. He spoke formally and respectfully to her, without the warmth he used to convey.

Today he had been subpoenaed to her courtroom, and another judge had been appointed to listen to her testimony exposing him. He was not the all-powerful attorney, judge, or politician. Today, he was just a subpoenaed witness called by his own niece who believed in the principles of justice, which she had always thought he represented. Today it wasn't his courtroom, but rather it was the courtroom for the hearing of his murdered sister, which had been delayed for twenty years due to his personal influence. He was, even today, on the opposite side, and he and all the others were aware of it. Yes, his expression was painstakingly grave, little wonder that it was. His wife venomously looked away in a huff, but today she was without threats and coercion.

Later the silent sheriff of 1964 made his appearance, and today was the first day they made verbal contact since her mother's death twenty years ago. "Hello, Shari," he said. "How are you?"

"Today, Dennis, I'm wonderful. Today I'm just fine," she answered, surveying her surroundings. Observing those seated in the courtroom thus far, her heart was so full that she mentioned it to her attorney next to her. "What if my heart literally bursts with gratitude, and I die right here on the spot?"

"Don't you dare die. It would give them too much satisfaction," he said tenderly, firmly, with a faint trace of a smile.

She laughed quietly, knowing that he was right and promised to postpone her own death until later. Then she resumed reveling this momentous occasion. In walked Uncle Darren, one person she fully believed knew the truth of December 18, 1964. He was the person on the death scene with her dad for an undetermined period of time prior to notifying others. He was the one who took active charge of the situation initially and served as her father's spokesman to her when she arrived two days later. Her father maintained total silence to all her questions and this uncle did all the explaining of everything. She'd long since concluded with certainty that he lied to her, although she still lacked the actual truth. Today, however, Uncle Darren wasn't in charge of anything. He was just another of the deceitful, subpoenaed witnesses. His face was hollow and pale, rigidly revealing clearly frightened eyes. Her breath seemed to halt midway in her throat as she looked at his face, for he so greatly resembled her father. "Hello, Mr. Lewis," she said, perhaps a bit sarcastically.

He curtly acknowledged her presence and her person, then quickly made his way to join the other men sitting silently on the front bench of the courtroom. It seemed nice to see the powerful men silent, subdued, even perhaps intimidated and frightened, at least for a brief while. They needed a few moments of what her entire lifetime had become. She wanted a picture of the courtroom, yet even more, she wished to be able to capture the momentum of this occasion for the future. She determined to absorb fully and appreciate every second of it as it gently transpired.

At that point, her attorney, who had stepped into the judge's chambers, returned with a strange expression on his face. "Your uncle Stan is still running the show. He is in the judge's chambers now, and the judge is leaving the decision to Stan."

"They are willing to order the death certificate," he continued, "to be amended from 'suicide' to that of 'undetermined' if you will accept that in lieu of a hearing conveying all the testimonies, arguments, and evidence."

Shari's feeling was a mixture of relief and sadness, for she had dual goals, and now they were being divided. Her immediate goal was to bear testimony of the truth with the resultant goal of succeeding in the amendment of the death certificate from "suicide" to that of "homicide." She wondered, *Is one more significant than the other, the vehicle or the destination?* Both are significant.

She also felt her old, very familiar fear of not accepting whatever Uncle Stan offered. They were willing to allow her partial goal of death certificate amendment—which they previously prevented and refused—in exchange for her forfeiture of evidence, testimony, and exposure of their own cover-up. In their own cowardly way, they were begging.

It had taken a long time to prepare her case, and she had a thorough case and, yes, she wanted the privilege of presenting it to its ultimate amendment to homicide. Yet, this was the town that valued protecting its own and maintaining the status quo above all else. She had dared defy them thus far, against great odds. Dare she continue further? Does she fear them or pity them? Is her wish to continue with testimony 'that which needs to be done' or merely that which she wants to do? She strongly suspected it was the latter, a determining factor that was undeserving of regulating her life. However, the death certificate needed to be changed! They actually accomplished that! So be it. She had enjoyed to the utmost the fulfilling satisfaction of seeing those subpoenaed, reluctant, wimpy witnesses and relatives come forth. Yes, she even enjoyed the concern that the hearing had aroused in each of them and what each of their expressions clearly conveyed.

The truth still needed to be brought forth, in full, but perhaps not today, not here, not in this courtroom. *I can wait*, she thought. The truth will find its own time, its own place and its own manner.

She strained for a moment trying to anticipate the future, which route truth might select. Perhaps that was none of her business. She had prepared so well her testimony that she felt as much sadness as an attorney who held an entire alphabet of court exhibits. She wished her father could have been diagnosed publicly in respect to him, for he was not the villain himself, rather, one sad link in a chain of ignorance. As she sat waiting for the papers to be completed in the judge's chambers, by her attorney, her uncle, and the temporary judge, she began reading the psychological evaluation of her father that had been prepared for court:

His First Twenty Years

He felt unloved and rejected as a child, and this feeling of low esteem continued into adulthood, masked in a schizoid personality. As infantile rage mounted, unable to relate to others, he learned to self medicate with alcohol. His infantile rage found ventilation when he was drinking, for then his aloof, withdrawn, introverted personality was no longer inhibited and his behavior became extremely violent, expressing itself in the destruction of his own furniture. The repressed infantile rage toward his parents was transferred to his wife on whom he had become dependent as an adult. Thus, serious wife batterings occurred frequently. By this point, alcoholic idiosyncratic intoxication (allergic to alcohol) had become his condition. His work was physically demanding and also mentally challenging. So, from Monday through Friday his rage was contained as employment preoccupied him, yet he was unable to enjoy relationships and felt inadequate in general (husband, father, man). The weekend drinking episodes served as a diversion from family life and provided relief from his inner rage. At forty, he was forced to choose between alcohol and his family. He relinquished the alcohol abruptly, alone and without medical assistance or psychotherapy for his long-seated emotional problems (predisposing his alcoholism). He was oblivious to the effects of alcohol on the central nervous system after twenty years of heavy ingestion. Alcohol hallucinosis was insidiously developing. The repressed rage remained, yet found ventilation in the form of fantasy and ideas of reference. He began avidly reading detective magazines, in which women were murdered by men. He and his wife stopped sleeping together. His personality was agitated, aloof and angry in general. He lost his business, the only real source of positive self-esteem and identity he had ever found, when a fire totally consumed it. He became more dependent, self-absorbed, angry, belligerent, with most of the verbalized rage vented onto his wife.

<u>Age Forty to Fifty, Alcohol Hallucinosis</u>

With work activity virtually stopped, murder-mystery reading increased; fantasy world replaced reality for him, offering him a solution to the rage that he had endured for so long from the mother figure rejecting/abandoning him as a child. He and wife planned separation and divorce, she stating her intent to take her half of their property and formulating her plans to live with her sister in Little Rock. His father became ill, and he began staying at his parents' home overnight, to help them out.

His wife was found dead, of a gunshot wound to the head.

Other bizarre behaviors included:

1. He spoke of people who did not exist.
2. He made numerous, strange trips, packing specific clothes.
3. Inappropriate responses: smiled when using the word 'murder' to family members.
4. Burned the children's and grandchildren's valued possessions.
5. Engaged in no family discussions regarding the death of his wife, their mother.

According to this profile, he may well have hoped to have been questioned, accused, even credited with such an achievement, as murder of his wife may have represented, to him.

Significant Items:

- He was firstborn to his parents.
- His younger sister died as an infant (cause unknown), whom he remembered well and talked about without hesitation. Only sibling he liked.

- Began working at his father's mill at age twelve -- his father's decision.
- Had no friends or social life throughout school.
- First day of school in first grade, he inflicted serious violence on another child who made fun of him.
- No mention of any meaningful events in family, childhood, or elsewhere.
- No positive word regarding other family members.
- Resented his father's helping his siblings in ways he was not offered assistance, even turned down when he asked.
- Had typhoid fever and missed one year of high school.
- Only boy in high school graduation without a suit, until another boy's dad bought him one.
- Only senior class member to get no class ring.
- Wanted to attend college and study math; enrolled and attended classes two weeks, then Dad reneged on tuition, forcing his withdrawal and return home.
- Watched younger brothers assisted with college expenses.
- Always wanted to know where and when he was born;
- parents withheld this information; no birth certificate.
- (Current records reveal three conflicting sites of birth, three different states).
- Talked often of his parents' preference for his siblings over him.
- Never ceased to do favors for his parents, never earning their approval.
- Remained his entire lifetime across the street and down the hill from his parents' home.

Shari looked at the diagnosis and realized that he had little influence in what he had become. So many components to an individual. With some minor changes, what might be different? The road not taken...

She vacantly starred at the last word, home. Their home was a factor in her dad's evolution. How would she diagnose their home of Clinton? She pulled out the yellow legal pad, which had become a friend to her. She let her pen wander over the pad and gave herself permission to write whatever came to her. She purposely used the derogatory term. She didn't care. It seemed to her these people not only fit the stereotype, but also were probably the basis for it.

Diagnosis of Hometown, Clinton: <u>Definite Redneck Community</u>

The value system there in 1964 was:

- Maintain the status quo at all costs;
- The "Politics" of the town is essentially in charge;
- A man's home is his castle (to hell with the other inhabitants).
- Drinking is macho, appropriate and admirable
- Wife-battering is macho, appropriate, and acceptable
- Racial jokes are macho, appropriate, and acceptable
- The silent laws of the town supersede the law of the land
- Victims invite their own problems
- Problems of the elite (politicians) must be avoided at all costs
- Keep up good appearances
- Keep outsiders uninformed
- Support fellow rednecks (stick together)
- Deny all contradictions to redneck philosophy
- Silence is essential
- Truth is trivial
- Truth is trivial
- Truth is trivial

CHAPTER THIRTY-TWO

THUS FAR IT HAD been imperative to maintain a running account of her life and that of her family, because she strongly suspected that something was terribly wrong from an early age. She could write only what happened, how she reacted to it emotionally, and what she observed in others. She always maintained the determination to someday sort it out and understand it all, knowing that it might take an entire lifetime. If so, the lifetime task would have been a constructive one, and the purpose would have been well worth it.

There was never a doubt but that the sorting out could be done only upon separating herself from that particular locality. She was not aware of a twofold mission during the first two decades of her life, only of the deep need to understand the meaning of everything. The confusion was enormously exacerbated as a result of her mother's death and the diminished state of her father.

At this point her mission assumed a second purpose: to understand it all in order to share it with others. She came to understand that the message of the wrongs and the ignorance must be conveyed to others to prevent nightmares such as her family experienced. Through her studies in sociology and psychology and professional work, she was involved in helping people and families and in preventing problems with families as much as possible. As she struggled with her own overwhelming sense of loss—of all family, of roots, and of a sense of dignity—she came to understand the plight of the survivor. He or she is much more than a victim. Rather, he or she is a victim stripped of dignity and existential foundation. Such a survivor seeks to retrieve his own dignity and his reaffirmation of human existence. As Dr. Viktor Frankl reminded her, "It must not have happened in vain." The survivor must come to fully understand the truth of his entire plight and bear public witness to it, thereby retrieving the lost dignity of his loved one(s) and of himself. This is the point at which he is able to love others as himself, no more and no less. He cannot tolerate injustice to himself or to others, and he can have no respect for hypocrites.

Recently a friend inquired, "So you're finished now? You got the death certificate amended from 'suicide' to 'undetermined,' and that's all you wanted, right?"

Shari remembered how anticlimactic it all seemed as she agreed to compromise in the courtroom. At that time she had no more money to go further in the court procedure. She was also forced to recognize that dear ol' Uncle Stan still did, in fact, regulate the court decisions there and that the legal system—at least at the state level—had not changed, nor would it change drastically as long as Stan remained around to "deal with things." Moreover, prior to that time, she had not been aware that one single factor offset all else in determining by the courts that her mother was definitely murdered. Her friend asked, "What is that one factor?"

"The fact that she was right-handed," Shari replied. "Pathologists agree that right-handed persons place the gun to the right side of the head rather than the left side in a suicide act."

"But didn't they know it was the left side?"

"Oh yes, it was common knowledge. They told me the left side, and I felt it behind the left ear, in the morgue. Even my picture shows me reaching across her face, feeling behind the left ear. Feeling that scratchy spot helped the reality to settle in for me. Much like viewing that gun that was used on her. Big and awkward."

"Yet all that isn't considered sufficient?"

"No. Nothing short of an exhumation and autopsy would be sufficient."

"So in failure of obtaining an exhumation, you accepted the amendment from 'suicide' to 'undetermined,' accepting the impossibility of the final achievement of amendment to 'homicide'?"

"That's partially true. I didn't wish to lose that important step of partial amendment, and I really couldn't afford to continue paying lawyers. I was pleased with the progress we had made and the article in the newspaper with my mother's picture, which conveyed partial exoneration. I feel we showed the townspeople that the issue was not at all resting in peace."

"Yet, with the court refusing an exhumation, then the evidence is lost, hidden six feet underground, right?"

"Not exactly," Shari heard herself reply, smiling with inspired warmth throughout her whole being. "For now it's just as well. You see, the evidence is actually protected six feet underground and will remain intact for another twenty to thirty years. A gunshot wound to the skull remains for about fifty years. Time is on my side, you see."

"But they still control the courts and the court controls the exhumation. They're never going to change their position and allow it, so you're stuck!"

"Only for the time being. There are other ways to obtain an exhumation aside from the legal system."

"You mean...?"

"Sure. Remember I'm from there myself and well understand their values. There are plenty of young men who would be honored by the opportunity to defy the courts and for the scary excitement of digging up a grave in the dark of night, especially if they were being paid well for it."

"But then, you'd be in defiance of the law!"

"Yes, ironic isn't it?"

CHAPTER THIRTY-THREE

"OLD" MUST BE THE feeling that ten years ago was only yesterday. At least that's the way it seemed to Shari when she was small and the grownups made such statements. But she had paused often during the past ten years, remembering that exciting court day. Still, she continued to enjoy learning from the people she worked with and keeping up with the busy lives of her children and grandchildren. It was fun being a grandmother, just as it was fun being a mother. She felt herself closely following her mother's brief example in both spheres, and thereby, she did a good job.

Then they learned that Cecelia's husband, Mark, was being assigned to a Korean base—a non-accompanied tour for two years. Naturally Shari had invited Cecelia and the kids to join her in California during his absence, and they had a wonderful time together, located nearby Aubrey as well. They remained close, and he had quickly become "favorite uncle" to Cecelia's two children. As vacation time crept closer, Cecelia and Shari planned a trip back to Arkansas to see "old acquaintances not forgotten." Cecelia wanted to route their trip through all the military bases, however, to visit her friends and see her own previous "homes" from the time when she was on active duty herself. Shari knew that would be fun and also economical.

They visited her friend Rose, who had been stationed with Cecelia in Germany. She and her daughters gave them a grand tour of Arizona, including horseback riding and tending to farm animals. Then they went on to Texas to military friends there.

And then the news broke: "Gunman shoots two dozen people, then kills self after driving his truck into busy restaurant at noontime!" They were as alarmed, appalled, and distraught as the rest of the nation. Those poor people! Just eating lunch—how horrible! Then in subsequent articles, they discovered that the gunman methodically put the gun to the heads of women and shot them. Some men were shot, but mostly because their movements seemed threatening to the gunman. But he was angry at women in particular. Yet these were women he did not know. That man carried his transferred anger onto more than a dozen women and executed them. Then he killed himself.

The morgues were suddenly packed. As they read the list of names, they selected one casualty to "visit" because her name had been Ollie and she had been guilty of having lunch with her daughter and granddaughter. Thus, her execution. But visiting her was something they both needed to do, Cecelia and Shari. Upon their arrival, she looked lovely in her coffin, a young, devoted grandmother. She wore a small hat, which helped conceal her bruise. As Shari looked at her, she softly said, "You need a hat, not a shawl, don't you? You know, dear, we have to hide the evil that men do in their society. Maybe that's why women's shawls and hats are available."

In her stillness it was as though she understood. Shari patted her pretty young hands that had worked so hard as a single parent to rear her children and that had started to enjoy the pleasure of the next generation. Her grandchild was only three years old. Cecelia was crying as she patted Ollie's face and hands also, and Shari heard her say, "I'm so sorry, so sorry. Kids need a grandmother who loves them. You were trying, weren't you? I'm so sorry."

Shari had already begun talking to Ollie's daughters who were tearful but composed. They had received guests for a couple of days already. One daughter, Susan, said to her, "You touched her. I saw that you touched her, and so did that other lady. I wanted to, but I didn't know whether I should or not."

"Honey," and she put her arm around the younger woman in a matronly fashion and somewhat as a mentor, "these are the last days and hours you'll spend with her—your mother—on this earth. Anything you want to do has to be done now, and you've touched her all your life. You certainly can now if you wish."

Shari had always been so proud of the time she spent with Mama at the morgue, and touching her had been the only comfort she'd received during the ghastly ordeal. She hoped Susan would decide to touch her mom, too. She leaned on her then and cried hard, hugging her as though they'd been lifelong friends. They sat down and Shari told her, "When I was about your age, a man shot my mother in the head too, and she too was called Ollie."

"Oh, my gosh. How did you stand it? I mean, sometimes I wake up and think I just dreamed it, and sometimes I think I can't stand to live with this for the rest of my life!"

"Susan, honey, God doesn't let us have more than we can bear. But you will need to work at it, for it sure won't be an easy thing for you. Be sure you get into counseling, individual and group, and talk about it, talk and talk and talk. And writing helps too. Write about it and get in touch with all your feelings in the months and years to come."

"It sounds like it's a different person, not me we're talking about."

"In a way that's true. You're still you, but what's happened will always be a part of you now, and you'll need to learn how to live with this."

"I wish you could tell Fran these things, for she was with Mother when it happened, and she's having a horrible time of it."

Her sister Fran was with other people then, so Shari knew they'd visit later. Susan was slender and pretty, with long, brown hair. She favored her mother. Fran didn't resemble them, but had dark, curly, short hair and spoke with a European accent. She had just arrived from Europe, and her mom was excited that Fran's husband was being stationed nearby. Expecting to see her daughter and granddaughter often, they'd gone to lunch. Then the gunman changed their plans and their lives.

"I'll be glad to see her whenever possible. We're here for a few days, but I'd love to visit with her and you, too."

Later, Fran called and invited them over. She and her husband were gracious, yet she was still confused with grief. She mentioned seeing whom she thought was "a policeman aiming his gun at the gunman while he was shooting people. But I think his gun was broken."

A news article mentioned that an armed officer did in fact arrive at the scene. But this officer made a decision not to shoot the gunman, who was then about halfway into his murderous rampage. Shari became absolutely enraged. "I don't care what his logic was! There was a man there that had the full capability of stopping that massacre, and instead he did nothing!"

She consulted an attorney friend with the question, "What can the relatives of the victims do about that man who chose not to intervene and save lives that day in the restaurant?"

"They'd need to find themselves a Rambo attorney."

"What in the world is a Rambo attorney?"

"The attorneys that go after this sort of thing—the really bizarre, wrongful deaths, hard-to-deal-with cases, like this one."

"So how does one find a Rambo attorney?"

"Most lawyers have a big referral book that lists them by state."

"Every state has Rambos, huh?"

"Yes, most major cities do, but not the smaller areas."

"Does Arkansas have Rambo guys?"

"Little Rock would."

"I want their names, those in Little Rock."

It had been ten years since her unsuccessful court petition for exhumation— although it seemed a much shorter time. Ten years ago, Uncle Stan still ran things, as her attorney had told her in the courtroom in Clinton. But Stan had died in recent years. Shari suspected that the court system might be more accessible to her now as a result.

"Check back with me later, and I'll have you a list of names, addresses, and phone numbers," her attorney-friend nodded affirmatively.

With her list, Shari and her daughter traveled on to Little Rock, and she visited attorney after attorney. She felt like an employer interviewing applicants. Then, finally, she liked the response she heard from Marvin Woods. "Stan Deevens was a dirty player. I knew of him by his reputation, he and the governor did a lot of damage to this state."

"Ah, I think I like you."

Marv was tall, thin, and in his late fifties, and he seemed more like a receptive nature rather than power crazed. "I heard about Stan dying a few years back. What did he die of?"

"I'm really not sure. He told me for twenty years he was about to have a heart attack. Maybe he finally did. But I heard that during his last few weeks or months, he couldn't speak anything except one four-letter expletive. Maybe that lone word was the summation of his life."

"How interesting. His words carried a lot of force for several years. He ruined a lot of lives."

"Yeah, I can believe that from experience. He didn't start out that way. He was my hero in many ways, the family's and whole town's hero. I wonder what happened to him later on?"

"A lot of the good ol' boys took themselves too seriously and never thought they'd ever lose their clout. But it comes and goes. I don't want what they had. I'm not willing to barter what they had to barter for it."

"Are you talking about politics in general?"

"Yes and no. Politics isn't always detrimental; but there's a good-ol-boy mentality that makes politics or anything else, destructive."

Marvin asked, "Do you still see your relatives up there, Stan's people?"

"No, I saw Stan and his wife, Bea, in court in '84 and that was the last time I saw him. We went to see her a year or so ago, but she stood in her doorway, arms folded, unfriendly, clearly not inviting them in. I miss my cousins. Stan had three children, and I loved them, but whatever they've been told about me probably has alienated them also."

"Your whole family sort of alienated you, right?"

It made her trust him to see that he accurately read between the lines. "For the most part. The only crime committed, as far as they're concerned, was me and my questions. As though some law prevailed that I didn't know about, so in my stupidity and ignorance I kept groping for the old law, wondering why it didn't still prevail?"

"You're guessing close now. That Governor Faubus' establishment actually did determine their own laws as they went and operated by them until they got caught."

"You mean the prison system?"

"That and other things. It's a different focus now in the state."

"Well, that's encouraging. But now I'm looking for a Rambo attorney so that I can straighten out one mess made by the good ol' boys. You know my concern. Will you take the case?"

"Maybe, but first you have to go see my buddy, because we work as a team."

The next day Shari found herself questioning this Rambo stuff. This new lawyer sitting across the desk was a far cry from Sylvester Stallone. *Oh, me of little faith,* she thought. Then, *could Marvin have been playing a trick on me?* Maybe he actually was a good ol' boy and this was a set-up to catch her... maybe.

Then Jessie Sloan broke her paranoia with his strategy line, "We'd have to approach it this way, because the town would be very resistant. We'd have to go real slow, but I think I can get it done."

"Wow! Really? Oh, that's exciting! Wait. You think you could get what done?" she asked, wanting him to be redundantly specific, in case she heard incorrectly the first time.

"I think I can get the court to grant the exhumation petition. I think we can get the exhumation and autopsy and then take it from there. Isn't that what you want?"

"Is it ever! It's just I've never heard an attorney say those words before, and I've waited twenty-eight years."

Jessie sat towering over his desk as though he ought to be on a basketball court somewhere, sinking easy baskets and picking up easy rebounds. But instead, thank goodness, he had chosen to dribble legal papers at a desk, probably following in his mother's footsteps. Maybe he's big enough not to be intimidated by the macho rednecks. But he grew up in the same area. How had he avoided it? His mother probably gets the credit for that, too. Mothers need credits. So he took Shari's case and her check. Sometimes she's wished she'd counted the thousands of dollars she's handed out to lawyers, but why start now?

> *Please help me Lord, to live each day as though it were my last*
> *To leave behind me no regrets or sorrows o'er the past*
> *Of all the work that I begin, I pray to carry through*
> *That when all time at last shall end, I'll have none left to do*
> *If I may live each day as though there'll no tomorrow be*
> *If I may look on each new face and yet no stranger see,*
> *If I can look behind me 'round me now and never fear*
> *That this might be the moment that Jesus would appear*
> *Then I can surely say my life has not been lived in vain*
> *And though I've lived in poverty, Eternity I gain.*

CHAPTER THIRTY-FOUR

THE MORNING OF THE hearing, they got off to a late start, and Shari worried that they might not make it in time. She wondered if they were one minute late, would they throw it out of court? Her daughter assured her there was nothing to worry about. Normally Shari encourages her to drive cautiously and watch her speed, but on this day, she trusted her ability and prayed as the speedometer tipped ninety-five.

They made it in record time and arrived at the courthouse at 8:59 A.M. Cecelia dropped her off and parked the car. As she came into the courthouse, Shari told her she couldn't find Jessie anywhere. She was afraid that perhaps he had to cancel and she hadn't gotten the word. Cecelia went upstairs, and as Shari frantically phoned his office, they came walking down the stairs together. He had been in a meeting, and she retrieved him from it. "Look who I found," Cecelia proudly beamed, and he smiled too.

He instructed them that they had plenty of time before their case was to be heard. Several cases preceded theirs that morning. As they sat in the courtroom, Shari was surprised that none of the relatives came to oppose the petition.

There was no response from her sister, Roberta; however none had been expected. Ten years earlier, her ex-husband, Chuck, attended the court hearing for exhumation petition. But Shari'd had no word from Roberta until afterward. She flashed back to that day in her small apartment when she'd received the phone call. Robbie had said firmly, "I never want to see or hear from you again, do you understand?"

"Certainly, I understand your words, Robbie. But can you tell me why you're doing this?"

"It's just something I need to do, and I want you to promise me you'll never contact me again."

"Robbie, of course I'd never impose, you know that. But please remember one thing. Remember what alcohol did to Daddy and to our family. So many things that happened began with his drinking. And you're a nurse and a good one. Don't let alcohol hurt you, too."

"Just don't try to contact me ever again."

"Honey, is this because of my court petition? I'm so sorry I lost it, but it was because of Stan that I lost it. Robbie, Stan was running things all the time—"

"Shari, I don't care. We'll never know what happened; only God knows, and He'll sort it all out eventually. I don't know why you feel like you have to."

"Robbie, He's not the only one who knows what happened. There are plenty of people back there who know, and you and I have the right to know!"

The silence on the other end was uncomfortable to Shari after a while. Finally she said, "Robbie, I love you—I've always loved you and I always will. Mama always loved you too. Don't ever forget that. And I'll hope and pray that you change your mind and contact me one day. If you ever feel like you'd like to, don't hesitate, 'cause I'd welcome you with open arms. But I'll leave it up to you, and no, I won't call or visit you ever again while you feel this way."

That had been a tremendously sad loss, for she'd loved Robbie so much. She was five years old when her little sister was born, and she called her "my baby," even arguing when her aunts laughed and corrected her.

She'd wished so desperately to show Robbie the truth of her mom's death, but she failed at the court hearing, and she felt that she couldn't afford to hold out hope any longer. She'd failed Robbie. Again.

Jessie said her brother had called his office, asking about her petition and saying he was afraid an investigation would reflect badly on his father. Shari wondered why it had never mattered for twenty-eight years how badly it reflected against his mother? Besides, she'd never known him and her dad to be close at all. Why this concern for Daddy's reputation now? He'd been dead two decades himself.

242

When the judge finally called their case, Shari walked to the front with Jessie, fully expecting to be rejected once again. It came as a surprise that the judge seemed somewhat indifferent to the case and even regarded her mother as a real person rather than a taboo character who deserved no mention. He inquired whether there was opposition from the state, and Jessie explained he had been appointed special prosecutor by the state to handle this matter. The judge smiled and said, "Oh, so you are the state!" He then uttered the most melodious words Shari had heard in a very long time. "I'm going to grant this petition. We will rule later on who bears the costs, depending on the result of Mrs. Lewis' autopsy." Mrs. Lewis' autopsy! Could this be real? Those words had hardly sunk in when she heard Jessie say, "Your Honor, we need this to be done within the week, because my client lives out of state and will have to return to her work, and I also have out-of- town business." The judge agreed.

The granting of the petition could have been savored for months before the exhumation. She was shocked. God had really outdone Himself on this one.

So many thoughts flooded her mind. So many years of torment and injustice. Could this really be the turning point? Her daughter cautioned her not to get her hopes up. She said all they had thus far was a piece of paper. It could still be challenged or appealed or something. The rest of that day they were elated. Shari spoke to several of the townspeople she had known but never told them why she was there.

The next day, Jessie called their hotel and asked for their help. He said in order to save time they should drive back to the courthouse area (they were temporarily housed seventy-five miles away) and get the order signed and certified. They eagerly complied. When they returned with the signed certified copy, Jessie took it and immediately left for the state medical examiner's office to place it in his hands. The exhumation was set for Thursday, 8:30 A.M. Shari looked up and telephoned some old and dear friends who lived in the area, Teddy and Mae, and they welcomed her and Cecelia. She also telephoned her dad's brother, Darren, who at last agreed to meet her and tell her all about what had occurred that day in December, twenty-eight years ago. He said he and his wife Connie would both meet with them. Shari was so happy -- after so long!

The following morning they went to visit the friends who had invited them so warmly. They spoke freely and fondly about Shari's mother. It felt so good hearing someone speak of her mother, the human being, in a loving way. She told them of their hearing and scheduled exhumation, for the next day. They were surprised but not shocked or appalled. They understood. They even said they would do the same for their mother. Then suddenly Teddy smiled, "Did you know Shari, that your mom sent me boxes of her homemade cookies, while I was in the service?"

"No I don't recall, but it isn't surprising - that's how she was."

He added other helpful reminders, "And when Ellis and I completed our military time, we were both approached by Harold C. Blevens. He encouraged us to join the state police. I wasn't interested, but Ellis was, so Harold C. recruited him."

"I vaguely remember he was with the police department, but what role did he play, do you know?"

"Sure, he was with narcotics. A lot of people never knew about Ellis' attempt to jump off the bridge in North Little Rock, but I remember it well. Stan helped keep that quiet."

"Teddy, were you at Mama's house the night she died?"

"Yes, we were both there."

"Can you tell me who was there and what was going on? And how did Ellis act?"

"Well, Ellis wouldn't talk to me. But he wanted to talk to my wife, Mae. It bothered me that he wouldn't talk to me."

Shari tried to imagine her brother upset and wanting a woman's shoulder to cry on, "So Mae, he was feeling pretty upset, I guess? Was he crying and talking about Mama a lot?"

"No, he didn't seem upset at all and he wasn't talking about your mother. He was trying to get me to persuade his ex-wife to talk to him."

"Oh. Was she there?"

"Yes she was."

"Who else was there?"

"It's hard to remember now," Teddy began, "but I know that Stan and Harold C. and Grover were all in the new room with Ellis and your dad."

Shari asked Mae, "Are you still in touch with Ellis' ex-wife?" She knew they were friends, but Mae hadn't been in touch with her all these years.

"I have no idea where she is."

After more visiting, they agreed to go with them to meet her Uncle Darren, but he and Aunt Connie never showed up, so they had a nice lunch with old friends, reminiscing. It was a first for Shari. Had Darren showed up as planned and told her the truth as he agreed to, they could have canceled the exhumation. She would have had what she so desperately needed all these years: the truth. But he didn't. She shouldn't have been surprised, however. She was just unrealistically hopeful. Later, Uncle Darren actually leveled with her concerning the multitude of lies he'd fed her from the start.

He said simply, "Our family always lied. My own dad told us for years that he had no sisters, then when I was grown, I met his sister. I don't even know why he did. But lying just comes natural, I guess." His candor that day actually made sense. It wasn't personal, it was just, 'his way of doing things.'

Thursday at 8:00 A.M. they waited at the cemetery. Still expecting something to go wrong, they waited. Cecelia had a borrowed video camera and Shari had her Polaroid camera. Jessie had insisted they keep it quiet and keep it out of the press. For now, they would. They were so nervous. Cecelia suggested they go into town to get coffee. As they sat in the little cafe, they spotted Robbie paying for gas at the station across the street. Shari wanted so desperately to call out to her, to run across the street, hug her neck and rejoice with her that after so long, progress was still being made in flushing out the truth of that day.

Instead, they just watched her. Shari still honored her request to her of years ago not to contact her. Robbie wanted no part of her ongoing investigation, having long ago lost confidence in her or in the truth ever being found. She had resigned herself to compartmentalizing the subject in that (1) Mama may have killed herself because of the kids, and because of her in particular since she was pregnant and married; or that (2) there may be another explanation, but we'll just never know what it is; or that (3) it doesn't really matter; God will sort it out someday. Although Shari ached to know, Robbie had been forced to those conclusions in order to stabilize herself. Shari was proud of her sister, so proud of her for maintaining. It was, of course, the way Denial works—the most common defense mechanism that people use in order to cope. For now, that was sufficient. Her hope and prayer and efforts, however, were that someday they'd know the truth and be freed of the need for such coping skills.

After a few minutes, mother and daughter left to go back to the cemetery. Driving past the funeral home, they observed the big, heavy earth- moving equipment parked out front. Their hearts were pounding. Could that be for Olive? Was this real?

Upon their return to the cemetery, Jessie arrived. He was obviously excited too. As they exchanged hellos, the trucks and backhoe started up the hill. As Shari looked across the cemetery, she saw tombstones everywhere. *They'll back out of doing it,* she thought.

Many other cars arrived and several men got out. Would these men laugh at this crazy woman who couldn't leave well enough alone? They introduced themselves: the newly elected coroner, police deputy, and other officials. They walked out to the gravesite with them. Everyone was very respectful. No one seemed to be amused at the whole thing. The coroner said he wished he didn't have to do this, clarifying that he, "wished it had been handled right the first time and wasn't now necessary. I wish she were not dead."

Another first! A man, an official, who wished her mom were alive. That meant so much. Soon, the backhoe operator cleared the area. He moved the footstones, then the small headstones from the babies' graves that were too close. The camera was rolling and the digging began. With every load of dirt, Shari felt dignity being restored. Even if there were nothing left of the casket or the bones, she appreciated this effort on her mother's behalf. The court felt Olive deserved all this trouble, the coroner left his office to be here; the trooper, sheriff-elect, and a deputy all felt Olive deserved this. Even Bill, the digger, drenched with sweat, was not opposed to what he was doing. They knew the story and didn't blame her at all for not "accepting it" and not "putting it behind me." God knows how she appreciated those men.

The coroner noted that he really had little expectation of anything being left of the casket and probably only a few pieces of bone and teeth would remain. The skull was the main part they needed, so they prayed it would be intact upon retrieval. Much to everyone's surprise, the lid of the coffin was indeed intact. The sides had fallen apart but the lid was intact. Cecelia was moving around with the camera trying to find the best angle. Their entire group was solemnly, respectfully, and pointedly attentive as Bill lifted the lid off the top half of the coffin.

They were prepared to see a skeleton with crossed arms like in the movies. What they saw was quite different. The entire area within the coffin was covered with brown pieces of foam! The only item clearly visible was the broach that Roberta had placed into her mother's hand at the gravesite twenty-seven years, seven months, and one day ago. Shari told them to lift it off if they could, but it fell apart. Yet Bill placed it carefully into a small box. Next he picked up the ring her mother had fondly bought herself and was buried with. Cecelia would later clean it up beautifully.

Bill then removed the pieces of foam, which had fallen from the casket lining. Slowly the skull was exposed. It had shifted, but was intact. Carefully, Bill lifted it out to place it inside the waiting container. The holes were visible. Two holes. One on each side. The one on the right was round and clean. The one on the left was small and the skull showed protrusion, bursting and crackling around that site. The coroner and others speculated that the big one on the right was the exit wound. Exit wound! Shari had never thought of that. She never felt the right side, only the left where she was told the bullet entered.

Where was the bullet? Of course, an investigation would have found that. Bill said he figured the hole on the right was the entry wound. He then proceeded to the removal of the remains, very gently and respectfully loosening the roots and earth that had begun to reclaim its own. It was sweet to see her mom's feet still in her little house slippers.

After Bill had freed her from the ground, he used the shawl she was draped in (the one they had used twenty-eight years ago to hide those bruised arms) to lift her out of the ground. Now the shawl served a good purpose. She was placed into a body bag and taken to the state crime lab. At last. Her mother's dignity as a human being was being restored.

But the coroner was expressly puzzled. "I wonder why she was buried in plastic underpants?" He went on to explain, "The morticians only use those if there is seepage from an open wound such as a patient who dies during surgery or suffers an injury or something in the lower area."

As they exited the cemetery, he told them he was surprised that none of the relatives showed up to "raise hell." They were surprised at that also, but then the deputy and other officials were here to permit this exhumation rather than a vigilante law calling the play, this time. At one point, a car drove up with her cousin and her friend, but they stayed in the car.

They were ecstatic as they left the cemetery. They kept pinching themselves to believe it had really occurred. Then they decided to stop at a local coffee shop to relax. Word was out, of course, as to what had just happened, and a kind gentleman approached them.

"Your mama was one fine woman," he stated emphatically, looking her directly in the eye. She nearly fainted, and her daughter hugged him. Cecelia knew the torment her mother had suffered all those years because no one even had recognized her Mama to be a person, much less dared to acknowledge the remarkably fine quality of person she was.

He commended them for their accomplishment, then added, "You really should talk to Lucy while you're up here." They had no idea why until he added, "She was the first one there when your mother died."

"Lucy?" Shari remembered her from years past, but never had heard her name connected in any way with the event of her mother's death.

"Lucy," he said definitely.

There was no need to say any more. They were convinced to go. Shari explained to Cecelia that she'd known Lucy back when she was a teenager and when she and her husband ran a business in town. They were both very impressive and likable people. Lucy was especially pretty. They telephoned her without delay, and she agreed to talk to them right away. When they arrived, she hugged them both and talked about everything under the sun, except Mama. Shari was suspecting this would be another don't-talk-about-your- mother visit. Finally, she mustered up the courage and asked Lucy what she knew about her mother's death.

Lucy took a breath, and tears came to her eyes. She shook her head and said, "Shari, I loved your Mama. We were babies together!"

Shari smiled. This felt somehow good and mysteriously hopeful. She asked, "What happened, Lucy?"

Lucy proceeded to tell her a story that would put an end to much of her pain and suffering, and all her nightmarish speculation as to what happened that day so long ago.

She began, "I was in my office. We'd just returned from lunch, and it was a few minutes after one o'clock when Darvell Lewis (also in the office) got a phone call. When he hung up, he said, 'Lucy, Olive is sick and they said they need me over there, but I don't have my car here.' I said, 'Well, if Olive is sick, come on, I'll drive you!'

"So we left in my brother's pickup. When we arrived, Connie Lewis was outside, sitting in her car, talking to Cecil and Darren, through her rolled-down window. She drove off immediately. Cecil caught up with me as I hurried toward the house, hollering, 'I didn't do it,' and I had no idea what he was talking about. When I went in, I saw Olive lying on the floor, dead. I knew she was dead because of her set stare. Her eyes were open. I closed them.

"The house was so hot! So hot I was afraid it would blow up! Olive was lying face up with her arms outstretched and legs together, straight. Her arm was so close to the stove that it was literally burning. I turned the stove off and said, 'What's happened?' There was not a drop of blood anywhere. Cecil kept running through the house yelling, 'I didn't do this!' Before long, Harold C. Blevens showed up along with old Dr. Hodges, long retired. He told Dr. Hodges to confirm suicide, 'So we can move her.' Dr. Hodges looked through her hair and eventually found a gunshot wound to her head, saying, 'Here it is.'

"Harold Blevens said, 'We're moving her,' and I said, 'No you don't. I worked at a hospital for eighteen years, and I know you can't move someone without an investigation.'

"Harold C. said, 'The doctor said she killed herself, so I'm authorizing them to move her. I am the law.'

"I called Stan Deevens out at the state prison, and he was out getting a Christmas tree. They reached him on his official's car phone. I said, 'Stan, Olive is dead.... She's been shot.'

"Stan said, 'The SOB killed her!'

"I said," I don't know, Stan, but you need to get here. We need you here!'

"When they rolled Olive over to get her onto a stretcher, a small amount of blood flowed from the back of her head. That's all the blood I saw!"

Shari asked Lucy what that meant to her—no blood?

She replied, "Well, she didn't die there!"

This she pondered and pondered as she felt a lump in her throat. It was shocking. She had never heard this before. Her mother had been moved? By whom? Why? Lucy was adamant. Shari also realized that Lucy needed to hear these things as badly as they needed to hear them. She was relieving herself of the burden she had carried these years, needing to testify of what she'd seen. Shari was being relieved of the burden of needing to know.

Lucy continued, "You can't shoot yourself, lie down perfectly flat, stretch your arms straight out, and die, with no blood anywhere on you or around you!"

Shari asked her whether she saw anything else unusual.

She said, "No, the house was clean except the lunch dishes were still on the table. Two places were set and one had been finished; it had been eaten out of. Cornbread was still on the table. Also, I saw her grocery list on the piano with a twenty-dollar bill lying on top of it. I had just seen Olive in the store a couple of days earlier, and she was buying Christmas presents and excited about the holidays. I knew this was no suicide. Anyway, I went home and made some banana pudding, rested up, and came back to the house later that evening. When I arrived, Kay Metagay walked out of the hall and pulled the hall door closed, 'cause the men were talking back there. It had been opened earlier, and I never saw the front of it. When she closed it, I saw blood splattered all over it, from about head height. I said, 'My God, look at the blood!'

"Kay said, 'Now Lucy, just go on and don't say anything about it. Just don't talk about it.'

"Then Stan came walking out and said, 'Hey, Sis, I know this is awful. We'll get it figured out.'

"I told him everything I knew and that I'd be happy to tell it to the police or an investigator. He said, 'OK,' but no one ever asked me. No police, no detective, no one until you asked me right now. Dr. Ball said I'd be a primary witness at the Coroner's Hearing, but there was no Coroner's Hearing -- ever.

"Your dad came up to me at the cemetery the next week, after your mother was buried, and he asked me, 'Lucy, do you think I killed Olive?'

"I told him, 'Cecil, I don't know who killed Olive, but I know that she didn't do it.'"

This precious lady had just been relieved of an agonizing and tormenting burden she had carried for almost twenty-eight years. We hugged, cried, smiled with relief, then hugged some more before we left. Shari felt more enlightened than ever before. The cornbread had meant Mama had been alive all morning and had fixed lunch at noon as usual.

The twenty-dollar bill meant Daddy was planning on her going to buy groceries that afternoon also; he put the money on the piano, as was their family routine. Money from Daddy went on the piano for Mama to go buy groceries or for their school lunches, etc. So Daddy was not an absolute monster, not a lurking, homicidal maniac. Now the whole scenario had changed from a nightmare scene of terror and hours of bloody torture (as her thousands of dreams had reiterated throughout the years) to possibly a simple argument and an impulsive act. Perhaps she reminded him of her plans to leave him right after the holidays and that she would take her "share." Whatever the words were, they culminated in her death (perhaps a quick, ghastly death).

Shari now imagined that Mama set his place at the table, and as he ate lunch they began arguing. Maybe she was preparing to go to town for groceries and he unexpectedly "popped" her in the head with the.38 pistol. Maybe she had no knowledge of what was about to happen at all. Just maybe. At any rate, how much easier it is to deal with this reality! That would account for the blood on the door, since she had to have been standing near it.

They went to the coroner's office and told him what they'd just learned. He said to call their attorney. They did, and he told them to get a sworn testimony from Lucy and to videotape it. Once again, they complied. Lucy was patient and cooperative in reiterating what she had seen and heard on that fateful day long ago. It was little wonder that people interested in deceiving them had ostracized them and excluded this valuable information, from the start.

During the next few days, they just relaxed. They yearned to relive the exhumation event again, (having never yet viewed their tape of the exhumation), so they decided to take their tape to a nearby K-Mart. It was early in the day, so they doubted they would bother anyone. They found a remote corner in the television department and found a VCR hooked up to a television. It was only a small TV attached to the VCR, but they were satisfied nevertheless. They'd learned to rejoice over even small things.

Cecelia inserted the tape and found her mother a stool to sit on. Shari eagerly watched, and the euphoria returned once more. Suddenly they heard other people moving around near them and when they turned around, they discovered that the VCR was hooked to every TV in the store! Everyone around was viewing the exhumation of Olive Lewis! Those who inquired were freely given the story in its entirety. They made several copies of the tape, and even though it was obviously not taken by a pro, it was still a unique and wonderful tape. The truth in visual and on audio!

Back at the hotel, there was a message from her attorney, Jessie. Her brother and sister were uniting to block her request to have their mom's remains cremated. Cecelia telephoned Ellis' home to discuss it with him, but he wasn't home. She spoke instead with his nineteen-year-old daughter (whom she'd never met, although they were first cousins). Teresa seemed eager to talk. She knew something was up but didn't know what it was. She had overheard her parents discussing Grandmother Olive being "dug up." When she inquired, they refused to tell her except to say that his "crazy" sister, Shari, wanted to dig her up. Teresa asked, "Cecelia, why does she want to dig her up?"

Cecelia answered that it was necessary because twenty-eight years ago, the laws of the land were broken and Olive didn't get an autopsy after her death.

Teresa asked, "But why did she need an autopsy, since she died of a heart attack?"

Whew! Ellis had lied to his own children for twenty-eight years. His own family knew nothing. So the cousins got acquainted over the phone and discussed the events of their grandmother in full. Teresa explained that she had been told that her Aunt Shari couldn't accept her mother's death and went insane out in California.

Cecelia responded, "Well, we did move to California, but that was ten years after our grandmother's death. During those ten years, my mom earned her bachelor's and master's degrees from the University of Arkansas and taught high school for two years. Then in California, she earned her Ph.D. and wrote a book."

Teresa agreed that Aunt Shari didn't sound crazy in her opinion. Then her dad came home and took the phone. "Roberta and I are not going to let Shari get a cremation. She's going to have to pay for a reburial, right back where she just dug her up from!"

"Well, Ellis, the coffin is ruined, so everyone thought it would be the simplest and most sensible to cremate the remains and rebury them.

Otherwise, bones would be dumped onto the open dirt. Is that what you prefer?" Cecelia asked him.

"Like I said, she can't cremate. She's got to rebury, and I told the funeral home I'll sue them if they do otherwise."

"I doubt if you have anything to worry about, Ellis. I sure wish I could meet you and your family. Teresa sounded really nice."

"Well, Shari and I never were close."

"Then too, there's nothing like a good murder cover-up to break up a family, I always say."

He stormed, "I can see that you're as crazy as your mother is!"

"Ellis, I have only heard my mother's version of everything over the years. But I'd be glad to hear yours, too. And I might change my own opinion after you tell me these things you know that convince you my mom is so wrong."

Bang! went the telephone.

Shari recalled that Roberta had told Cecelia when they last talked on the phone that she understood that the exhumation was something "Shari needs to do." She had so appreciated that, for it sounded like the sister she remembered and loved, who was warm, sentimental, and caring. Undoubtedly, the two of them together could have stopped the exhumation also, had it been up to Ellis. Perhaps Roberta permitted her that. She was grateful to her.

Now on the cremation issue, she needed to side with Ellis. No problem. The next few days dragged on as they awaited the autopsy. It had to be delayed but finally was scheduled for Friday. They arrived early Friday and waited for their attorney. Upon his arrival, he asked them to wait. Eventually, he returned, saying words that rattled her very being—words that cut through her like a knife.

"We won't know much for several weeks; what we do know, is that she was shot on the right side, and the bullet is still lodged in the left side of the skull." He went on to state that they wouldn't know much more until tests were run.

Cecelia and Shari hardly spoke till they got to the car. How could she have been mistaken about that? Shari was told Mama was shot on the left side, and she had felt the scratchy spot on the left side. It felt like an emery board or plaster, and she assumed the morticians had filled in the hole of the entrance. Actually she was feeling the exit wound, and the bullet was still in that wound! She was feeling the bullet that killed her! She suddenly hurt all over.

So the three-month wait began, to eventually receive the results of the extensive, elaborate autopsy. They were invited by the crime lab to call—weekly if they chose—as is routine procedure. Meantime, Shari began a long period of introspection. What was it all for: the search, the questions, the struggle? What did she accomplish? Does she prefer murder to suicide? She didn't think so. She believed anyone could commit suicide under certain circumstances. But was Olive in those circumstances? More and more questions continued to emerge.

Three months later the autopsy report appeared, although it was dated three months earlier, as though there had been no wait at all. The autopsy states that the wound to the head behind the right ear is consistent with other self-inflicted gunshot wounds to the head.

Case closed? What else is there left to do? Is there anything left to question now? Any other evidence that matters? What could have prompted a healthy grandmother to leave the people she cherished, the world of love, joy, future? Did she see no future? What about the plans to leave Cecil and move to the city with Aunt Faye? What about the little outfits on her sewing machine? What about the grocery list on the piano and the lunch she'd cooked? And the bruises on her arms? It doesn't add up to suicide.

But could a murder look so much like a suicide that it would fool even the scientists? Stranger things have happened. He had motive. He was losing Olive to liberation and emancipation and losing half of his possessions to her, leaving him open to humiliation by the townsfolk.

Cecil had opportunity, too. The gun used was assumedly his father's. But he was not a professional killer. Could he have outsmarted the scientists? Possibly. For twelve years, he had saturated his mind with detective magazines about murders of women. He read them religiously. He knew what the police, coroner, and forensic people would look for. He may have fantasized the killing many times. In a sense, he was a pro. After all, Shari had found the lady-killer magazine hidden in his desk, describing the woman killed with a.38 behind her ear then placed in front of a stove so that heat would offset the rigor mortis process. Simple coincidence?

Hardly, now. This autopsy report alone could not have convicted Olive, but in addition to the town's cover-up and refusal to acknowledge other evidence, Olive lost (seemingly, for now).

Who won?

Shari suddenly felt engulfed by the familiar loneliness she'd felt through the years, the need to vindicate her mother and the still deeper need to reach out to her and receive from her.

> *Life is tiring, ooh so trying but is just a test*
> *Once inspiring, now desiring, but to find some rest.*
> *Some peace midst all life's burdens,*
> *Some sleep through darkest hours,*
> *Some comfort in some safe, sane place*
> *Far from man's cruel powers*
> *It wasn't in Thy plan, oh Lord,*
> *Nor was it in ours so*
> *That to the trials which crush so hard*
> *Our spirits sink so low.*

CHAPTER THIRTY-FIVE

SHARI READ AND REREAD the autopsy report. So brief and conclusive. "Consistent with suicide." She dialed the number she had been given for the state pathologist, as families are permitted to do after an autopsy.

"Hello, Dr. Churn, this is Shari Lewis and I've just received your report from the autopsy you did on Olive Lewis, and I have a couple of questions."

Silence.

"Dr. Churn, I'd like to better understand this. What were the consistencies you refer to in your finding?"

"Everything. It's clearly a suicide."

"But, please help me to understand. Could you elaborate just a bit? I have waited a very long time and gone to a lot of trouble and expense because it's important to me."

"Like I told you. It's consistent with suicide. I'm confirming the original finding."

"The legal status of her death is Undetermined. If you change it to suicide, I need to know the basis of your decision."

Dr. Churn's response showed how irritated and impatient Shari had apparently made him. "I've told you, my conclusion is suicide, and everything is consistent with suicide."

"Dr. Churn, are the findings also consistent with some homicides?"

"Well, of course. But my conclusion is suicide."

"If it's consistent with suicide and also with homicide, why would it not remain Undetermined? What would be a reason to change it?"

"I am confirming the original report: Suicide. Now goodbye."

Within a few days, Shari received a letter of reprimand from her own attorney, scolding her for having telephoned Dr. Churn and "trying to get him to change his finding." Suddenly, light dawned. Why the resistance to her question? It was a sensible question. Families are permitted to call and make such inquiries. She was only asking a professional person to be responsible, to be accountable. After all, she'd paid thousands of dollars for this event, and she was entitled to ask her questions. She looked at the response her attorney had received from the former coroner, Dr. Ball: "I have lost this person's file. I have no knowledge of her." Yet he told her attorney on the phone, "She was depressed, and I was treating her for depression."

Being in the mental health field, Shari was well aware that a general practitioner is not qualified to diagnose or treat someone for clinical depression, a mental illness. He would instead refer the person to a psychiatrist.

Then she remembered her visit with her sister to this same Dr. Ball back in 1964 and her specific question to him three days after her mother's demise: "Dr. Ball, was Mama depressed?"

"No, Olive was not depressed. She was never depressed, and this was no suicide, rather the most blatant murder I've seen.... She had taken her insulin shot as usual..."

Shari thought of what her mom was doing in her Christmas preparations, their phone call, her shopping list, hot cornbread. Just how could the clever Dr. Ball fit depression into her bustling, joyful Christmas holiday? And why, years later would he want to?

He clearly recently fabricated that little tale of "treating her." Why? Was he scared now that Uncle Stan wasn't around to protect him? Yet what persuaded the Arkansas State Pathologist to do such a thing? He wasn't from her hometown and wasn't involved in the initial cover up. Why was he tenaciously adamant about thirty-year-old loose, unattached bones? Thus she began to contact other state pathologists and coroners to find out about this cut-and-dried "consistency" business.

Commonly, fifty-year-old, arthritic grandmothers put handguns to the back of their heads, at Christmastime, for the purpose of suicide, in the 1960's? *We'll see...*

Meanwhile another name had surfaced, of another person who had arrived at her mom's home as she lay dead in her living room. This was the County Health Nurse in 1964, Bertha Lynn Childs. Shari needed to visit Bertha Lynn again after these many years. She was both friend and relative to Mama and she, too, as Lucy, was glad to share her experience from 1964. Shari couldn't help but marvel at the courage of these precious women. They were glad to talk with her. They had expected to testify at the Coroner's Hearing about all they had seen and heard. But there had been no Coroner's Hearing, no investigation at all. They didn't even know that their information had been kept from her for three decades!

"Olive had telephoned me the night before and told me she'd baked a cake. She asked me, 'Could you stop by sometime tomorrow and have coffee and cake? Besides, I have you a little gift, so we could have our Christmas visit.'

"She also asked me to bring a clipping out of my newspaper of her niece's engagement picture. I put it in my purse as soon as I hung up the phone."

Shari blurted, "She had made Robbie's birthday cake, Bertha Lynn. That day she called you was Robbie's birthday."

"Well, I told her I'd be there with bells on and that I had her a Christmas present too. Shari, Olive and I had given each other Christmas gifts since we were girls in school. You may not have known that, did you?"

"I don't recall now, but then you went to see her next day?"

"I sure did. When I walked in and saw her lying there dead, I went out of my mind. They told me later I was hysterical and screaming. But that was Olive, and I loved her—had loved her all my life."

"Bertha, you being a nurse and all, did it look to you like she'd killed herself?"

"Pooh! Heaven's no, girl. That was no suicide, and Dr. Ball and I talked about that as we leaned over her, checking her body, later on. We talked about her arms and hands being streaked and all."

"What do you mean, streaked?"

"They'd washed her, but fast and hadn't done a very good job of it. There were red bloody streaks all over her. It looked awful! That poor thing."

"Why didn't an investigation take place? All these years, I didn't even know you were there. How I'd love to have talked to you years ago. Bertha, I didn't think anybody even cared or grieved for her. But you did, didn't you?"

"They never told you, huh? They sure kept it quiet. I never thought about you not being told, but yes, honey, I was sure there, and I loved your mother."

"Who are *they* actually?"

"All I know is that Stan Deevens was my cousin, just as Olive was, and I hated him for keeping it quiet and letting it go as a suicide. Not very many people believed it, but a few just accept whatever the paper says. Olive sure deserved better."

"Bertha, how was Daddy acting when you went there and she was dead?"

"Like he always acted, just standing around with his mouth shut. Cecil never had much to say."

"But did he look or act guilty? Did he act different?"

"Nah, not really. He and Robbie came to have supper at my house a few times after that. I felt so sorry for that little seventeen year old. I didn't know how to help her, but I sure wanted to. That wasn't fair to her, to drop it on her."

"Bertha, weren't you afraid of Daddy? Why would you invite him down to visit?"

"Honey, I knew him, too, when we were all kids. He was still just Cecil; he was always strange. He talked to my husband some, but there was no reason to be afraid of him. He didn't have the nerve to do that, Shari."

Shari was stunned. Stunned. So many new facts bombarding her brain. Dr. Ball was *there*, at the house, examining her mother's body alongside Bertha Lynn. He'd always told her he didn't see her till she was at the funeral home. So Shari and Robbie weren't the only ones to whom Dr. Ball had confirmed murder! And Bertha had hated Stan too (at least for his mysterious handling of that event). And Mama sure wasn't depressed—so Dr. Ball was expanding his lying base. Yet Bertha would be a good witness against him, being an RN! It was such a blessed relief to have additional proof of Mama's murder and it was just wonderful to visit with Bertha Lynn. Growing up Shari'd always liked her, and now she was so glad to learn that this dear friend had talked to Mama that night before and even saw her there in the living room the next day. She was grateful to Bertha for the courage to share these things with her. They visited more generally awhile, and then even her parting words were comforting to Olive's eldest daughter.

"I'll never accept suicide. No way. Your mother was a precious lady and my good friend and my cousin. I don't know what happened to her that day, but I sure know what didn't happen."

Much later Shari wondered why she hadn't thought in time to ask her, "If you don't believe Daddy killed her, then who could have done it?" But she did get to ask that question to another older lady. Neida was also a friend of her mom's for years and her friend, too. Neida's husband had recently died, and she was just barely beginning widowhood. Shari hated to upset her, but she really wished to talk with her about "it." Neida knew she'd traveled a long distance, and she confidently reassured her, "I have no qualms about talking of your mother. She was a remarkable lady, and that was awful what happened to her, both the death and the cover-up."

"Do you have any doubt in your mind that there was a cover- up?"

"Goodness, no. I've just always wondered why."

"Well, they did the autopsy and the pathologist conferred with Ron J.'s suicide finding."

"Oh, I'm sure they convinced the pathologist that's the simplest thing to do."

"Ron J. said he was treating Mama for depression."

"Your mother wasn't depressed a day in her life."

"Then who are 'they,' and why did they cover it so well?"

"I think 'they' is mostly your Uncle Stan, and I always wondered why he covered it, because I know he loved Olive."

"Do you suppose it was because of his desire to run for governor of the state later on?"

"No, because he looked bad, politically speaking, to cover up the murder of his own sister."

"Then it had to be the prison stuff he was involved in. People have suggested to me that he probably didn't want Daddy in his own prison. Do you suppose that's why?"

"No. Stan could have handled that OK. He could have made it hard on him, or he could just ignore him, but he could handle it."

By that point, Neida was soul-searching with Shari, reaching along with her for the truth. She seemed to pick a spot high above her head in one corner of the wall to focus on as she struggled to wrench out an answer. Shari had to add, "I've been told, too, that Grover Lewis had threatened to expose Stan and Governor Faubus if they allowed an investigation to incriminate Daddy. Would that have stopped Stan? Was that his reason?"

Deeply pensive but very assured, she slowly turned her gaze back to meet her eyes. "No. Stan was a politician and he knew that, in politics, sometimes you lose. He wouldn't have covered it for that reason. Besides, the prison scandal broke the next year, and he just got himself elected judge. He didn't suffer much. No, he wouldn't have, for that."

"Then he must have been afraid he'd kill Daddy himself, if Daddy was in prison and Stan saw him every day."

"I think if your dad had done it, Stan wouldn't have lost any time in getting him behind bars."

"Then you don't think Daddy did it either? You don't think Stan was protecting Daddy—for whatever reason?"

"Honey, I don't know. I've thought about it, and I just know Stan wouldn't have covered up for Cecil, not for anything in this world."

Shari knew she was right, but her heart was pounding. "Then why, why, why? And why did he continue to cover it all through the years while I begged him and the governor to investigate it? Neida, Stan just kept saying, 'For the kids' sake,' while I was telling him it was hurting Robbie and me so badly we could hardly stand it. Why the double-talk?"

There was a painful, very serious pause, then a solemn reply as Neida met her eyes with grave sadness: "Ellis. He would have done it for Ellis."

Shari looked at her in utter bewilderment as the walls began to sway gently. She felt a twinge of nausea in her stomach. For a brief moment she wondered, *Perhaps ignorance is bliss after all?* Those words, "For the kids' sake." Now she understood what Stan meant! It never mattered about Robbie and her.

She kept looking at Neida, waiting for more. The older woman continued slowly, revealing a number of small but significant facts.

"There were some people I worked with at that time who were scared to death of Ellis."

"Scared of him? Why?"

"I told them I couldn't believe there was need to be, for I'd watched him grow up. I watched all you kids grow up, and I just remembered him from the ball games and things."

"Neida, he's the one who first told me it was suicide and that it was because of Robbie. But I told him I knew that wasn't true and he got real mad at me. Then he stopped talking to me at all, all these years. He's even told people I was off in California, gone crazy. That's why I came back for the class reunion—because I learned he was discrediting me, and I didn't know why. And I still don't. How does it all fit?"

"All I know is that from the time it happened, we knew it was something highly volatile for Stan to cover up Olive's murder, and that's the one reason that does fit."

"You know, at the '77 class reunion, Ell ignored me, and Stan did too. I'd come all the way from California and wanted to see them so badly, and they never seemed to see or speak to me. Then when I asked Ellis to come up to Robbie's and visit, he and Stan came together, and left together."

"Ell was the son Stan never had."

"He was the first grandchild to the Deevenses. Mama's first two babies died, then she had Ellis."

"Ellis was the golden boy."

"Oh God, I'm just remembering so many things now. Ellis had just divorced for beating up his wife, just what Mama had predicted. And Ellis had threatened to jump off the Broadway Bridge in North Little Rock. He'd taken off his shoes and socks and the press came and everything. It came out in the newspaper but... Stan had them delete the name. Nobody but them and just a few others knew who the 'suicidal young man' was."

"So Ellis was the suicidal one? That's interesting, isn't it? How was he treating your mother around that time when she died?"

"She told me herself on the phone that week that he was angry at her, blaming her for his getting diabetes. Oh, and Aunt Faye told me that he'd doubled up his fists at Mama several times. But she wasn't scared of him; she just told him how bullish that was, being she was his mother and all."

"And then your Aunt Faye suddenly died, didn't she?"

"You know, Stan and Bea told me I caused Aunt Faye to die by talking to her about Mama. I thought they meant I caused her heart attack!"

"Maybe one of you had to go before you put it all together. How old was she anyway? I knew she was young."

"In her forties. Do you think...?"

"No way to know, Honey. I wouldn't doubt it. Those power-crazed men have been known to do such things. Just no way to know."

"Neida, I can't tell you what this means to me, to talk with you. We may be wrong about everything, but oh God, it helps to be able to talk with you now. It'll take a while to sort it all out, but there's so much to think about. Thank you, thank you, thank you for talking with me."

"Shari, you're welcome in my home anytime and you're welcome to talk about anything you want to. I don't buy into that town's status quo, secretive stuff myself, I never did. I think it's silly, and life's too short to waste it with such nonsense."

"That's why I always liked you. But as for the secretive stuff, is that the Brotherhood stuff? I've heard that in the South, the Brotherhood group is synonymous with the Ku Klux Klan. Do you know if that's true?"

"Yeah, I think so. Do you know if Cecil and Ellis were members?"

"I know Daddy was for sure, 'cause I used to try to get him to tell me their secrets. He only told me Grover was their president, or chairman, whatever, and I have his Brotherhood ring. Oh, and Stan was buried with his Brotherhood apron, so he was, and I don't know about Ellis, but I bet, I just bet he is."

"Chances are. They play that little game seriously and do protect each other. They consider themselves to be superior to everyone else."

"I know Stan took credit for the town remaining white, even after Governor Faubus fought so hard to prevent integration in the schools."

"They don't consider American law to regulate them; they make their own law."

"Do you know if Harold C. Blevens is a member and Darren and Ron J. and—"

"Probably so, dear. That helped seal the cover-up. After that, they were all in it together and stayed steadfast."

Neida and Shari went for a walk, then ate, watched TV awhile, and went to bed. Next morning, rested and refreshed, Shari thanked her again for such an inspiring visit. Neida's hug and open invitation meant more to her than words could convey.

Just when I grow weary of trying or of holding up
Or of holding onto, or of believing in
Some step forth that I'd never realized were with me
All along.
Their strength strengthens me anew and my own strength
Perhaps, strengthens them too
And together in love, we know it isn't pointless to believe in
And to hold onto these things.
For these people are the things-and-the-principles that matter
And they make life valuable as God intended it to be.
And because this is where I found you to be
And because this is where you are today
You're a lovely person and a very special friend to me.

CHAPTER THIRTY-SIX

AFTER NEIDA'S ASTOUNDING REVELATION, Shari became curious about a former friend of Ellis who lived a short distance away. She had not seen Leland for three decades and now she began to wonder why. After all, he had been her brother's good friend and had spent oodles of time at their house years ago. He was much like a brother to her. She wondered whether he had come to her mom's funeral at all. Certainly she had not seen him during the Christmas season that year of 1964, even though many of their friends had been in Clinton for the holidays. She decided she would very much like to visit with him again, after so long.

She was apprehensive about phoning him. Would he be happy to hear from her? Cecelia encouraged her just to call and play it by ear. Her heart was pounding as she dialed the number. His phone rang several times, and she was almost relieved that no one was home, but then she heard, "Hello?" It was a man's voice.

"Leland?" she said.

"Yes," he replied.

"Hello, Lee. This is Shari Lewis. Remember me?" He didn't answer. "Leland, are you there?"

"Yeah, I'm here, but I can't believe you called. How long has it been, Shari?" He sounded friendly. She could feel herself calming down as they began to talk.

"I'm in town and would love to see you if you have time," she said.

"Where are you staying, Shari?"

"At the Holiday Inn on Willow Road."

"I'll be there in about an hour."

She was shocked. Not only did he not bawl her out and hang up, but he also was glad to hear from her and wanted to come see her.

"OK, see you then," she said and hung up the phone.

Cecelia was grinning from ear to ear. "He doesn't have two names, like Billy Bob and Debbie Faye?" she teased gently. "Most Southerners use two first names. In any case, it sounds like you're going to get your wish."

Shari looked at the clock, then at the room, and finally at her daughter and her grandchildren playing nearby, thinking how brief an hour's time really was.

"He's coming here in one hour! Do you think we can be ready by then?" She still suspected that something would surely prevent what she most desperately longed for.

"No problem." Cecelia sweetly picked up the phone, motioning to the menu nearby. "We begin by settling the kids in with breakfast, and they'll enjoy room service." She proceeded to order as both Mark and Nikki caught on, scurrying to her side to offer their input. Shari's grandchildren traveled with them regularly, as they continued their 'investigation' over several states. Even with Mark's diagnosis of autism, he fared very well, always having the specific food he needed at the rigid timing required, preventing him from becoming tense and frustrated.

As Cecelia dressed the children and found some cartoons on the television to entertain them, all Shari had to do was get herself dressed, yet it seemed a major task. Cecelia straightened up the room a bit, then put the finishing touches on her hair and makeup.

When room service arrived, Cecelia helped the kids get their breakfast arranged and soon the children had forgotten about the grownups altogether. She poured Shari some coffee, saying, "Now you can relax."

Just as she sat down with her coffee, there was a knock on the door. Shari jumped and nearly dropped her cup.

Her daughter smiled as she breezed toward the door. When she opened it, Shari felt she'd gone back in time.

He still looked like the all-star athlete she remembered, and she felt close to him again, instantly. Age had not changed his warm smile or his soft blue eyes. He grinned, coming in with open arms.

"Shari, you haven't changed a bit," he said. "I'd have known you anywhere!"

She laughed. "Oh, Leland, you haven't changed either. You still have all the charm you always had!"

He laughed warmly, then waved toward Cecelia and the children. "Who are all these folks? I thought she was you when she first opened the door."

Shari beamed. "Well, thank you. This is my daughter, Cecelia, and my grandchildren, Mark and Nikki."

He quickly brought out pictures of his family. Shari commented on how lovely they each were, and they caught each other up on their lives as best they could in a short span of valuable time.

"Lee, you surely know I want to speak with you about my family and my mom's death."

His eyes looked away ever so slowly, then he fidgeted in his chair a bit. Despite his size, she could still see both his parents in his features and mannerisms. His face seemed strained, and she knew they both felt the tension of talking about it.

She thought perhaps she should change the subject, but she couldn't. She had to know how he felt. "Lee," she began. "How long has it been since you've been back to Clinton?"

"Shari, I haven't been back there since 1964, December." She was shocked. So terribly long. "Why not?" she asked.

He shook his head and looked down.

"When was the last time you saw Ellis?" she asked very carefully.

His eyes continued to look downward and he said, "Not since then, December, 1964."

"Why do you suppose you never went back or saw Ellis?"

"I just couldn't, Shari. I guess I got busy and never found time."

A safe answer, she thought. She tried to muster up all the courage she could; then she asked, "Lee, what did you think happened to Mama?"

He took a breath. "I don't know."

"But what did you think happened?" she pressed.

"Shari, why are you asking me this?"

"Because she was my mother. I loved her; you loved her too, didn't you Lee? Am I right?"

He squirmed again, then slowly raised his eyes level with hers.

"Yes I did, but why are you suddenly asking now after so much time has passed?"

"Suddenly? Lee, I have been asking for nearly thirty years. I begged Stan, the governor himself, and many of my relatives, but nobody would ever answer me. I finally took the matter to court and exhumed my mother's body. That took a lot of time and money. Nothing was suddenly." She scarcely believed she was sharing all this with someone she hadn't seen in so long.

He looked square at her now, appearing more courageous. "Shari, what do you want to know?"

No one had ever asked her that before. She answered, "Leland, I need to know what happened to Mama."

"What were you told, Shari?"

"Ellis said she killed herself because of Roberta. The Deevenses said Daddy was a monster and murdered her. The Lewises said Mama went crazy and killed herself. Which of those stories would you have believed, Lee?"

He quickly replied, "None of 'em."

She smiled, relieved, feeling they had connected. "Thank you. Me neither." She took a breath and asked, "Lee, did you hear anything back then, or did Ellis tell you anything?"

His warmth seemed to surround her as he leaned forward and said, "Shari, I'm very sorry about all this. It must have been horrible for you all these years. I guess I thought you knew."

She nearly jumped out of her skin. "Knew what?"

"Shari, I'll tell you what you need to know, but I won't ever take a witness stand or anything."

She knew this was serious now, and she knew they would continue this conversation to its monumental conclusion. With a breath of respectful, even reverent patience, she heard the simple statement part her lips, "Lee, all I need is the truth."

He nodded in agreement and, with a surrendering sigh, very respectfully began sharing what he knew. "I was home from school that morning, Shari. All the schools were out for the Christmas holidays. Around noon or later, my phone rang. It was Ellis. He was talking so fast and loud I could hardly understand him. He told me to pick him up at the pond near your house. I didn't know what was going on, but I went. When I got there, Ellis was a wreck. I'd never seen him like that—ever. He was wearing a T-shirt and jeans. It was so cold I wondered why he didn't have on a coat. He seemed to be hiding behind a tree while cars passed, then he ran to my car and jumped in. He was crying and just blubbering. He said, 'Drive, Leland!' I asked him, 'Drive to where?' and he blurted out, 'Back to school! I want to go back to school! Or anywhere—just drive!'

"I drove off wondering what in the world was going on. Ellis was crying and hollering all the time. I finally pulled off on a dirt road and asked, 'What is wrong, Ellis? Tell me!' He opened the door and ran out into a field. I chased him, and he stopped and said, 'It's Mama.' I remember I grabbed him by the arm and said, 'What about her?'

"He said with his hands over his face, 'I think she's dead.' I was shocked. I asked him, 'What are you talking about Ellis?' He was blubbering and ranting and raving. I threw him down to the ground and said, 'Ellis, talk to me. What has happened?'

"He looked at me and said, 'I didn't mean to Leland. I didn't mean to.' By now Ellis was slumping down onto the grass, beating the grass with both fists. I asked, 'Didn't mean to what, Ellis?'

"'I shot her,' he said weakly. I thought I would faint, but instead I pressed him to go on and make some sense. He was just hysterical. I'd never seen him like this, and it kind of scared me, I tell you. Finally I asked him, 'How, Ellis—how did it happen?'

"He sobbed like a little kid, said he just wanted to die, told me his wife left for good. Said he called her and she said she was done with him. He was really upset, Shari. Never seen him like that before. He said he went into the kitchen and your Mama was making dinner. So he got himself the pan of beans and cornbread and sat down. Your Mama knew he was upset and all, but she didn't say anything. Ell said she'd seen him on the phone earlier. He told me he got real mad and went back to the phone again and called Betsy again. He said he told her he couldn't live without her and that he was going to kill himself. She hung up on him. That really did it. He said he put his police gun to his head. He was all mixed up about what happened then. Said he heard your Mama holler, then the gun went off. He told me she fell and blood was all over the place."

Leland paused, then continued. "I couldn't believe what I was hearing, Shari. I said, 'Ellis, are you sure she was dead? Maybe the bullet just hit her arm; maybe she just fainted or something.' But he said no. That's when your daddy came in all cussing and screaming. He went up to your grand-dad's to get Darren and then Ell called me.

"Shari, I cried and vomited. I couldn't believe my close friend was telling me this. I couldn't believe it and didn't believe it. I just knew she was injured but OK. After a while we drove to a phone. I called your mom's house and Harold C. Blevens answered. He asked if I knew where Ellis was. I said no, I didn't. But he said he knew I had him, so keep him out for a few hours. I asked about your mom, but Harold C. hung up the phone.

"A couple of hours later, we went back to your house, and there were several cars there. I wanted to drop Ellis off and leave, but before I could, your Uncle Stan came out. He came around to my side and reached in and turned off the engine and took the key. Then he said, 'Come in the house, boys.' We went to the back bedroom and Stan asked, 'What happened, Ellis?'

"Ellis started blubbering again. Stan tried to calm him, and Ellis told Stan the whole story that he had told me. Then he started crying and saying, 'I can't go to jail, Uncle Stan. Please don't let them take me to jail, please!' I thought it was strange. We still didn't know about your mom."

Shari thought, *Mama never was the main issue. As far as they were all concerned, she already didn't matter.* She certainly didn't want to interfere with Leland's statement, however, and he went on, oblivious to her inner dialogue.

"I asked Stan, 'How's Olive?' And Stan looked at me with a sick, puzzled look and just said, 'She's dead, son.' I got up off the bed and said, 'I'm going home,' and Stan said, 'Sit down, boy, we have to talk.'

"I realized that I was involved in something I didn't wish to be involved in at all. I asked Stan why I needed to stay, and he told me to just stay with Ellis awhile. I thought he meant because he was upset or something.

"Then Harold C., Stan, and Cecil went into the next room, and there were some other men already in there—Grover Lewis and some more. They shut the door behind them. About half an hour later, Stan came and got us and we went inside. I was scared to death, everyone was looking at us real strangely. Then Stan sat us down on the foot of the bed. Ellis began begging, 'Please Stan, please. I'll kill myself for sure if I have to go to jail, Stan, I'll kill myself.'

"Stan wiped tears from his eyes and put his hand on Ellis' shoulders. Then he looked up and said, 'Ellis, your Mama was my sister, and I loved her very much. Now I know this was an accident, and I know your Mama wouldn't want you to go to jail. You do need help, son. It could have been you dead instead of her. Either way, it's an awful tragedy. Now, you can get help by pleading temporary insanity and the court will send you to a hospital. I know, because I am the court in this town.'

"Ellis immediately jumped up and, still hollering, tried to run out. He was yelling, 'No, no, I'll never say that, Stan. Everybody will know. Betsy will know. Shari will know. Robbie will know. I won't do that, Stan. Please, they'll all think I'm crazy, Stan. They'll hate me. If anyone knows, I'll kill myself for sure. Please, Stan, please!'

"He was frantic, totally out of control. Stan was cursing and shaking his head. Stan said, 'I just don't know what to do.' I had never seen Stan Deevens not know what to do. But he was like, whipped down and confused himself. I knew he was real close to your mom, but he mumbled like he was talking to himself or just thinking out loud, 'No matter what, it won't bring Olive back. She's dead.'

"All this time your dad never said a word, he just watched all the others. Then all of a sudden, Cecil said, 'Well, I don't really care who you say did it, so long as it isn't me. It better not look like I did it!'

"Then Harold C. said to Stan, 'You could just say she did it herself.' Stan looked at Harold C., clinched his teeth and fists, and, Shari, I just knew Stan was going to hit him. He glared at him for a few seconds, and then Harold C. said, 'Stan, it's either suicide or homicide. It's your call.'

"Stan looked back at Ellis, who was crying into the rumpled bedding now where he lay face down, pounding the mattress with one fist. He put one hand on Ellis' shoulder and Ellis reached for him, 'Please, Stan, please don't let them know I did it!'

"I couldn't believe it when Stan breathed deeply and said, 'OK.' Then Stan looked at me and said, 'What do you think, son? Can you go along with this, or do you want to see your best friend spend the rest of his life in prison? It could happen that way, you know.'

"Shari, I didn't know what to say. I loved Olive, but I felt like a little kid in that room. What was I among all those powerful grownups? Finally, I told Stan I wouldn't tell anybody, and when I did, I felt a weight being placed on my shoulders that has never been lifted. He looked me square in the eye and said, 'Are you sure now? Because once it's done, there's no way to undo it without all of us getting in big trouble.'

"I remember hesitating for a minute, and Harold C. spoke up and said, 'Actually, Leland, you could be considered an accessory, you did pick him up and stay with him.' For the first time ever, I saw Harold C. as a state policeman, not the hometown boy.

"I was so confused. All of a sudden I became so angry at Ellis. *Why did he drag me into this?* I wondered. Then Stan said, 'Well, son?'

"I said, 'OK, Stan, whatever you say.' But then I thought of you girls, and I asked Stan, 'What about Shari and Roberta?'

"Stan said, 'Don't worry, son, I'll take care of them.'

"Shari, I left after that, and I never went back. Not to the funeral, not to class reunions, not to see Ellis. In fact, I've not laid eyes on Ellis from that day to this one. I always sent my mom and dad tickets to come out here to visit, but I never went back."

"Lee, did you ever tell anyone?"

"No, Shari, I never even spoke of it till now."

She hardly knew what to say after all this revelation. She looked at Leland and he looked exhausted. That made sense, since he had just unburdened himself of a thirty-year secret. He then looked over to her and said, "Shari, I feel so ashamed."

She wanted to say, "Don't worry, it's OK," but she couldn't. She could not absolve him of his guilt or shame. After all, he did help cover up her mother's murder. She couldn't say it was OK. She just looked him in the eye and said, "Lee, I do understand your position back then—Ellis being your friend and all. But Mama was... she was my mother. She was convicted of her own murder! She was deprived of the dignity she deserved. Roberta even took the blame at barely seventeen years old and pregnant! She was given the blame by a bunch of men who didn't even care about Mama. Our lives were hell on earth for a very long time."

"How is Roberta anyway, Shari? I've wondered how she handled it all."

"I'd love to be able to tell you that she's just fine, that she just put it behind her and went on with her life. That is the asinine advice that so many people gave me all these years. But God knows, we're just not made that way. People certainly can go on with their lives, but their lives may be hell on earth, without some closure. There has to be some logic, some understanding, to make their tragic loss palatable. We needed to know the truth. But we didn't have it. We were given lies and silence and inconceivable innuendoes. Robbie went on with her life. She just turned against men. It hurt me when she decided to leave her husband and her pretty house, to live in an apartment with a woman. But I respected her right to make her own decisions, and I still do."

"Do you see her often?" Lee's genuine concern was apparent.

"No, I don't see her at all. She and I used to visit often, and we both would try so hard to put the pieces together and figure out what happened. But I let her down when I took my first petition to court and lost it. I guess she gave up on me ever getting to the truth. At least, right after that, she told me she never wanted to see me again. But I wanted more than anything to show her that our Mama's death had nothing to do with her."

"Shari, I know I can't undo the damage all this did to you, and I know I could never make it up to you. I'd give anything if I could."

I just had to measure his sincerity. "Anything? Even testifying in a courtroom if necessary?"

He closed his eyes and said, "No, Shari, I can't do that. I have to think about my family and what it would do to them."

She couldn't help but smile sadly at that statement. How often she had heard what 'it' (the truth) would 'do' to someone or their family if they got involved. She did, however, appreciate him for at least telling her what he knew.

She didn't know what else to say except, "Thank you. From the bottom of my heart, for my mother and for Roberta and for my children and myself, thank you at last for this, the truth."

He picked up his coat and said he needed to run. She thought that was an ironic choice of words. He looked spent, and she was certain she did as well. As they said their goodbyes, they both smiled.

"Stay in touch, Shari," he said, as he hugged her and her daughter one last time before walking out the door. The women sat speechless, in a state of shock after the whole story had finally been given to them after so many years of searching.

Shari awakened. She hadn't realized she'd fallen asleep, but Cecelia explained that she'd collapsed in exhaustion shortly after Lee's priceless visit. She'd replayed their discussion in her sleep, needing closure so badly.

"Mom, are you OK?" Shari heard her daughter asking as she reluctantly rose and reached for the warm, soothing coffee.

"Sure. But you know, I'm still remembering things, things that help complete the puzzle."

"Yes?"

"I remember I was sad to have to miss Ellis' wedding; Betsy asked me to be in the wedding yet we lived out of state and Nat didn't want me to make the trip back. I told Mama I would have to miss it regretfully and her answer surprised me."

"What was her answer?"

"She just smiled and said, 'Don't worry about it, Honey. They plan to have a nice wedding and Betsy'll have a nice shower too... I've already bought some crystal, a pretty Fostoria pitcher I plan to take to her shower... '

"I replied to Mama, 'Oh, I wish I could go with you to the shower too!'

"She said to me, 'Shari, I plan to dress up nice and go to the shower and dress up nice for the wedding, but mostly for Betsy's sake. She's a little sweetheart of a gal. Sometimes when she's spent the night in the new room, I see her sleeping there in the morning and she looks like a little doll with golden curls lying on the pillow.'"

Shari knew her mom thought a lot of Betsy, and did she. But she had to know what Mama meant.

"What do you mean you're going to go 'for her sake?' Aren't you going for Ellis' sake too?

"Mama replied, 'Not really. There's no doubt in my mind that this marriage will be short lived because Ellis will be mean to her. He's mean and self-centered and I know for sure he'll mistreat her. She's an only child and from a good family and they won't put up with his meanness. I used to put up with stuff years ago that even I wouldn't put up with in today's world. No, Ellis is a bully and I think he's in for a rude awakening. I love Betsy and I know she's crazy about Ellis, but he doesn't really care about anyone but himself. So, I'll dress up and go to the shower and we'll go to the wedding and grin with them all. But there's no doubt in my mind, it won't be a marriage to last.'"

Shari hadn't really thought about their future, but with Mama spelling it out, she could see the truth of her words. She explained to her daughter that after that conversation, she didn't feel too badly about having to miss the festivities.

Cecelia was hanging on every word, then, "So your mom wasn't surprised when they broke up, was she?"

"Heavens no. She told me that one day they stopped at her house to get Betsy a shirt of Ellis' or Daddy's to wear home, because Ellis had roughed her up so much in the car, while he was driving, that he'd torn her dress and she needed a big shirt. Mama said Betsy was crying and really upset. Mama worried about her until she learned that she had, sure enough, gone back to live with her parents."

"Did they get divorced then?"

"I'm not sure how long it was, but fairly soon after that incident. Mama said Ellis tried to see her, demanding to her folks that, 'She's my wife and I have a right to see and talk to her,' but that her dad told him his rights stopped when he used his fists on her. Her dad was a doctor in Little Rock, if I remember right, and he said, 'We didn't raise her to be mistreated by anybody. She's getting a divorce and that's it.'

"Right after that, the Broadway Bridge incident took place. I lived out of state, but Mama told me everything that was happening with them. Mama and I both appreciated Betsy's dad for taking the stand he did. I wish all dads did the same."

As Shari sipped her coffee and pondered it all she added, "And you know something else? I suspect that's what they were arguing about that day... I can accept this, for I must "

She realized the men were covering all the bases even now as they had begun back in that bedroom—her bedroom!—the day her mother lay dead a few feet away. Now she better understood the recent autopsy report that followed her costly exhumation. It was consistent with all other deeds of the men these many years—to simply confirm each other. Pity she hadn't thought to have hired an out-of-state pathologist to do the autopsy! She scheduled a visit to Texas to visit the state coroner there. Honest, objective professionalism would be refreshing.

He gave a very different interpretation, or conclusion, of the autopsy findings. He began by explaining the situation. "Well, when an autopsy is done, everything is taken into account, for example, where the body was found, any bruises or cuts, and so on. Then various tests are run on different organs. Now, without all the vital body parts and organs present, it is very difficult to be exact in determining cause of death.

"In the case of your mother, however, we have an entirely different situation. In this case, we have only a skeleton that has been buried for twenty-eight years. It's absolutely impossible."

Shari abruptly interrupted. "What if the skull has a bullet in it?"

He smiled knowingly. "Doesn't really matter. I could confirm that the skull has a bullet in it and I could measure the size, angle of entry, and the particular distance it lies from the posterior or the anterior and many other things. But what I could not do, nor could any other human being do, is determine what the person died from twenty-eight years ago. Perhaps she died from the bullet. Perhaps she was poisoned, stabbed, strangled, and after death occurred, was shot in the head with a gun. It is simply too late to determine exactly what caused the person's death.

"Now, if you tell me you are satisfied that she died from the gunshot head wound, but you want me to tell you who shot the bullet into her head, again I have to tell you, that is impossible. Any thinking person can understand that. We could talk about statistics, commonality of homicides and suicides with the type of gun used, the area of the wound, the gender of the victim, those sorts of things. We still would only be speculating, but the accuracy of the foundation of our statistical base would tend to support a plausible speculation."

This was music to her ears! She could not retrieve her autopsy report quickly enough to present to this honest, objective pathologist. Once she handed it to him, he studied it carefully. She felt a twinge of dread that he, too, might immediately retreat from his honesty and try to support his male colleagues. He might feel annoyed that she had put him on the spot in this way, and he could refuse to go on record in dispute of another in the field.

Instead he looked up, eyes twinkling and said, "Man, this is a crock!"

She was absolutely elated. She even loved his verbiage.

"Whoever did this autopsy must have consulted a psychic! He not only determined that it was the bullet that killed her, he also determined who put it there. Wow! I am impressed!"

Then after additional perusal, he looked up and said, "Did he have records from a previous autopsy?"

"No," Shari answered emphatically, never having forgotten that no autopsy had been done following her death, even though it was required by law at the time.

"Then there is simply no basis for his determination. Just because there is a gunshot wound to the head doesn't mean that it was the cause of death, not when the victim is a twenty-eight-year-old skeleton. Gunshot wounds to the head are consistent with many suicides and also with many homicides. Since the hands could not be tested for powder burns, there is no way to determine suicide. That word never should have been used."

Out of sheer curiosity, she ventured one heartrending question, "How commonly are gunshot wounds in this area of the head, behind the right ear, found to be suicides in females?"

"I've been in this business many years, and I've never had one, nor have I known of one."

At that moment she realized she need never again plead her mother's defense. No, never again. The records are clear; they were simply disregarded with her precious mother's death.

She asked him, "What would be your findings if you did this autopsy?"

"Well, based on what they had to go on, I would probably say, 'Gunshot wound to the head. Cause of death: Undetermined.'"

As Shari left the doctor's waiting area, an African-American lady met her eye and nodded sympathetically, having overhead part of her previous discussion. She sat down beside her, aware that they had a great deal in common.

She soon knew Shari's entire story, and she told her how many times she had cringed for the agony of the Black women in early years who had helplessly watched as their husbands were strung up from a tree by a noose, in front of even their children, to dangle there until dead. And at her screams, the white men had simply scoffed, "Now woman, you got a choice here. You can hang there beside him, or you can take your kids and go home, keep your mouth shut, and go on with your life." As Shari shed quite tears together with the compassionate woman, she knew she was proud to have more in common with her than with the men in her own family and from her own hometown.

I can accept this, for I must
And my tears in time will dry,
But I know that deep inside my heart, This
ache - will only - very slowly... die.

CHAPTER THIRTY-SEVEN

IN HER YOUNGER YEARS, Lucy was beautiful and stately. In recent years she had become widowed and also suffered some medical problems. But she had an adorably sweet smile and was still a beautiful lady. Shari wanted to buy her a pretty, frilly gown and take it to her. She also wanted her to reiterate her experience of December 18, 1964.

It had become clear to Shari that she didn't seem to incorporate all the newly revealed information until quite some time later. There was so much to absorb, so many facts and feelings to process. Even to think of the best questions to ask was still difficult for her. But then she'd never planned to be an actual investigator, and to investigate one's own mother's murder can still mean crossing an emotional abyss even after three decades. But it needed to be done and if not by her, then by whom? She set out for her next journey across the states.

In Lucy's room, the women talked and even though she was much older now, she never floundered.

"Honey, you don't walk in on a sight like that but once in a lifetime. I'll never forget what I saw."

"Please tell me again what you told me before," Shari quietly implored. "It is so important, and I am deeply grateful. I have to be certain I'm getting it all correct."

Lucy began, "I had just returned to work from lunch and the phone rang. I answered it, and it was for Darvell. I gave it to him, and when he hung up, he said, 'They said Olive is sick and they need me to come up there to help, but I forgot, I don't have my car here.'

"I replied, 'Well, come on, I'll drive you. If Olive is sick, I want to help too.' As we passed the hospital, I looked for Cecil's car, thinking he might have taken Olive to the hospital. But it wasn't there, so we went on to the house. When we arrived, there was one car, and it belonged to Connie Lewis. She was sitting in the car in the driver's seat and her husband, Darren, and Cecil were talking to her through her window. It was rolled down."

"I never knew she was there. She denies it, you know," Shari stated. Lucy continued.

"Well, as soon as we got out of the car, she drove off fast. She never spoke to me again after that day. Even when we'd meet on the sidewalk, she just looked away."

"I wonder what she was doing there?"

"When I went up the front steps, Cecil followed me, saying over and over, 'I didn't do it, Lucy, now I didn't do this!' I didn't know what he was talking about; I just wanted to go in and see about Olive. And there she was—poor, poor Olive, lying there in her housecoat, eyes staring, arms burning "

"Wait, Lucy," Shari interrupted. "Mama didn't own a housecoat. She never did wear one. She put on her house dress every day at five in the morning when she started breakfast."

"Well she had on a housecoat that day, a floral one, pink I think it was."

Shari was puzzled by that, knowing it'd have to be deciphered later, but she'd never seen Mama in a housecoat. Maybe she had just begun wearing one since their last visit in September? Even so, cooking lunch in a housecoat? Not her mother, no way. She planned to call Robbie and ask her—she'd know that for sure. Maybe her sister would be ready to talk to her now.

Lucy continued on vehemently spewing out the details that had lain silently in her mind and heart too many years, wanting someone to seek them out. Knowing much of these facts were already on videotape from their previous visit, Shari had the instinctive certainty that they'd missed something.

"The cornbread was on the table and the beans, still in the cooking pot, were sitting on the table," Lucy described, "and two places were set, and one plate was eaten out of. The utensils were there, and you could tell the meal had been finished from the one plate."

"Lucy, wait, stop," Shari interrupted. "Let me set up a similar kitchen scene. Here's a rectangular table like ours was. Here's the entrance from the dining room to the kitchen. Where were the plates set? Can you remember? I know it's been a very long time—"

"I remember well. The plate at the end of the table had been eaten out of."

"Wait, show me what you mean." Shari sensed Lucy was confused, perhaps, but when she set up the table, she'd see that Daddy had eaten lunch.

"Honey, I remember your kitchen. I walked inside the door and at the end of the table, on the right, was the finished plate."

And her words bumbled out, "But that's not Daddy's plate!"

"Then your dad ate from a different place that day or he didn't eat lunch at all."

Shari knew that Mama didn't set pots from the stove onto the table, so the cooking pot on the table seemed strange. But even more importantly, "Daddy was so regimented. He never, ever ate a meal except from his own spot."

Lucy smiled a patient, empathetic, somewhat consoling smile as Shari reminded herself that Mama's place was at the side of the table directly across from Daddy's. And she absolutely never ate before Daddy did! Oh God, it was true, wasn't it?

"Whose plate was it, Shari?" Lucy asked ever so softly, meeting her gaze, giving her little choice but to answer with strained effort.

"Ellis."

"Honey, I never thought it was your dad that killed Olive. He was a real wimp except back when he drank, and he hadn't drunk in years. How many years had it been?"

"Thirteen years. I was nine. Lucy, do you know what Ellis was doing—where he was, and what he was doing during that time?"

"Word was that he'd just flunked out of college."

Shari remembered Mama saying, "Ellis is enrolling in this new school; maybe he'll make it this time." She had gone with Mama and Daddy to visit him in Little Rock while he had an apartment there and a part-time job and attended school at the university. But when they arrived, they learned that he'd left school, quit his job, and moved out of his apartment suddenly, without notice. He'd gone to another college after that, then on to another one. Yes, Ell was impetuous, impulsive, erratic, volatile, but... the truth was, she was running out of arguments.

She still remembered how she used to feel so sorry for her brother when Daddy spanked him. (Daddy never spanked the girls; he felt that was best left for Mama to do.)

He'd use his belt to spank Ell and it seemed like he never wanted to stop, and he hit him terribly hard. Ellis just jumped up and down on the bed, screaming and screaming and screaming. Shari would usually try to tell Daddy, "That's enough, Daddy, he won't do it again!" To her brother she would offer, "Don't cry, Ellis, don't cry."

But neither one ever heard her. That's why she never wanted to tell on him for anything she could tolerate. Even so, when he doubled his fists at her she would be scared, but not too scared to assure him that, "If you hit me, I'll tell Daddy."

As Lucy talked on, now Shari began to imagine a different scene—not of Cecil eating lunch and getting into an argument with Olive, but rather, of Mama's firstborn, her golden boy. Maybe they both argued with her. Maybe they... *no, no more pictures.* But if it were Ellis, where did the gun come from? She'd always assumed that it was Grandpa's and that Daddy had brought it to the house; maybe it was and Ellis found it. Maybe.

She suddenly remembered that Ellis had worked for a while in the State Police Narcotics Division, recruited by Harold C. Blevens! She wondered what kind of gun the "narcs" used back in 1964? And Harold C.'s statement to her in 1982 when they talked, had been, "No one was there when she died except Cecil, so we didn't question anyone." Those men sure knew how to throw her off. Those gun-totin' 'Brotherhood members' sure knew how to fool little girls, confused and grieving over their mother. Was that supposed to be macho? They meant for her to suspect Daddy, knowing she was scared and intimidated by him, and that kept her attention from wandering onto anyone else—very clever and very successful.

"Lucy, how many cars were in Daddy's drive when you arrived?"

"Well, there were two driveways, remember? Connie's car was in one so I drove into the other one."

"Did you park behind Daddy's car?"

"No, I didn't park behind anyone; just my car was there."

"Was Connie parked behind Daddy's car?"

"No, just hers was in the other driveway."

"Then where was Daddy's car?"

"What do you mean? Wouldn't he have left it up at his planer mill?"

"No, he said he drove up to Grandpa's and got Darren and they drove back to the house. Then you arrived, less than an hour later, and Connie was there in her car, talking to both of them. But what happened to Daddy's car meantime?"

"Interesting. Who knows?"

Shari remembered the "wet spot" upstairs that Robbie saw later that day. And Ellis moved to the new room, suddenly ceasing to use his room upstairs, which had been his pride for twenty-four years. Why? And the housecoat... and the intense heat... and the broken bathroom stove... and the metal file cabinet—Daddy had instructed Robbie to get the papers out of it after he died. But she found it already opened and empty. Ellis said Darren had opened it. Darren said, "Oh no, it was Ellis, and there was an insurance policy which Ellis cashed."

Suddenly her mind was racing. All the new evidence pointed to Ellis. It was so clear—so obvious. She said, "Lucy, my dad didn't kill Mama, did he?"

She shook her head. "I never thought he did. If he was gonna kill her, he'd have done it back in his drinking days. He was hateful to her, but he wasn't mean. He wasn't a monster."

"So it really was Ellis, wasn't it?"

She took a long deep breath, closed her eyes and said, "Well, it wasn't Olive and it wasn't Cecil, but that's all I'll say. I wasn't there when it happened, so I can't say for sure."

Shari could tell Lucy was tired, so she thanked her for her time and the nice visit. She wished her well and left, feeling certain that at last she knew the truth.

Oh the joy is full and the peace sublime
And the love of God so good,
And I surely know as I am known,
For through-it-all I endured.
My tongue hath not the words to say,
But my soul it crieth out

As the Comforter helps to convey...
There ne'er was cause to doubt.
Oh my Lord - You heard me in the night
When all other ears were deaf
And though I saw no peace in sight
You gave peace within myself.
You're the Mighty One - The Abounding King
You're Majesty o'er all
The Lord o'er All - The Prince of Peace
The Victor o'er my soul.

CHAPTER THIRTY-EIGHT

SHARI HAD ALWAYS SHARED a strong bond with her nephew Ken, so when they finally met again after a long time she welcomed the reunion. They visited at his naval base in northern California and then drove to visit with friends in an adjoining town, talking and laughing all the while. After catching up on both their lives, they decided to return home for a light dinner. Most people who knew Shari, know they're free to say anything they wish to her, just like she does with them. Ken also knew this, and the irritation was clear in his tone when he announced, "You question everything. Don't you think you carry it a bit too far? You can't talk without questions. Can't you stop being a psychologist for a while?"

She knew they were both tired, but she also knew that was an important issue with him, and it wasn't exactly the first time she'd faced it. As she listened to this fine, young man, at first the words stung in their familiarity. Then she felt a smile forming.

"I don't ask questions because I'm a psychologist, Ken. I became a psychologist because I have so many questions, so much I want to learn and understand. I think in questions."

"But you can't seem to just talk without asking a question. It gets on people's nerves."

For the first time she realized that the people who had rejected her along the way—her relatives and friends from home—had done so not exclusively because she sought to find out what happened to her mother but also because of her individual personality. That realization helped, for it actually was a relief to be rejected on her individual merits.

"Honey, my personality has never changed from the time I was very small. I used to wonder about many things, but I didn't dare ask my questions for several reasons. Now as an adult, I permit my questions. But I only learned to do that after separating myself from my hometown and relatives back there, where questions weren't acceptable. In going to school, going to therapy, and working as a therapist myself, my questions were not only permitted, but even welcomed and helpful. Now it's a way of life that I really enjoy. Besides, I get paid for it."

He laughed. "Do Aubrey and Cecelia question everything too?"

"All our lives together, we've questioned everything together. We discuss books, sermons, people, and events in terms of 'what purpose did that serve?' or 'what do you suppose he or she meant by what they said?' Some of our questioning was serious, and a lot of it was playful, but it was always conducive to our growth. How can it be bad when Jesus endorsed it? All the people I know and admire do likewise in order to learn and create, and it just makes life more interesting. I mean, what else do families talk about, if not questioning?"

"I kind of do see your point. Our family didn't, but then our family doesn't count. Let's see, what do normal families talk about?"

"Of course your family counts. You're each very special and precious people, but your family life was certainly dysfunctional. It's OK to use the words, 'I came from a dysfunctional home,' because it's true. You certainly did, and you know that's no putdown, coming from me."

He laughed again. "You mean you did too, huh?"

"Absolutely. I came from a dysfunctional home within a dysfunctional neighborhood in a dysfunctional town and a dysfunctional state. I'm seriously scrutinizing the country now."

"This is so wild. I mean, who'd believe all this? But I really do know what you mean. How do you suppose everything got so messed up, or where did it really start? Do you think our town is worse than other towns, or Arkansas is worse than other states? Hmm, now what do I mean by worse? See, I thought of that question before you did, didn't I?"

"Yes, you did. And do you see why you did? Just because you came from a place where it isn't the normal or popular thing to do doesn't make it impossible for you to do it. You can follow the norm and people won't get mad at you, or you can do whatever you need for your own learning and growing and understanding and peace of mind, and some people might get mad at you or make fun of you or—"

"But I'll still gain the learning and growing and understanding and peace of mind, right? Not exactly a bad tradeoff, I'd say."

"Well, you, young man, have just defined healing and the process of therapy itself. That's why I never felt I had a choice but to seek that. Yet now I can better understand why I was considered a nuisance to the others. And the strange thing is that it really does help. I can let them go easier now."

"Is it the same with my Mama and with Uncle Ellis? Letting them go?" Ken wondered.

"Sure. They both rejected me. But I couldn't understand why. Now it's clearer. We've turned out very differently, and they just don't like my difference and that's OK. I don't have a problem with that. You know, after all these years, we still made similar choices to those we made when we were little."

Ken sat there practically mesmerized; Shari suspected that they would never have that gulf of difference between them again. He was "open-receptive," as they say in psychology.

"When I was nine, we left Daddy and moved to Little Rock because of his drinking, you know. Well, I chose to go with Mama then, although Daddy asked me to stay with him. Ellis chose to not go with Mama, and Robbie was so little she didn't get a choice. When Mama was killed I chose to represent Mama, Ellis chose otherwise, and—"

"And this time she, my mother, had a choice."

"Right. I respect her right to choice. That's why when she telephoned me and told me she never wanted to see me again, I accepted it, although it tore my heart. I told her I hated to hear that, but if she felt that way, I would respect her wishes. I only urged her to remember what alcohol did to our family, and since she was a nurse not to let herself be fooled by it. Then I told her if she ever changed her mind, I'd welcome her back, because I'd always loved her and always would—as I remember Robbie. And that was over a decade ago and she's not beating on my door yet, so I guess she hasn't changed her mind."

"Seems such a pity. Like you all should be able to visit and all. I remember the visits we had together when I was little, and oh, I enjoyed them so much! I loved it when you all came, and I hated it when you left.

I pretended that Cecelia and Aubrey were my sister and brother, rather than cousins."

"They feel the same way. We all loved you from day-one of your life, and that's never changed. We always will love you. You're my third kid!"

"Shari, how much do you think Christianity plays here? I mean, isn't there more to it than just different personalities from the same family and town?"

"Very good question, my child! I figure Christianity is the big 'It' or accounts for about 200 percent of the difference. Some people think Christianity is a passive affiliation and that church is a nice place to go. But I think Jesus' teachings and His life's example prove that it's much, much, more than that. He stressed our need for truth, understanding, justice, humility, and—"

Ken chimed in. "I'm thankful that I know Him and I don't have any interest in redefining Him as passive. I like knowing that He is the big 'It' in my life, that He's very personal to me, and our relationship involves every word I say, everything I do, and every thought I have."

They hugged, and Shari felt her tears of gratitude for this nephew-kid of hers and for all the marvelous things God had done in their lives. They spent the next couple of days just touring all the sights of San Francisco—the little crooked streets, the revolving restaurant, the famed old military base. Then they relaxed at Fisherman's Wharf.

"I'm so proud of you, Ken. You've grown up to be such a fine young man, and yet your life has been extremely difficult. I'm just so proud of you."

"Well thank you, Ma'am," he said grinning. He put his hand on her shoulder and added, "Before you leave, we're going to get the best coffee you've ever tasted, and then we're going to talk one more time about that taboo subject... you know?"

"I can certainly be bribed with good coffee."

It was indeed good. Later when their visit was ending, Ken surprised her with an entire bag of coffee beans so that she could continue to enjoy his San Francisco coffee for a long time to come. As he settled himself in comfortably, as if for a long haul, he presented his concerns.

"I really do want to know all that you've learned about our family saga, Shari. I never met my grandmother, yet I want to know. The only reason I don't talk about it with Mama is that it's so horribly painful to her, I could never bring it up."

"The lack of truth is what caused her the pain. Your grandmother was a Christian, and we all die. It wasn't Mama dying but the way she died and the lack of truth, plus the blame being dumped onto Robbie, that's what caused your mother the pain."

"You know what? This is all for her."

"What's all for her?"

"Me and everybody else back there were thinking, 'Shari won't let it go; Shari has to keep digging. Why can't Shari go on with her life and let it go after these decades?' You know, that is a very long time, and besides, who ever heard of an exhumation after that long?" He leaned forward, nodding playfully.

"In archaeology, they do it all the time," Shari replied. "Even after much longer periods. And did you know that Abraham Lincoln exhumed his little boy twice while he was still president, just because he missed him so much?"

Ken shook his head as if amazed by both the archaeologists and President Lincoln. He went on, "But you have gone on with your life. You and Aubrey and Cecelia. You're all happy and healthy, you have fun, you have interesting careers. But more importantly, you're settled about your mother and your dad. I thought you were supposed to be obsessed or something. But you're not. You're doing this for her, for my mother."

"Good point, my child. Accurate observation. But it's also been for other reasons as well—such as myself, my children, for my mother's good name, and just for general principles. Heck, it just needed to be done by somebody and who else was investigating?"

She couldn't stop yet. "But you've also hit on three other points: First, another good example of how some people distort truth to their own liking. The relatives you're talking about like to diagnose me as crazy, obsessed, etcetera, yet I'm the one who went ten years to college and earned the license and credentials to diagnose! What they're doing is simple projection and denial; they know better, but they can confirm each other and feel convinced they're right. If they see they have the power to convince others, then they're certain they're right!

"As for Robbie, you may be correct. I've always felt I owed it to her to show her that Mama's death had nothing to do with her. Maybe it's the last of the big-sister feelings or surrogate-mother role, I don't know. But I thought, and still do think, that it was the cruelest deed in the world to dump that on Robbie, and maybe I felt Mama would want Robbie to know the truth. Sometimes I felt I just started and never knew how to stop, or felt that to stop in midstream was senseless when I almost had it. I never dreamed it would take so long. But it's been well worth it. Mama and Robbie are worth it."

"And point three?"

"You said you just wanted to know, even though you never met your grandmother. You want to know. That's only natural. The unnatural part was that Ellis never wanted to know, and she was his own mother. The only reason he wouldn't have desperately wanted to know what happened, the way Robbie and I wanted to know, was because he already did know! And he had a vested interest in obscuring from us what he knew!"

"That is strange," Ken commented. "I never thought of it like that. Hmm. Well, you can ask all the questions you want. Now I understand it and you better. Now it's like, Why not?"

Aunt and nephew hugged each other warmly. "Shari," he went on, determined to use their next few hours to wrap up the loose ends. "Do you think you would have liked them, considering you have only one brother and sister, if your circumstances had been different?"

"Well, I always liked Robbie. As for Ellis, I was close to him when we were little, but after that I never felt like I knew him much, so I've never missed him much."

"When did you stop speaking to him?"

"Oh, I didn't. He stopped speaking to me. Remember, he was the one that told me Mama killed herself because of Robbie, and I argued with him about that. Then he got mad and let me out on the curb in front of the mortuary early in the morning, before dawn. We never had a conversation after that, actually. We just passed each other in the rooms of the house the next few weeks. After I'd gone on back to Kentucky, he got married. I'd never met her. Then later when I lived in Little Rock and taught school, as did he, he ignored me in public, like at basketball games when my school played his. I took the kids to visit him a few times, like when he and his wife had a new baby, but he'd just yell at my kids and talk hateful."

She reflected for a moment, then continued. "In 1977, I was living in California and telephoned Uncle Darren and blurted out over the phone, 'Darren, I know Daddy killed Mama. I know he did!' It took a lot of courage for me to make that phone call, even after all those years. To say the words to Daddy's brother was a big step for me."

"And he said " Ken prodded, waving his hand for her to hurry.

"He said, 'Yes, Shari he was down there, but not by himself. He wasn't alone. He didn't do it by himself.' I was so shocked that I didn't think about the rest of what he said. I just hurriedly called up Robbie and Ellis to tell them what Darren said. I just knew we three would now talk about it together for the first time ever and get it all straightened out.'"

"What did Ellis say when you called him?"

"He said, 'I'll have to think about this. I'll call you back.' But he never called me back. He's never telephoned me once in thirty years. But later that year our classes had a reunion, so I flew back there to attend. He and Stan were the emcees, and both of them ignored me all evening. So when it ended, I patted Ellis on the arm and told him, 'We're staying up at Robbie's, can you come up there to visit? Stan stepped up and answered, 'Sure, we'll all come.' And the four of them did, they and their wives. Stan brought his banjo, played a few songs, told a few jokes, and they all four left together."

"And you three kids still never talked at all?"

"Nope. That was the last I saw of him. You know, except for that call to him and the night he drove me to the morgue, we've never discussed our mother once?"

"And he was the one that told you it was suicide, wasn't he?"

"Yes, he and Aunt Pearl together told me just cut and dried, 'She shot herself.' And as Ellis drove me to the morgue, he told me it was all because of your folks getting married and pregnant."

"I wonder how he knew that?"

"How he knew what?" Shari asked her nephew.

"Ellis said your mother killed herself over my mom and dad getting married, but how was he supposed to know all that? I mean, my mom and her friend had left for school that morning, and your mother was fine, and didn't you say she had cooked lunch as usual and even written out her grocery list? So if she's doing her normal routine until noon and she's found dead an hour later, when did Ellis learn all this information? Unless she left a suicide note explaining that, how's he supposed to know that? Was he supposedly there and she told him this, then killed herself?"

Shari hugged him jubilantly. He really looked at her strangely now, tilting his head to one side, in an awed stance. "What is going on with you?"

"Your question, child, your question! It's a darn good question! Just how was he supposed to know this?" Then she realized it was a story that only a man could contrive, any mother knew better. "I shocked my mom when I got married by marrying the worst person ever and dropping it on her over the telephone, two thousand miles away. Yet she recovered nicely. Mama adored your dad and wanted them to get married, so that was clearly a concocted story. But you see, Ellis was, I truly believe, the last person to see her alive."

She shared with Ken about her recent visit with Lucy, and how others had noticed that Ellis' plate was eaten out of. They talked about the disappearance of Daddy's car right after he parked it from going after Darren, and they talked about the "wet spot" upstairs that Robbie herself had looked at only hours after Mama died.

"You know, Ken, one other thing I wondered but never consciously questioned. And that was why your folks stayed upstairs at our house later, rather than in Mama's new room? Mama had designed it to be like a little studio apartment. It had a couch, TV, tables, all the amenities of a lovely parlor. But on one side of the room, there was also a pretty bed, and Mama had picked luscious, decorative rose brown. I told her it looked like chocolate. She had said, 'With a closet and a bathroom, it's like a little private quarters.' It was perfect for a young married couple to start out in, and if Mama had lived, Chuck and Robbie would have definitely been given that pretty room. God, how I wish they would have had that chance! But instead, they slept upstairs, in that old, dusty attic."

"Do you know why they did? Why didn't they use the new room?"

"I never asked. But I would bet you money that was a decision that Ellis made for them. Because Ellis took the new room as his room after Mama died. I stayed there for three weeks after the funeral, and although my kids and I had always stayed in the new room during our visits, this time, Ellis had the new room. I slept in Mama's bed instead, with the kids.

Ellis always had taken whatever he wanted, and it wasn't questioned, so I didn't question that either. I just thought it strange, but he used to lick the top of the biscuits in the pan at breakfast, so he'd get all of them, and that worked too. Ellis had loved his upstairs for twenty four years. Yet that week, he arbitrarily decided to take the new room and did, putting me in Mama's room and Robbie and Chuck upstairs in his own room with the 'wet spot' on the floor."

"What do you think caused the wet spot on the floor upstairs?"

"Well, considering that Roberta was informed the wet spot downstairs was where they washed up the blood, then I would tend to expect a similar explanation for the one upstairs, such as where they piled the bloody clothes and rags, maybe towels and sheets, until they could dispose of them."

"Yeah, really. No wonder he never wanted to room up there again."

"By the way," Shari suddenly remembered, "do you happen to know what Robbie did with that empty casing? Ellis was so angry at her the day of Mama's funeral because she had found it, and he was yelling at her through the new room's bathroom door to give it to him. I told her to keep it if she wanted to. Now I understand better why he wanted it."

"You know what, when I'm with her next visit, I'll ask her where it is," Ken replied.

"Even though she'd rather you not bring up the subject?"

"Sometimes maybe we need to allow some pain in order to really end the pain, the right way. I think she can handle thinking about it for a worthwhile reason."

"The truth that sets us free, pretty worthwhile, huh?"

"For sure. For sure."

Somehow, as they closed that chapter of their lives in San Francisco, they knew they had entered a healthier chapter of life, and Shari was very thankful. It had been a heartwarming visit, and now her eyes weighed heavily against the lids, welcoming sleep. Just as she was about to surrender to the peaceful oblivion, her eyes suddenly popped wide open again.

She was observing, in retrospect, an event from months prior, which was now vivid with particular meaning. She was remembering her last class reunion. As word had drifted to her through numerous sources that her brother was discrediting her by announcing that she was deranged somewhere out in California, she was bewildered, disheartened, and finally disgusted. After a while, she decided to combat his words the best way she knew how, remembering fondly Einstein's words:

"Arrows of hate have been shot at me, but they cannot touch me for they come from a world of which I have no part." She learned that Ellis' and her graduating classes would be holding another reunion soon, as in 1977, and she decided to attend, unannounced. Cecelia agreed to accompany her, primarily hoping to meet her Uncle Ellis.

The two flew in from separate coasts, meeting in Little Rock for the small, hometown gathering to be held in Clinton. The plans included an all-day picnic, an evening banquet, and morning church services the next day, giving all the class members ample time to visit. Shari and her daughter arrived late morning, and the crowd already was large. She could hardly believe her eyes! There were all her old buddies, who were now a bit gray and wrinkled but otherwise the very same.

As they walked toward the pavilion, Cecelia asked her mother, "I wonder if Ellis has arrived yet? Even though he hung up on me a while back, I'd really like to meet him in person."

No sooner had she spoken than Shari spotted him across the way. She hurriedly said, "There he is in the green shirt and cap." Cecelia saw him also.

It seemingly took forever to make their way the few yards to the pavilion food bar, hugging necks and screeching, laughing, and crying over names and recounts of old events from their teen years. By then, however, the green shirt and cap had simply disappeared. Assuming he'd be back, Shari continued visiting until the day ended and people were exiting the picnic to prepare for the evening banquet. She thought, *We'll see Ellis at the banquet.*

Cecelia was disappointed too, but I reassured her he'd be at the banquet, probably master of ceremonies as he was at the reunion in 1977. The banquet was enthralling with so many old familiar and very loved faces in one big room—even Shari's sixth- grade teacher was there! But no Ellis.

After the banquet ended, mother and daughter noticed a small restaurant they'd never visited before and decided to end their evening there with a cup of coffee. Inside, a young lady approached her and asked, "Are you Shari?"

She proceeded to tell them that she'd spent the night at Olive's home that last night, which had been the night of Robbie's birthday. Shari vaguely remembered hearing about that, many years ago, but well remembered this person as her sister's close school friend.

She asked, "How was everything?"

"Oh your mother was a lovely person. I remember she cooked my breakfast and sat with me as I ate. We discussed something from the county paper the previous day, and we laughed about it."

"Did anyone ever contact you, like an investigator?"

"No, no one did. But then I was young, sixteen or seventeen." She was not only her sister's friend, she was also her mother's friend, and now Shari's.

She wondered whether her brother Ellis would be at the reunion church service in the morning. How could he stand to miss such a wonderful opportunity as seeing all these friends, many of them former classmates? But then, how could he leave without speaking to her, his former sister, and to her beautiful daughter, his only niece who wanted to meet him and had just told him that on the phone a few weeks earlier?

But as it turned out these sixteen years later, her only brother ignored her again. A familiar replay of the 1977 event, minus Uncle Stan. At the conclusion of the morning service, as many people were exchanging goodbyes, several individuals approached Shari, asking about her brother. She made absolutely no association at the time, being curious as were they, as to why Ellis would miss their grand meeting. Still she was pleased to have attended, after being informed that he was reporting her 'deranged in California.'

She thought of Ken's earlier question, "How would Ellis know?" and smiled inwardly at the question. Considering Ell never telephoned or visited or wrote to her once after they moved to California two decades ago (or invited her to visit him), how would he know about her in California? As with Mama's death, he just "speaks the words," needing no basis in truth whatsoever. A few people seemed to be testing her as to whether or not she was, in fact, deranged, to which she felt great amusement. Naturally she was analyzing them reciprocally (with the credentials to do so). But others questioned in a different way, and she answered spontaneously and unguardedly. She was surprised that some people wanted to know about Ellis' first marriage, but she answered their questions. To some, she responded that she simply didn't know him, as he was a bully at home growing up and Mr. Wonderful in public, and she never understood that, except to know that she didn't know him.

By the end of the day, her eyes grew heavy again, for they had served well in "seeing more than that which meets the eye." As sleep overtook her, the feeling was strong that she was getting to know Ellis better all the time, even after all these years, and from a remarkable distance. He didn't want to face them that day, Cecelia and her, nor did he wish to face the lies he'd spoken to their mutual friends. But now she understood the whys of the lies and his need to discredit her in advance of whatever she might be about to discover and reveal in the near future. So easy to wreck a person's character when that's the motive. Suicide—only one word was needed for Mama, because she couldn't speak in her own behalf. Shari could, however.

All those negative statements dispersed in her absence would, assumedly, serve as well, if left to Ellis, except that she attended the gathering and with her delightful daughter. So glad, yet so sorry that it was necessary for such a cause. But it was good to see old friends. The irony was that she wished only to dispel Ellis' efforts in that particular task—not knowing why he would exert such an effort in the first place. She thought smear tactics served politicians, but why a brother would indulge in them against a sister was incomprehensible. However, since she couldn't very well discuss it with him, she knew her presence there was needed.

But as she and Cecelia were about to depart for home after the Sunday morning church service, one of her former classmates approached her. Shari had noticed him nearby, edging his way about and seemingly listening to her conversations with those who inquired about her family.

"Shari, these things you've been discovering, we've known all these years," he said, matter-of-factly.

"You have?"

"Yes, we've always known. But now that you know too, what will you do about it?"

"Well, I'm not sure yet."

"Shari, you need to go on with your life. Just leave these things alone— what you've been finding out. Just leave it alone and go on with your life."

She thanked him for his concern and commented on what a nice event the gathering had been and how good it was to have seen him. "Your folks, too," she said, nodding in their direction.

As she walked away, she thought, *Just what qualifies him to ask me to forget my mother?* Ironically, his inferences about what she had just found out were simply premature, for at that time, she had not yet discovered what he assumed she had, but in short order, she would. Nevertheless, why did he assume it was his place to advise her anyway? And why was that same advice, thirty years later, still being meted out to her now, by the next generation? Is this the prevailing condition of their country, as it was in 1964? Had nothing changed? This was too much for her to try to absorb and assimilate all at once. That night as she let herself drift off to sleep, she welcomed the truly wonderful refuge from a turbulent family saga.

One question yet, I wonder still, Lord, how You loved and why
And came into this world so cruel, in agony to die?
"For God so loved the world," You say
and within the world was me,
That you sent your only precious Son, to redeem
at Calvary Help me love Thee Lord,
with all my heart, soul, strength, and mind
For Thy goodness merits all my love, if my soul
Thou grace wilt find

CHAPTER THIRTY-NINE

PEOPLE START MAKING CHOICES as to their existential purpose in life when they're very young. A question often asked in a psychosocial or psychiatric intake interview is, "What is your earliest memory?" For many people, that is when the "self" begins. Whatever base is established early on is, for the most part, maintained throughout life. Some people experience and perceive themselves as being inferior, or as being victims, while others feel superior in some ways. Some like the role models they're given and gladly develop similarly. Others, lacking healthy role models, live in resultant pity or anger. Others choose to add new ones or to change role models altogether; they have to seek out the new ones to follow. Some separate-individuate from early experiences and choose their own identity, a new way to travel that leaves the familiar far behind. They carry some memories and some loves with them, but they sense that they no longer "belong back there," where they originated.

Shari remembered her uncle's philosophy of long ago: "We all read numerous books in life, some comedy, some mystery, some romance, some horror. Life compels us to read some of these, but eventually we choose those we indulge in. So whether we see life as a journey or as a great library, we need to respectfully consider our relationship to life. We're responsible for what we contribute during our stay here, and we're responsible for whatever we become."

Sometimes even Shari wondered why her book had to be written. Writing was her early therapeutic outlet, and her inspired poems provided the much-needed diversion. She chose Christianity even before she fully comprehended it. She knew she could trust God, while it was unclear which people could be trusted. God's words and Jesus' life made sense, while her neighbors' and relatives' values didn't. She loved her parents, but they, too, were recognizably limited by the Southern-redneck mentality—the thinking that seems to grip so many who live there. So she chose other parents, friends, heroes, and role models to learn and model from. As far back as her memory goes, understanding seemed crucial. Who can say whether a child prays for what she needs or for what she wants? Shari knew only that her prayer was answered, accompanied by peace, acceptance, forgiveness, and fond, fond memories.

In some ways she's merely lived a story. She often wished the story would end with a happy ending, but it had to be completed in order to be told. And it had to be told, as it could not be silenced. Perhaps thousands of people are silently living such stories, lost in the conspiracy of silence, and with society's habit of "victim blaming" they never become liberated from their stories to really live. As Dr. Viktor Frankl discovered, one must complete his personal saga and find the meanings thereof to be existentially, quintessentially, authentically, and autonomously himself.

Some of her former friends remain encapsulated within their own stories, and their friendships dissolved. Those who remain are dear and trusted, for they've risen beyond stories, both others' and their own. They're incapable of pettiness, gossip, or being judgmental. Instead, they're the salt of the earth and never, ever discourage authenticity in another with the stale, moot, self-serving phrase, "Let it go and put it behind you, and go on with your life."

As she stopped by a bank in Clinton, a man who'd known her warmly shook her hand in greeting and asked, "Shari, have you come home?" Both of them knew that she'd returned to her hometown periodically for decades, yet his question was not amiss. For she had in fact, come back as her mother had stated in the poem she wrote so many decades ago. Shari and her friend at the bank both knew that she had come back from the confines of her very perplexing storybook to complete it.

When she was a teenager, a very popular song was *I Can't Stop Loving You.* Though it was a romantic song, now it took on a more global meaning for Shari, for she can't stop loving those whom she loved back through the story, nor would she wish to. The childhood memories, both wonderful and tragic, are now just respectfully filed away. Her family members, living and dead, will remain special to her, and she wishes them well. The town and its familiarity will never fade entirely, for all those components created, in her subjective opinion, an Oscar-level performance that remains unsurpassed. Yet even after such a premier is shown on the screen, when the lights come on, the tears are wiped away, the illusion dissipates, and the audience files outdoors into the light of reality.

She doesn't wish to reside in the theater or to eulogize an illusion. The stage, the props, the directors, actors and observers have served their purpose, and now the act is over. It's time to go home.

As her banker-friend warmly greeted her, "Have you come home?" Yes. For home is what she shares with her real and true friends wherever they may be. Home is where the heart is indeed, for in Him we all live and move and have our very being.

Years ago, when asked who her favorite television characters were, without hesitation Shari named The Fugitive, The Hulk, and the lead character in the Kung Fu series. In that they were all Davids, she found her favorite name, for David was also her favorite Bible hero as well. He did a lot of wrong things, yet his heart was good. He truly loved God, and God had a special love for him. When he discovered the error of his ways, he repented with a vengeance. God's special love for David shows us that it isn't our errors that matter the most but that we learn to repent from them and to seek Him.

As Shari found herself losing her home ties, she found ties forming with other groups, groups she's pleased to be a part of, and groups in which she's welcomed and feels she "fits." She's happy if her sister and brother have done likewise. She doesn't feel a grudge toward anyone, because with the writing and telling of her story came the forgiveness necessary for healing. Jesus said, "I am the Light. I am the Truth. The truth will set you free." He gave her the truth that she needed, and she hopes others will seek truth in Him also.

Yet she recalled how she and her dad had such a difficult time understanding the simplicity that comprises Christianity, Jesus Christ, the Savior of the World and the Pardoner of Sin. Yet He cannot pardon until we humble ourselves and ask for it with heartfelt repentance. So many churches assume that everyone knows that. But Shari didn't understand it until that preacher in Tennessee said, "Believe."

She doesn't know what decisions her dad made in his last moments, but she hopes he, too, had given his heart to God through Jesus Christ. His dying moments were difficult, hopefully not indicative of belief and commitment to the illusionary god of secretive power clubs, to vending machine prayers, to an impersonal creator. Perhaps his trip to Robbie's home with the message to her that, "I've put some papers in my metal file cabinet for you to read after I'm dead," was his attempt to confess, repent, and even reveal the truth—to set Robbie free of the horrendously burdensome lie he helped impose on her years earlier. (He never anticipated that someone would intercept his attempt, and Robbie would neither see the papers intended for her, nor learn their contents). So maybe, just maybe, he may have tried to tell this story, in his own way, and bring justice to the scene at last. And maybe, he also repented.

These are our needs as people, for truth, repentance, mercy, justice, and finally forgiveness. Shari can forgive the person who took her mother from all who loved her and needed her. She could have forgiven earlier had she known the truth earlier. She can forgive only because she is forgiven by Jesus Christ of sins far worse than murder. What is much harder to forgive, however, is the evil that demanded silence through deception and intimidation for so very, very long. For personal redemption we must repent and confess. A real Christian or friend can only encourage another to seek this course, certainly not to live an insidious, debilitating lie. This is a blatant contradiction of both friendship and Christianity. For that secretive darkness, the ultimate betrayal, slowly destroys the soul of man.

As children, we instinctively try to conceal our error, and thus, avoid detection and punishment. But as adults, we need to mature from that childlike level of decision to a responsible level. Perhaps her brother continued too long, trusting and following those role models he followed in his youth. As Paul once noted in his New Testament writings, "When I was a child I thought as a child but when I became a man, I put away childish things." We must be very careful of whom we trust ultimately, for our very soul is at stake.

Shari feels no animosity toward her mother's actual murderer, because their childhood home had become a setting for someone to murder and someone to be murdered. Her mother first prepared her for that when she was ten years old. In a way the routine of three children running in terror and hiding in the weeds while their mother was beaten became the stage that fostered a sociopath. But, while their ignorance about alcoholism and autism contributed to the family dysfunction, they were not a family lacking in love. Their love and respect for each other, despite their differences, transcended the obstacles they shared. A childlike, nonjudgmental innocence surrounded each of them, her parents, siblings and herself; paralleling their frustration, and leaving them all vulnerable to the evil, calculated others who took control of them, of their home, their family, their tragedy.

But because of love, it had to transpire, and because of love, it had to be survived, understood and transcended. Because of love it had to be told and now because of love, it is finished. "To everything there is a season and a time to every purpose under the heaven. A time to keep silent, and a time to speak."

Ironically, the same people who ordered her so frequently to "Put it behind you and go on with your life," are the very people responsible for propelling this work on to completion.

Arkansas law states, "The greatest drive in the human being is the drive to survive." Survival includes the mental, emotional, spiritual, and physical. One cannot "go on with her life" until she has found the answers, restored the dignity, permitted the grief process, and found truthful, restorative healing for the pain. It took thirty years to do this against the efforts of those who could have and should have been helpful in facilitating the process, but thanks to their inadvertent and unintended encouragement, the puzzle was finally completed.

The significant factor that the controllers ignored was that Olive Lewis was a good, fine person, and many loved her. Such quality and love can never be totally silenced, because the time comes, eventually, when the secrets are brought to light. For the time comes to speak the truth, the whole truth and nothing but the truth. Whether this can occur within the legal system depends on those in charge of the legal system.

In summary, after all the dehumanizing treatment, ultimate insult-to-injury-occurred, when Olive was accused of killing herself! Because in order to support such an absurdity, she had to be re-characterized and redefined as:

a) mentally ill, such as psychotic or suffering from multiple personalities, OR
b) emotionally fragile, impulsive and hysterical, OR
c) a violence-prone individual, OR
d) conniving and sadistic, particularly toward her children, to plan such a Christmas, OR
e) all of the above... VICTIM becomes VILLAIN, redefined as different, inferior, within her skin.

Mental diagnoses are made ONLY by skilled clinicians such as psychiatrists, psychologists, social workers, psychiatric nurses, with a minimum of master level education, training and specialized licenses. Additionally, these diagnoses are made over a lengthy period of time, with ample supportive documentation and meted out to only "living, breathing patients."

This lady, Olive Lewis, was initially diagnosed as she lay dead, in her own living room, by uneducated, untrained, unlicensed townsmen, with one common purpose: concealing the truth. The fact that various men were gathered in her mother's living room, doing these things, violating this decent lady's privacy, her body, her life, her reputation and eventually her roles of mother and grandmother—her entire essence   is not a minor part of the despicable acts done to her.

Olive Lewis, fifty years old, was a lady of exceptionally fine character, having endured trials many people never even imagine. The violence done to her 'character' with cooperative deception was equally gruesome as the violence done to her body. The word suicide, combined with moral 'implications,' were used to transfer guilt and blame from these calloused men onto the victim's own seventeen-year-old daughter, at her birthday, during Christmastime, just prior to her high school graduation, in the excitement of her new marriage and at the point in her life when she was the happiest and totally deserving of happiness! And because she was in grief, young and innocent, it worked. The contemptible epitome of Male Cowardice.

Little wonder it cost Roberta her first child...

Yet, all who participated in this vicious exploitation, including officials, would continue on with their lives, without repercussions, while those who loved their mother would suffer all the repercussions. Additionally, these participants would even instruct her to, "Leave it alone, ask no questions, go on with your life." (Obviously, for the officials' sake, having committed a hideous crime.) Shari was instructed to 'protect them' with her silence.

Finally, it is astounding that the System of Justice can be so easily manipulated by a few individuals, that even with volumes of proof, it is still so difficult to expose them.

It has been suggested that the men who initially made the decisions which escalated into these inhumane acts may have moved swiftly, without a real 'plan' other than to hide the truth in what at first seemed like a fairly simple task. But they were dualistic thinkers, limited to choosing one of two possibilities, in this case, between Homicide and Suicide. In the intent to hide a homicide, it seemed they felt it necessary to call it suicide instead (which is dualistic, as in 'either-or,' 'up-down,' or 'in-out').

There were just too many excruciating insults. Had Shari and her sister been lied to, but in a way that did not violate their mother's dignity and their own loving relationships with her, they could easily have been fooled. Had they been told that a stranger came in to burglarize, shot her and ran off, they would have believed it. Had they been told she fell off the back steps, had a heart attack, an insulin reaction, or a number of other things, they would have accepted it, grieved together with each other and their friends and nurtured their wonderful memories.

But what they did to that fine lady and inextricably to her daughters was of such dehumanizing proportion that only the Truth could possibly heal. Only the truth, the whole truth and nothing but the truth. Those who were violated are not the only ones in need of healing, however. Shari's mother is in heaven. She and her sister have yet to reunite. Her mother's friends finally were able to give their testimonies for her. But those who are responsible are in greater need of healing.

Years ago, after her Christian relationship began, Shari was so happy that she wrote letters back to some people in her hometown to tell them about it and shared her poems about the event with them. She was stunned at their response.

"How can you dare say you just became a Christian? Why you were already a Christian—you were active in church all those years through school!"

They equated regular church attendance synonymously with 'being a Christian.' Yet in those early years she had missed the essence of Christianity. She loved church, God, hymns and the Bible but she didn't know about Jesus. She thought He was only God's son and a nice person... perhaps many others also lack that same significance.

It's inconceivable that anyone who has that personal relationship with Jesus (Who described Himself as The Truth) could possibly participate in the deception and indignities done to her mother, her sister, and her.

She used to wonder why He said from the cross before He died, "Father, forgive them, for they know not what they do." She thought, *They knew they were crucifying Him*! But did they lack the depth of understanding of the actual evil they were doing?

Those who discover Jesus first as Redeemer, Who gave up His life, shed His innocent blood for their sins to redeem them and make them worthy by Grace, to be His personal friends forever, those who form a personal relationship with Him and find Him to always be a help in some way in every situation, those become the Christians.

In 'skipping' this portion of one's development, one is inevitably limited in his maturation process. In failing to commit oneself to his Savior, he will eventually commit himself to something else. Without a commitment to Truth, one can easily be led to join forces with others in acts of deception, or become the blind led by the blind.

In society today, there is a high interest in violence, and a low interest in tenderness. There is a high interest in 'victim-blaming,' and a low interest in moral development.

The solution would be: A low interest in violence and a high interest in tenderness. A low interest in victim-blaming and a high interest in moral development.

Why does one individual choose to behave violently while another does not? And why does that same individual feel compelled to act violently on one occasion and not on another occasion? And why do some adults succumb to peer pressure?

Lawrence Kohlberg explains how people function at different levels of moral development, not to be confused with moral behavior. They differ in the reasons behind the choices of their action, in certain situations. These reasons are always related to the level of maturity from which the individual is functioning (or in some cases, the group or community).

The levels of maturity of functioning are as such:

Pre-conventional level of development is called "fixated," for this is the appropriate functioning level of adolescents ten to thirteen years old. Here, the individual feels small, weak and dependent on others for receiving pleasure or pain. In an authority relationship, he feels himself inferior and he relates on a reactionary level to his environment and to people. He is unable to empathize with others at this level. His primary reason for choosing behaviors is his own personal pleasure or pain; his primary reason for abstaining from pleasures is the threat of punitive consequences greater than the amount of pleasure expected (punishment vs. reward).

Conventional level is next, and he may or may not evolve into this level of moral development or mature beyond the pre-conventional level. At the conventional level, there is a preference for involvement with others, a growing sense of self-respect and a general concern for the social order.

Post-conventional level would be next, of which a serious empathy for others exists, a more global concern for humanity, a respect for laws, justice and ethics in general.

Principled-level is that level at which wisdom rules the individual's thoughts, decisions and actions. This level is basically devoid of immediate gratification, selfish interests and disregard for others' rights.

Most criminals are fixated in the pre-conventional level. Many criminals never go to jail.

CHAPTER FORTY

SHARI THOUGHT OF HER dad who needed a friend so badly that he found solace in alcohol. Everyone who drinks alcohol is not alcoholic. But those who develop a relationship with alcohol, who find alcohol to be a trusted friend who can be counted on to always 'help' in some way, those become the alcoholics. He was unable to be social with people; he was unable to effectively communicate his thoughts, feelings and needs. But he had them. Her mother had been the one person who loved, respected and assisted him by helping him through the years, maintaining his simple routine, which gave him a sense of calm. But she did not understand autism nor did she understand alcoholism. Thus, they both did the best they could with these unnamed conditions. These diagnoses would be helpful for future generations.

The condition of Post Traumatic Stress Disorder has become known in recent years and recognized to have permanent, haunting and disabling effects on its victims who receive no intervention. But the extreme condition of PTSD is that which involves trust, self-identity and enmeshment of family members. A distinct set of symptoms emerge which merits our attention, for in our society today, these victims are increasing and need to be recognized. This condition is Survivor's Syndrome. It was first noted among the Holocaust victims upon liberation, who had lived in a 'reversed world,' devoid of basic civilization. Their Existential Foundation had been lost and their lives were hopelessly identified with both real and symbolic death.

These symptoms can be recognized, understood, respected and transcended. It behooves all of us to be aware, because it may one day be a loved one or oneself, who becomes a victim of Survivor's Syndrome.

SURVIVOR SYNDROME: Definition of Symptoms

TRAUMA: The psychic reality of the individual involved in it; it is brought about by the overwhelming of the stimulus barrier and the resulting dynamic disarrangement, rather than by any external situation. Trauma occurs inside the individual. Trauma is not an event.

DEATH-IN-LIFE: An immediate reaction to trauma, characterized by a ghastly stillness and a sense of slow motion.

AFFECT LAMENESS: Suppression of all affect with other common patterns being: somatization, loss of ability to enjoy life.

EMOTIONAL ANESTHESIA: A minimum of object cathexis whereas seemingly a wall is erected between the patient and others.

DEATH-TAINT: A hostility generated toward the survivor and which he feels himself to carry: "psychological contagion."

PSYCHIC CLOSING OFF: Mental paralysis, i.e., "If I feel nothing, then death is not taking place."

COLLAPSE of the PERSONALITY: A state in which the individual has lost his ability to trust in others, or to display any initiative.

UNDER-LIVING: The incapacity to enjoy life or seek (or accept) happiness.

SURVIVOR HUBRIS: The need of the survivor for a constant experience of surviving.

NON-BEING: Loss of identity.

PSYCHOTIC CULTURE: An environment in which regression and deforming of the ego are the only reality-oriented adaptations available to the people living in such an environment.

INAPPROPRIATE DEATH: When the loved one was not killed right off, but had a lingering death, the survivor develops the notion that it was actually indecent; an ambivalent situation develops in which he identifies with the victim, yet has such horror of the circumstances, that he rejects the victim, with subsequent tremendous guilt.

SURVIVOR GUILT: Pathological mourning in which the survivor is stuck in a magnification of the guilt which is present in every bereaved person. The repressed aggression toward the lost object prevents the completion of the work of mourning.

PSYCHOTIC NIGHTS: The sudden, frightful awakening in the night, to a haunting, taunting melee of murderous introjects, in which it seems that rage is about to consume the survivor.

HAUNTING: (noun): The persecutor introject.

SURVIVOR SYNDROME: The condition in which the individual is left in a state of mourning, not only for the dead, but also for his former self, who existed prior to this infringement of an overwhelming nature— this death imagery upon the self. Thus, he is bound to the dead and bound to his grief.

PERSONLICHKEITSWANDEL: The lasting change of the total personality in all its relations to the world 'within' (to one's own self) as well as to the world 'without' (society, interpersonal relationships, etc.) having fully incorporated and accepted the reality of the trauma.

Picture and caption here.

Would her own mother be forgiving toward those who violated her and put her family through so much pain? Shari believes she would if it resulted in others entering the kingdom of God in Truth. If it opened the eyes of exaggerated blindness and softened the hearts of people who lied easily, she would forgive. If the pain would eventually propel her daughter and granddaughter to learn about autism so that Cecil's autistic great-grandson, Mark, would benefit, if it were the only way her own children would come to understand, believe and accept Jesus as their personal friend and savior, she would welcome the violations.

CHAPTER FORTY-ONE

SHARI VISITED A SCHOOLMATE OF long ago who pointed out to her that actually, all her efforts had been futile because, "God simply doesn't need us to effect truth or justice. He is fully able to do that Himself, and He very well may. One of those men (perpetrators) may become spiritually convicted and give a deathbed confession. It happens sometimes."

She knew her friend was right, for she knew of such things happening. Yet she left there wondering why we have policemen and detectives at all? Why do we ever need lawyers, doctors and teachers? She wondered sadly whether Martin Luther King, Jr. had died in vain and Mother Teresa and Billy Graham had wasted their lives, for certainly God could comfort suffering without human hands and evoke salvation without human evangelists. Paul, on the road to Damascus, was a vivid example of that. And conviction could have corrected racial inequities as well. Then too, Jesus fed the thousands, so, why do we even need grocery stores?

Ideally, we would have responsible leaders who have such a high regard for integrity that justice would always prevail, that lies and cover-ups would not occur. That, when a person for unknown reasons does the unthinkable deed of murder, officials would be swift to do their jobs. They would wish to administer justice to the murdered victim, her family and the person who killed her, so that the living could go on with the work of healing in a normal and dignified manner. And the guilty party could face his deed, openly, receive the help he needs, and mature from that point, rather than spending a lifetime maintaining his facade.

Where have these leaders gone, those wise, principled leaders so desperately needed by the ordinary people living ordinary lives? What have become their 'higher priorities,' replacing the priorities their jobs dictate, for which they took an oath to uphold and for which they receive their financial income and retirement benefits? What drummer are they marching to?

Shari thought of the Serenity Prayer—desiring the 'serenity to accept the things I cannot change, the courage to change the things I can and the wisdom to know the difference.' Then she recalled the visit with her schoolmate. She was right, in that God doesn't need people in order to bring about justice, but He does require something on their part. God could have simply changed the hearts of the Egyptians and never used Moses at all. That would, however, have placed God in the position of the mighty dictator, which would defeat His purpose of giving them a free will. He could have destroyed Satan in the Garden of Eden, thereby never needing to involve Mary, Joseph or Jesus. God uses people who are willing to be used, not because He needs their help, but because we need to be useful at some point in each of our lives, for a higher purpose. We need to expand our involvement in life to include more than just a routine existence. No matter what our position in life, we need to extend beyond ourselves. We need to try to right some wrong or heal some wound or comfort some hurting person. This is the "action" of our relationship with God. To do less leaves one open to apathy and lawlessness.

Shari's lengthy quest has been a journey of learning and healing... her 'reachable' star. Could she have been doing something more worthwhile with her time? She thinks not! She is happy to have made the truth of her mother's murder better known. She's less naïve now, having become far better acquainted with the people she once thought she knew but didn't really know and has no further desire to know. She has come to know well the quality of people she respects. Her children and her grandchildren have benefited. Clients of all walks of life have benefited, simultaneously.

It was extremely gratifying to find other friends, loved ones and mourners of her mother, and experience the warm bond with them, even after so long. These dear old ladies were not a part of the cover-up, they were simply women who loved Olive but were as powerless against the men in their town as she was against the policeman's gun. Women are not taken seriously in our society, nor is their pain. Unless they are represented by a man or serving a man's cause, they are simply deemed insignificant in general.

Even in Jesus' final hours of trial and prosecution, there were at least a few powerless women struggling to save Him, every step of the way—perhaps the few that remained at the foot of the cross long after He had breathed His last breath, and the same few that tended His grave and ached over the injustice that had transpired. Shari wonders, did those women fail in their efforts? Were their efforts wasted? What might they have done with their time and energy that would have been better than trying to prevent injustice and to persuade the authorities toward integrity? Could they possibly have begun to go on with their lives in the midst of their pain, short of exhausting all effort, however futile?

When her own ache began many years ago, in December of 1964, Shari began the task of asking, seeking and knocking, out of desperate necessity. She believed that one day she would know what had transpired, and that her sister and brother would also know and they'd know together. She believed they would be better for knowing and understanding, and that the truth would set them free to 'go on with life,' and live more abundantly. Only because truth liberates, understanding transforms, and love heals.

Mother Theresa once said, "God did not call me to be successful. He called me to be faithful."

As I stand here on holy ground
And look o'er the years of this life,
Hardships were simply expected,
Of torment, struggle and strife.
I wasn't aware that life could be different,
That old things could be passed away
The glass appeared ever so darkly,
Concealing that new brighter day.
But then, there are those before me
And those who will come later on
Who seek a better beginning,
Long to know as they are known.
These are the ones I shall heed now

And with them, Lord, follow You.
Wherever the path may lead us,
However narrow the way through.
I thank Thee, Dear Lord, for things now understood
And more that will be revealed
That our mission on earth need not end incomplete
Till Truth and Love surely have healed,
Till Truth and Love surely have healed.

CO-AUTHOR'S NOTES BY CECELIA MAURER, OLIVE'S GRANDDAUGHTER

THE EVENTS IN THIS story began before my birth and culminated with the murder of my grandmother, Olive Lewis, when I was only two years old. Throughout my childhood, teens and into my adult life, I was always aware that the pain of my grandmother's death and the mystery that surrounded her death was never far from my mother's consciousness. I always prayed that God would someday let my mother know the truth about her mother's death. However horrible the truth may have been, it had to be better than the torment she was going through not knowing. Sometimes I would hear her muffled cries in the night or come home from school to find her exhausted with her eyes red and swollen. Most times, however, she was coping well and giving my brother Aubrey and me a wonderful childhood. I enjoyed these times although I knew they were temporary.

Aubrey and I never wanted to add to her pain so we rarely if ever gave her reason to worry. We would call before it was time to, or be home long before curfew. We often chided her about her long "be careful, stay together, don't wander off from the group, look both ways, and don't talk to strangers" speeches we would hear before going out. We did, however, heed her advice and are still here to tell about it. I guess we all knew that dangers were real and didn't just happen to 'other people.' We never enjoyed the luxury of a false sense of security.

My mother had heard so many people tell her to go on with her life. She and we did go on. We had happy holidays and special birthdays and often little surprises for each other. When we made mistakes we tried again; if the situation was hopeless we moved onto another situation. Most importantly of all, we approved of each other and we appreciated each other. We knew we weren't perfect but we all felt we were as close to it as we needed to be. We validated each other as valuable individuals, so none of us ever felt totally alone.

As the sequence of events unfolded and we all finally came to know the truth, we also came to know that it was a story that had to be told. However, none of us relished the idea of writing a book. My brother had graduated from college and had begun his career as a teacher. I was a full time college student and mother of two small children, and my mother was working full-time in her private practice. None of us had time to write a book. Therefore, it soon became obvious that this would be a collaborative effort. Aubrey forced my mother and me to become computer literate and hoped this might be the extent of his involvement. It wasn't. My mother and I compiled the story from the zillions of notes she had made over the years, her doctoral thesis and the many interviews we conducted—usually involving a cross-country trip with my kids in tow. As we got a chapter together we sent it off to Aubrey, whose job it was to correct our mistakes and offer suggestions. He also had to edit some of the photographs and get the whole work put on a computer disk.

I wish I could say that we "whistled while we worked," and never let our frustrations get the better of us, but that wasn't the case. There were several occasions when we all agreed to forget it and that it wasn't worth the headaches involved. Then a few days later one of us would call the other with some new and great inspiration and we would be off and running again.

I would like to thank my grandmother, "OliVee," for her guidance from above, throughout this ordeal. I do not have any personal memories of her, only some old home movie films which are barely visible. However, I believe with all my heart that she was with us to lend support and inspiration. Some parts of these writings were truly inspired.

I also think that my grandfather, Cecil, has played a big part in my son's life, and mine. My son, Mark, was diagnosed with autism when he was three years old. My mother took us to some of the best psychologists in the field (still asking, seeking, knocking) and we were given some excellent advice. The more we learned about autism the more she was reminded of her father, who was quiet, good with numbers, and had an above normal IQ but lacked in social graces. He didn't have friends and did not socialize. There is a great deal of information on autism available now that would not have been available to him as a child. We believe that he fits all of the criteria for High Functioning Autism (HFA), and would have received that diagnosis had it been known then. (The closest known diagnosis then was Schizoid Personality, according to Tony Attwood, noted expert on Autism/ Asperger or HFA.).

One of the problems HFA individuals face is that they do not understand or perceive the world the way other people do. This often results in their making social blunders and misreading social cues. They realize that they are not like other people and feel that they are just 'wrong.' This leads to poor self-esteem and in time can lead to self-loathing. Many HFA individuals who went undiagnosed into their 40's or 50's have reported that they often turned to alcohol or other drugs to dull the pain and the shame.

I believe that this explains a lot about Cecil Lewis and his behavior. He was not a monster. He did not hate his wife or his kids and he didn't kill anyone. He was a misunderstood child, boy and man.

Now we understand, and when I see my son happy and healthy with high self-esteem and all the confidence in the world, I know that his great-grandfather must be smiling. Mark will have opportunities that he never had. I feel, however, that as Mark moves through his life, Cecil will be able to share in his accomplishments from the other side.

This book was a magnanimous effort but now that it is finished we all agree that it was definitely worth that effort. It is our prayer that others may find strength in its pages.

And, we're glad our mom didn't try to just 'put it behind' her and 'go on' with her life, without this lifelong quest!

www.ingramcontent.com/pod-product-compliance
Lightning Source LLC
Chambersburg PA
CBHW070905120626
46546CB00001B/145